Measuring EU Inflation

John Astin

Measuring EU Inflation

The Foundations of the HICP

Head of Price Comparisons Division, Eurostat, 1991–2002

palgrave
macmillan

John Astin
Canterbury, Kent, UK

ISBN 978-3-030-68805-9 ISBN 978-3-030-68806-6 (eBook)
https://doi.org/10.1007/978-3-030-68806-6

This Palgrave Macmillan imprint is published by the registered company Springer Nature Switzerland AG
The registered company address is: Gewerbestrasse 11, 6330 Cham, Switzerland

Preface

This book has been brewing in my mind since quite soon after I left Eurostat in 2002 when somebody suggested that I should write a history of the HICP. It sounded to me at the time a very good idea. The HICP had been "my baby" during my relatively short time with the European Commission, and it had been not only a speedy success but an enduring one. It was, to quote a comment by the then Director-General of Eurostat, "probably the most important project that Eurostat had done to date". And who should write such a history other than the person who had been responsible for its development?

But after I had retired from Eurostat in 2002, I was immediately engulfed in a welter of consultancy assignments which kept me occupied for many years. Later, I was again involved in a project of CPI harmonization, this time in a large group of developing countries, and I realised that my experiences with the development of the HICP gave me a solid foundation for that project. Now I have time to think once again about writing the HICP history—hence this book.

Why have a history of the foundations of the HICP? Isn't it perhaps the driest of dry subjects, which will interest almost nobody? I don't believe so. In fact, the project made economic and statistical history. It was perhaps the first such major project of international statistical harmonization in the economic sphere. The HICP is now produced in almost all European countries, with a combined population of some 530 million people and a GDP of over €15 trillion. It is also produced by the USA, mainly for comparison purposes. It is a key measure for the administration of the euro area by the European Central Bank (ECB), which from the start has used it as the principal measure for its inflation targeting, and hence for setting the interest rate for the euro area. The HICP, to be sure, has had its critics, but it has been described in recent years as being the "state of the art" indicator of inflation. As the CPI, it is the most widely used inflation index in the UK.

With this background, it is surely a duty to put on record the story of its development.

It would not have been such a success story without the dedicated and highly motivated team which I was fortunate enough to lead in Eurostat.

We had an established staff of seven or eight, often supplemented by short-term appointments of temporary staff. The HICP section was headed by the indispensable Alexandre Makaronidis. Other statisticians who spent several years in the section included Carsten Olsson, Daniela Schackis, Patricia Klees and Ambjorn Berglund. Our administrative staff, who ensured that our statistical work was properly organised, included Angèle Costanzi, Marie-Noelle Barbier, Silvia Santos, and in particular my faithful and efficient secretaries Franca Lanzillotta and Claire Moorat.

Two directors of Economic Statistics were in place during my time on HICP work, Alberto De Michelis and Bart Meganck, to whom I owe a debt of gratitude for their support and advice.

Not to mention the hard work put in by national CPI experts who turned up regularly for the unremitting delegate meetings in Luxembourg, when every single word of every draft regulation was put under the microscope. One of my main recollections of those days was the gradual harmonization of not only the CPIs but of our own relationships. Before the HICP project began, most of the national price statisticians had scarcely met each other (or us!) except maybe at infrequent international conferences. As time passed, we grew to know and understand each others' ways of thinking, and it was a constant pleasure to me personally to realise that this project had sparked such new understandings between our teams.

This book is not a technical manual about CPIs in general, and not even the HICP in particular. It is not intended to provide comprehensive technical explanations of all the complex statistical concepts, techniques and formulas used in the HICP; there are other sources for such information. The current HICP Methodological Manual[1] gives a detailed description of the HICP as it is today. What this book aims to do is to describe the processes involved in constructing the HICP and especially the legal acts which define it. This covers a wide range of topics, including legal matters, language problems, common terminology—("item", "weight", etc), sub-indices, coverage, to name but a few. In the course of this descriptive narrative, it has often been necessary to explain—sometimes in detail—some of the technical considerations.

Above all, the book is intended to be a work of reference for existing and future researchers and CPI practitioners wanting to discover exactly how (and why) a major process such as the HICP was conceived, born and developed. There are perhaps many lessons to be learned from the whole experience.

Kent, UK John Astin

[1] HICP Methodological Manual *ISBN 978-92-79-76861-3 Eurostat, Luxembourg, 2018.*

Acknowledgments

This book—and indeed the whole HICP project—owes a tremendous debt to three colleagues who worked with us on the project in the early years. Don Sellwood had been head of the statistical unit responsible for the UK's Retail Prices Index, and came to Eurostat for several years to guide the initial development of the HICP. He has also provided me with helpful advice in the preparation of this book. The late Professor Ralph Turvey (formerly Director of the Statistics Department at the International Labour Organisation (ILO) in Geneva) provided his services as a consultant for several years, and his sharp and logical mind helped all of us to make the right decisions. The late Professor Peter Hill, former Head of Economic Statistics and National Accounts at the Organisation for Economic Co-operation and Development (OECD) in Paris, gave us the enormous benefit of his wide experience on this aspect of our work. We also benefited very considerably from the consultancy services of the Swedish statistician Jörgen Dalén, who provided a wide range of in-depth statistical analyses.

I would like also to acknowledge the valuable contribution of my wife Alina, whose experience as head of the Polish CPI gave her the ability to act as a sounding-board for the sometimes scatter-brained ideas I had while writing this book. It is all the better for her advice, though responsibility for any errors or omissions is entirely my own.

Organisation of this Book

The book traces the history of the early development of the HICP. It has fifteen chapters, the first five of which are roughly chronological, from first ideas to definite plans following the 1992 Maastricht Treaty,[1] to the preparations for the first "Framework Regulation" and to the establishment of a special expert Working Party (WP). The WP, and its subsidiary Task Forces (TFs) met on many occasions in the following years. Up to the end of 2001 the WP had 33 meetings over 58 days, with a total of 416 papers. The TFs held 33 meetings over 55 days, with 267 papers, in 12 countries. These meetings were to a large extent drafting technical regulations and guidelines on most aspects of CPI construction.

Chapter 3 describes the construction of the first regulation—the so-called Framework Regulation—which set the scene for a long series of technical implementing regulations. These five chapters comprise Part I of the book

Part II (Chapters 6–11) is essentially about technical aspects of the HICP, where the focus is on subjects rather than on a timeline. There is inevitably some partial overlap between Chapters 1–5 and 6–11, as general statistical principles are first dealt with, while the details follow in the technical chapters.

Part III comprises the final four chapters, 12–15. They deal with other matters concerning the HICP, such as the publication of data; the

[1] Treaty on European Union, 1992, ISBN 92-824-0959-7.

monitoring of compliance with the regulations; issues connected with data handling and processing, and so on. There are chapters describing the wider context of the HICP, such as the structure of the European Commission, its reports to the Council on progress with the convergence criteria laid down in the Maastricht Treaty, as well as the crucial matter of funding the process. Chapter 13 deals with the aggregation of the national HICPs of the member states, while Chapter 14 is concerned with the expansion of the EU with the forthcoming accession of a dozen new member states, mainly from eastern Europe. Chapter 15 concludes with some thoughts on future directions of the HICP.

The book covers the years when the author was responsible for the HICP development, 1991–2002. There are some references to later work, including the nine regulations adopted since 2002.

There follows a glossary of terms which may not all be familiar to readers, and finally, of course, an index.

Contents

About the Author

John Astin has been a professional statistician, working in the public sector, since 1972. His career falls into two parts, firstly with the British Government Statistical Service where he worked at the Inland Revenue, the Central Statistical Office (now ONS), the National Economic Development Office (NEDO) and the Department for Trade and Industry, where he became head of statistics. He then joined Eurostat, the Luxembourg based statistical directorate of the EU, where he spent twelve years as head of the unit responsible for price statistics. One of his main tasks was leading the project to harmonise EU national consumer price indices, leading to the creation of the HICP—the subject of this book. He left Eurostat in 2002 and continued to work as an independent price statistics consultant, work which took him to many places around the world. He was a founder member of the UK National Statistician's Advisory Panel for Consumer Price statistics (Technical).

Author's Note: In the days before 1993, the organisation known today as the European Union (EU) was known as the "European Community" (or "Communities") abbreviated to EC. I have kept this name in references to works in that earlier period, and moved to "EU" for later periods.

List of Tables

PART I

Concepts, Design and Preparation

CHAPTER 1

Background to the HICP

1.1 Early International Studies by the ILO

For many years, the International Labour Organisation (ILO) had been urging its member states (which included the EC member states) to use the recommendations for CPI compilation set out by the ILO at various times. Discussion on the question of CPI design and practice began at the ILO as early as 1925.[1]

In 1947 the subject reappeared on the agenda of the Sixth International Conference of Labour Statisticians, held in Montreal. At that time, a comprehensive resolution plus a series of related resolutions were adopted, setting uniform basic concepts and procedures for the construction of cost-of-living index numbers.

In 1962, the ILO published a document "The computation of consumer price indexes (special problems)".[2] This was a comprehensive paper that sensibly addressed many of the issues which later had to be faced by Eurostat in its CPI harmonization project.

Since then, following meetings of the Conference of European Statisticians—a body under the wing of the United Nations Economic Commission for Europe (UNECE)—especially those in 1981 and 1986, the ILO

[1] ("Methods of Compiling Cost-of-Living Index Numbers", Studies and Reports, Series N [Statistics] No. 6, ILO, Geneva, 1925).

[2] Available on the ILO website, ILO.org.

J. Astin, *Measuring EU Inflation*,
https://doi.org/10.1007/978-3-030-68806-6_1

has issued several editions of its recommendations, taking due account of the latest research and expert opinions. Thus, the ILO had, over many years, provided the basic toolkit for any country wishing to establish a CPI or to improve the methodology used in its existing CPI.

1.2 Later Studies Undertaken for Eurostat

The European Commission is the executive arm of what is now known as the European Union. (For more details see Chapter 15.1). It has directorates that cover a wide range of technical and administrative areas. One such directorate is Eurostat, which is responsible for nearly all of the Commission's statistical output. My job was head of the unit dealing with consumer prices, purchasing power parities and the annual cost-of-living changes to Commission staff salaries.

In 1974 Eurostat, then known as SOEC—the Statistical Office of the European Communities—commissioned a report, "*Consumer Price Indexes in the European Community*" by Dr. Josef Stadlbauer of Heidelberg University,[3] aimed at assessing the prospects for harmonizing EC CPIs.

Stadlbauer began his report with a strong statement about the importance of the CPI as an economic indicator:

> *There is hardly another statistical figure in economics which is of such national and international significance as the consumer price index. Its annual rates of change are regarded in all countries as an indicator of trends in the general level of prices and therefore of the purchasing power of money in general. . . This index is thus an instrument of economic analysis and is used as a criterion for assessing the effectiveness of past economic measures and for shaping such measures in the future. This applies to both national and international comparisons.*

The present author can only reiterate this statement; it applies even more strongly in the present world, and particularly in the monetary union at the heart of the EU.

[3] Eurostat, Consumer Price Indexes in the European Community—Comparison of existing indexes and approaches to their harmonisation, Josef Stadlbauer, Luxembourg, 1975.

Stadlbauer devoted much of his report to describing in considerable detail the methods used by each of the EC member states (then 9) in compiling their national CPIs, showing that there was very considerable scope for harmonization. However, his conclusion was pessimistic as far as the prospects for CPI harmonization in the immediate future were concerned. To quote from the foreword to his report:

> *The attempt to put forward practical proposals in an initial harmonization stage [has] proved Utopian; the national significance of such an economically and socially important parameter is so closely linked in the various countries to their respective requirements and historical development of price statistics that for political reasons the National Statistical Offices cannot make short-term radical changes in methodology on their own account. Even comparatively minor changes in the method of calculating the index, such as an increase or reduction in the number of prices recorded or reporting units surveyed, require parliamentary approval in a number of countries. Against this background this study can only provide a basis for discussion with respect to constructing uniform indexes and therefore unrestrictedly comparable index information within the Community.*

So the report was filed away for possible future reference. Meanwhile, the ILO devoted considerable efforts to the theory and practice of CPIs, in particular two seminars in 1981 and 1986, organised jointly with the European Conference of Statisticians (a UN body in Geneva).

Another important landmark for CPIs globally—not just in Europe—was the 14th International Conference of Labour Statisticians convened by the ILO in 1987, which resulted in the publication in 1989 of an important manual,[4] edited and largely written by the late Professor Ralph Turvey, then Director of the ILO Statistics Department. This manual, while not directly leading to the development of more comparable CPIs, certainly provided much of the groundwork for later harmonization.

In parallel with this development, in 1987 the Single European Act came into effect, with the objective of establishing a single market in the EC by the end of 1992. This vitally important legislation moved the goalposts for economic statistics in the EC. It was no doubt this new impetus which in 1989 prompted Eurostat (still the SOEC) to commission a second report *("Consumer Price Indices in the European*

[4] R. Turvey, "Consumer Price Indices: an ILO Manual", International Labour Organization, 1989.

Community") on the prospects for CPI harmonization, this time from Prof. Rudolf Teekens, of the Institute of Social Studies Advisory Service in The Hague.[5] As well as updating the Stadlbauer report, in particular the inventory of national CPI methodology in the (by now twelve) EU member states, the Teekens Report was considerably more optimistic about the prospects for CPI harmonization, given the new economic circumstances. Quoting a 1987 EC report, "*a large market without internal frontiers could not be completed or operate properly unless the Community had instruments enabling it to avoid imbalances interfering with competitiveness and inhibiting the growth of the Community as a whole*".

Teekens quotes more from the above EC report:

> *It is quite obvious that the monitoring of consumer prices across the member states of the Community can only be a powerful instrument to serve the above purposes if it is based on a harmonized CPI calculation in all member states . . . . One cannot pursue a Community policy, unless one has at his disposal statistical instruments which measure the same phenomenon in the different countries in a comparable way.*

But the Single Market Act, powerful incentive though it was, turned out to be insufficient to persuade member states to make the necessary leap forward and decide to embark on a CPI harmonization project.

The required stimulus was provided just a few years later by the Treaty on the European Union—known widely as the Maastricht Treaty—of 1992.[6]

As we shall see in the following section, it was the Maastricht Treaty which not only made the task of harmonizing EU CPIs desirable, but essential—and moreover with a tight deadline. CPI harmonization immediately rose to the level of high priority in the European Commission—and in Eurostat particularly.

Why was this? Put simply, the Maastricht Treaty established the foundations of Economic and Monetary Union (EMU); this would require the creation of a single currency zone—the euro area—and a single currency—the euro. Member states would not be able to enter the euro

[5] R. Teekens, "Consumer Price Indices in the European Community", Luxembourg, 1989.

[6] Treaty on European Union (Maastricht) 1992, ISBN 92-824-0959-7.

area automatically: they would have to fulfil certain stringent conditions. These were known as the "convergence criteria". Among them was a requirement to have a level of inflation below a certain ceiling—and to enable this criterion to be workable it would be necessary to have national inflation measures that would be comparable to one another. In short, harmonized CPIs were now a necessity.

1.3 The Maastricht Treaty: Convergence Criteria

We cannot proceed much further without examining the wording of that part of the Maastricht Treaty (the Treaty on European Union) which underpins the HICP. It is found in the 13th protocol, which establishes the convergence criteria—those economic conditions which countries are required to fulfil as qualifications for entry to the euro area. Adopting the single currency is a crucial step in a Member State's economy. Its exchange rate becomes irrevocably fixed and monetary policy is transferred from the national central bank to the European Central Bank (formerly the European Monetary Institute, EMI). The economic entry conditions are designed to ensure that a Member State's economy is sufficiently prepared for adoption of the single currency and can integrate smoothly into the monetary regime of the euro area without risk of disruption for the Member State or for the euro area as a whole. In short, the economic entry criteria are intended to ensure economic convergence prior to joining the euro area. The criterion for price stability was one of four convergence criteria laid down in the Treaty, the other three relating to interest rates, excessive deficits and exchange rates.

Article 1 of Protocol No 13 states:

> *The criterion on price stability referred to in the first indent of Article 109j(1) of this Treaty shall mean that a Member State has a price performance that is sustainable and an average rate of inflation, observed over a period of one year before the examination, that does not exceed by more than 1½ percentage points that of, at most, the three best performing Member States in terms of price stability. Inflation shall be measured by means of the consumer price index on a comparable basis, taking into account differences in national definitions.*

The Maastricht Treaty was signed in February 1992 and entered into force on 1 November 1993 (The essence of Article 1 was later incorporated into the 2008 Treaty of Lisbon).

The key phrase in Article 1, at least as far as the HICP is concerned, is "*on a comparable basis*". At the time when the Maastricht Treaty was signed, each EU member state compiled its own CPI, which had developed according to the perceived needs of each country—often with the principal objective of having an index which could be used to uprate the wages of employees in order to preserve their purchasing power (a "compensation index"). The result was that a simple comparison of national CPIs did not necessarily give an accurate comparison of relative rates of consumer price inflation. We needed to get to the situation where it would be possible to state, for example, that the rate of inflation in Germany was 2.7% and in France 3.1%, in the knowledge that the two figures were drawn up on a comparable basis and that consequently it could be said with confidence that the French inflation rate was 0.4 percentage points higher than the German rate.

During this period, Eurostat itself used to publish monthly statistics showing the latest CPIs of each country, without any attempt to adjust for methodological differences. Eurostat also published weighted average figures for the EU as a whole—but as the latter were calculated on the basis of the non-harmonized national data, they were rather meaningless.

A few examples of methodological differences between member states were mentioned in the Teekens Report (para. 4.1):-

> *Both Germany and France seem to have limited their index population, while Luxemburg continues to concentrate on low income households (about 3% of the resident population). Moreover, the member states have not much progressed towards a harmonisation of the classifications. With respect to the field of observation of goods and services one can say that the same problems and difficulties which were identified by Stadlbauer persist at present. There is still no uniformity in the treatment of (imputed) rent and the treatment of insurances and taxes did not converge significantly over the decade. There was little progress in the alignment of base years and periodicity of family budget surveys across the nine. Finally, the way in which quality change, substitution and seasonal products are treated by the nine member states does not show much convergence over the last ten years.*

1.4 Consultations with Member States

My job in Eurostat started in early 1991. Consumer price indices formed only part of my division's work on price comparisons. A large part was concerned with the gathering of data and subsequent calculation of purchasing power parities (PPPs) for EU member states and some other European countries. (PPPs are effectively spatial price comparisons rather than temporal ones.) Another important part of my job was internal to the Commission: the calculation of the data needed for the annual pay review and fixing of equalisation factors to assure that the salaries of staff working in different places around the world had equal purchasing power, regardless of the official exchange rates. Of these three aspects, CPI harmonization was, in early 1991, the third priority. After all, Maastricht had not yet been signed. That happened a year later, in February 1992, and from then on the pressure for harmonized CPIs began to mount strongly.

But in fact we already began early in 1991 to lay the groundwork, on the assumption that monetary union would happen sooner or later. At that initial stage, we did not have the Maastricht protocol and we had to use our own initiative in deciding what type of statistical indicators were likely to be needed in respect of having comparable indicators of inflation throughout the EU. We already knew (from the Stadlbauer and Teekens reports [see above]) that harmonizing national CPIs would be a difficult, if not impossible, job. Perhaps there were other indicators, less politically sensitive, that could be harmonized instead? To help test the waters on this, I embarked on a round of visits to several countries, including France, Germany, the Netherlands and the UK. My aim was to speak to central bankers and the national statistical offices. The bankers, because they could be regarded as the future main users of a harmonized inflation index after the creation of the euro area; the statisticians, since it would be their job to compile the necessary data and send them regularly to Eurostat.

I was given plenty of advice, though not always in the same direction. The central bankers were all in favour of a harmonization project. I asked them which of the possible indicators would be the most appropriate and useful to harmonize. Possibilities included, as well as the CPI, the producer price index (PPI) and the national accounts consumer expenditure deflator. The main arguments against using the PPI were that it was an indicator with little public impact, and also that it excluded services—one of the largest sectors of the economy in most countries. In principle, the consumer expenditure deflator might be appropriate, but it was produced only quarterly, and this time lag was probably unavoidable. For a future European central bank, it was surely going to be necessary to have an indicator produced at a frequency of at least once per month. So the general view was that efforts should be focussed on harmonizing national CPIs. Of course, the later Maastricht Treaty specified clearly that it was indeed the CPIs that were to be harmonized.

The national statisticians were more or less of a similar view, though there was some scepticism about the practicality of harmonizing such a national treasure as the CPI! Some no doubt recalled the earlier hesitant steps following the Stadlbauer and Teekens reports. Surprisingly, with hindsight, the idea of creating a new harmonized CPI alongside and separate from the national CPI did not seem to have occurred to anyone at this time. Nevertheless, there were emerging signals from member states that a more European perspective on CPIs may be useful. For example, the UK's RPI Advisory Committee (RPI—Retail Prices Index) being the main CPI in use then, had been asked to take account of the practices in other EC countries, and for the first time a representative from Eurostat (myself!) had been invited to be on the Committee. Furthermore, several EC member states had started thinking about the desirability of being able to compare their country's inflation rate with others'—on a like-with-like basis of course.

1.5 Establishment of the CPI Harmonization Working Party[7]

By December 1991 Eurostat was in a position to prepare a definite harmonization proposal to the heads of statistics in the member states. These senior statisticians were known collectively by the term DGINS, an acronym standing for "Directors-General of the National Statistical Institutes" (in the French original version). The DGINS meetings first began in 1953, and for many years their purpose was "for mutual information and for fixing the guidelines for future actions". It was, in other words, a high-level talking shop, without any legal status or power. They met at

[7] Two small points of explanation: The term "Working Party" was regularly used by Eurostat as a synonym for the more formal and correct title "Working Group". Throughout this book I refer to it as the "Working Party" or WP for short.

regular intervals in Eurostat, at meetings chaired by the Director-General of Eurostat. They, of course, were responsible for proposing the meeting agendas, and thus they had first to be persuaded that the time was ripe for a CPI harmonization proposal to their national colleagues. This was not a difficult task, as they were in any case pre-disposed to such a plan. But of course the document which had to be provided for the crucial meeting had to be drafted with extreme care. A poorly prepared case would have risked a negative reaction from the DGINS, and possibly set back the project by some time. On the other hand, the pressure for harmonization was growing as a result of the Maastricht Treaty.

The Director of Statistics of the European Monetary Institute (EMI—the forerunner of the European Central Bank [ECB]) was by this time invited to participate as an observer in the meetings of the Statistical Programme Committee (SPC),[8] and his presence would clearly have encouraged the members of the committee towards a positive view of CPI harmonization. The SPC is a Regulatory Committee established by Council Decision (89/382) in June 1989. It will be frequently referred to throughout this book. It is now known as the European Statistical System Committee (ESSC). Although the SPC comprised more or less the same officials as in the DGINS (which continued in name as simply the Directors-General of the EC NSIs), it had a different legal status—see Chapter 15.1.

In fact, in December 1991 (two months before Maastricht!) the SPC formally gave their approval to the recommendation of Eurostat to begin preparation for CPI harmonization by establishing a new Eurostat Working Party (WP). The WP concept was a long-established method for discussing proposed legislation, and associated matters, by experts from the relevant official departments in the member states. The delegates were usually, but by no means always, drawn from the staff of the national statistical institutes (NSIs) and would usually be experts in the particular subject under discussion. WP meetings were chaired by a Eurostat official (usually the head of unit dealing with the issue), and meetings would be held as frequently as necessary to move the business forward on an agreed timetable.

It was necessary for a great deal of groundwork to be laid before calling the first meeting of the CPI WP. For a start, it was necessary to recruit

[8] Committee of Directors-General of EC national statistics institutes.

suitably experienced staff. This book rarely refers to named individuals, but it would be wrong not to mention the vital role played by our senior expert, Don Sellwood, who came to Eurostat from the UK in April 1993, just in time for the final preparations for the first meeting of the CPI WP in June 1993. Don performed a most valuable—indeed, indispensable—role in every aspect of our work, based on his previous experience in charge of the UK Retail Prices Index.

Draft terms of reference or mandate for the new WP were proposed by the SPC at their December 1991 meeting. It is useful to quote the text of this document:

> *The proposed mandate of the Working Party on the Harmonization of CPIs is to draft guidelines on the construction of Harmonized Consumer Price Indices suitable for inclusion in a Regulation. In order to achieve this the Working Party should take account of the range of current practices and the constraints arising from precedent and from legal and institutional requirements in member states. Proposals should be practicable for all member states and should involve minimum cost consistent with the required accuracy of the indices which the Working Party should attempt to establish on the basis of their many uses. It should also make proposals for the construction of a pan-European index based on the harmonized CPIs. The Working Party may decide to delegate part of its work to sub-groups or task forces where this is likely to lead to a more rapid conclusion. It will also consider the participation of members of the CEIES as observers at its meetings.*

The CEIES was the European Advisory Committee on Statistical Information in the Economic and Social Sphere, established in February 1991. Its task was "*to assist the Council and the Commission in the coordination of the objectives of the Community's statistical information policy, taking into account user requirements and the costs borne by the information producers*". Its membership included all of the SPC members, other senior Commission officials, and representatives from all member states.

In 1992 the CEIES formed a subcommittee to examine the question of CPI harmonization. The subcommittee, under its chairman, Ullrich Heilemann, presented a report to the CEIES at its meeting in March 1993 (see Chapter 15.4 for further details).

The recommendations of the CEIES turned out to be an extremely useful starting point for the forthcoming discussions of the WP.

It was intended that the draft mandate from the SPC should be discussed by the future WP and amended if necessary. Any changes would need to be approved by the SPC. The final mandate also made a requirement for the WP to report regularly to the SPC. The WP was also required to make regular progress reports to the Committee on Monetary, Financial and Balance of Payments Statistics (CMFB). This was a committee established in 1991 as a forum for coordination of statisticians from the national statistical institutes and Eurostat on the one hand, and the national central banks and the EMI (later European Central Bank) on the other.

In the next chapter, we get down to brass tacks, as the saying goes. In other words, we began meeting as a Working Party and starting to tackle in great depth the huge problems that we would be facing in harmonizing EU CPIs.

CHAPTER 2

First Meeting of the HICP Working Party

2.1 Invitations and Agenda

Invitations to the first WP meeting were sent by the Eurostat Director-General, Yves Franchet, in May 1993. It is interesting to see some extracts from this letter:

> *You will be aware that in December 1991 the DGINSagreed that a separate working party should be set up to consider the harmonization of consumer price indices. They recognized the urgent need to have comparable inflation indicators in the creation and realisation phases of economic and monetary union.... I now believe that we are in a position to take the work forward with the help of NSIs. I am, however, conscious that two previous attempts on our part to obtain agreement on a programme of harmonization made little progress and am concerned that this should not happen on this occasion. To this end I attach great importance to the first meeting of the Working Party, where we will discuss the broad issues, identify the main obstacles and decide how they can best be tackled.*
>
> *You will appreciate the problems we face, and I would like to stress that Eurostat has no set ideas as to their solution. We appreciate that the CPI is*

Now known as the Price Statistics Working Party.

J. Astin, *Measuring EU Inflation*,
https://doi.org/10.1007/978-3-030-68806-6_2

> *among the most sensitive of all national statistics and that each country will have its own peculiar constraints and requirements with regard to harmonization. Indeed some countries may find it impossible for political or contractual reasons to make significant changes to the method by which their national CPI is compiled. It may therefore be necessary for these countries to consider a separate harmonized price index.... I also hope that we can reach a consensus on a pan-European index based on the harmonized CPIs. I very much hope that countries will send a senior member of staff.. to the first meeting of the Working Party so that we are in a position to assess the issues, to agree the line of approach and to set the programme of work.*

The first meeting of the new WP was held on 15 June 1993, and was attended by 21 CPI experts from all 12 member states—at that time comprising Belgium, Denmark, France, Germany, Greece, Ireland, Italy, Luxembourg, Netherlands, Portugal, Spain and the UK. In addition, 11 CPI experts from 6 member states of the European Free Trade Association (EFTA) attended: Austria, Finland, Iceland, Norway, Sweden and Switzerland, as well as a representative of the EFTA secretariat. Several other international organisations were represented: the International Labour Organization (ILO), the Organization for Economic Co-operation and Development (OECD), and a representative of the secretariat of the Committee of Governors of Central Banks of the Member States. The United Nations Director of Statistics was also invited, but was unable to attend.

Representatives also attended from other European Commission departments: from Economic and Financial Affairs (DGII) and Personnel and Administration (DG IX). The meeting was chaired by John Astin, the head of Eurostat's Price Comparisons Division (who went on to chair all the 33 subsequent meetings prior to his retirement in 2002), and the meeting was opened by Eurostat's Director of Economic Statistics and Economic and Monetary Convergence, Alberto De Michelis.

This first meeting, held in one of the Commission's Luxembourg conference rooms in the Jean Monnet Building (recently demolished!), was for a single day, as were most of the early meetings. Later they were extended to 2 or occasionally 3 days, and sometimes held in other countries. Here is the agenda:

EUROSTAT
B3

Luxembourg, June 1993
HCPI 93/1

Meeting of Working Party
on Harmonisation of Consumer Price Indices
15 June 1993
Jean Monnet Building, room M5
Luxembourg
Beginning : 10H00

AGENDA

1. **Introduction by chairman and adoption of agenda**

2. **Terms of reference and legal background**
Discussion of draft Terms of Reference - political legal and budgetary constraints - -Maastricht -Article 64- Regulation 3830/91 on EC staff remuneration - possible regulation on CPI's-
Pan-European Index and comparability with CPI's of O.E.C.D. and E.C.E countries.
Objective - Agreed terms of reference for submission to DGINS in September.

3. **Modus operandum**
Discussion of membership of WP - distribution of papers - frequency of meetings-timetable - use of task forces - use of consultants - participation of CEIES.
Objective- Agreed method of approach.

4. **Technical Agenda**
Discussion of differences between CPI's & any idea of scale of these - coverage, (expenditure
or consumption approach) - concepts (formula etc)- practices (price collection; revisions, publications) - derivation of weights (family budget surveys).
Objective - Agreed topics for study with priorities.

5. **Next steps - Programme of Work**
Discussion of compromises that may be neccesary (eg. to change CPI or to have two - to exclude housing -to exclude imputation) -membership of task forces, their tasks and guidelines for them to follow.
Objective - Agreed membership of task forces, tasks and guidelines.

6 **Miscellaneous**

Note: Papers covering the various discussion points will be sent before the meeting. Delegates may wish to consider to which task force topics they would most likely want to contribute.

As the agenda shows, the topics discussed were mainly non-technical.

The objectives were to decide what had to be done, how to do it, and who should do what.

Papers had been prepared prior to the meeting (and, as always, distributed to delegates by fax and/or post) on all agenda items except No. 3. One must of course recall that in 1993 we did not have such a thing as a website—nor did we have emails!

Nearly all of the documents were available in English, French and German. The first meeting—and indeed many others in the early days—benefited from interpretation into and from nine languages (nowadays they are monolingual—in English).

Of course, in the time available for the meeting, technical topics could not be discussed in any detail, and most of them not at all. But they were pointers for future examination, and delegates were asked to suggest further topics. Orally, Eurostat amplified the above points to draw out the essence of the issues. For example, before designing a new index it is desirable—if not essential—to determine how the index is likely to be used, and for what purposes. Would a diversity of uses give rise to conflicting requirements? What compromises may be necessary? Do all of the technical aspects need to be harmonized? Is the gain in accuracy which may be achieved by a certain type of harmonization likely to outweigh the cost of achieving it? Could it be that the types of weights needed for the new index would have repercussions on the data requirements in the Household Budget Surveys—the main source of CPI weights?

A list of detailed topics was later prepared for the first Task Force meeting; these are given in Chapter 2.3. All of these issues are dealt with in the technical chapters of this book (Chapters 6–11).

But the main purpose of this first WP meeting was to convince the delegates from member states that this time Eurostat was in earnest about achieving CPI harmonization—and that it must be done quickly. The Eurostat Director of Economic Statistics said that the monetary union could start as soon as 1997 (though this later turned out to be slightly optimistic—it began on 1st January 1999). He reminded the delegates that the DGINS had identified the HICP project as a top priority, and that strong support had been received from the Central Bank governors, as well as from the Commission itself. He emphasised that Eurostat had no pre-determined ideas, but was fully open to the views of delegates and from potential users of the HICP.

2.2 Terms of Reference

The first point of the agenda was the need to refine the draft terms of reference for the WP which had been proposed by the DGINS at their meeting in December 1991 (see Chapter 1.5).

Eurostat began by explaining the differences between the various types of instrument which could be used to manage the HICP. For the benefit of readers who may not be familiar with these instruments (and there have been several changes in the intervening years) these are outlined here.

Below the lowest level of legal enforceability is what were commonly known as "Gentlemen's Agreements". These were informal and legally unenforceable agreements. In practice, what this meant was that the DGINS would agree among themselves—preferably but not necessarily unanimously—on a set of rules concerning a certain topic. From the point of view of an individual country, it would be somewhat perverse if that country ignored a particular Gentlemen's Agreement when its own Head of Statistics had signed their name to the agreement. But there could be no legal redress if it was in fact ignored.

One step up from the Gentlemen's Agreement was a Commission Directive. A directive is a legislative act that sets out a goal that all EU countries must achieve. However, it is up to the individual countries to devise their own laws on how to reach these goals.

Next up the chain was a Commission Regulation, followed by the most stringent rule, a Council Regulation. Both of these regulations carry the force of EU law—which, incidentally, takes precedence over national law in any dispute. Chapter 15 contains more information about the relationships between the various EU bodies and the principle of "comitology".

At this first meeting of the WP, there was some discussion about the nature of the "guidelines" mentioned in the draft terms of reference. There was a feeling, shared by many in Eurostat, that legal regulations would force the imposition of detailed rules which might be too complex and onerous. It could be that most technical issues could be dealt with by means of Guidelines, but these may need to be backed up by a legal regulation. On the other hand, it was pointed out that some countries could find that the authority of a regulation may turn out to be a helpful means of getting changes made which might otherwise be resisted by the national government, such as where certain items (e.g. alcohol or tobacco) have been omitted from the national CPI for more or less political reasons.

This issue was by no means resolved at the first meeting, but it was at least identified as a priority topic. This was the first big question posed by the WP and discussed at length in Task Force 1 (TF1)—see Chapter 3.3.1.

This important decision cleared the way for the WP to develop the HICP in ways independent of CPI models in member states, thereby creating a much-needed open-mindedness in those responsible for the development of the HICP. At the same time, however, it was agreed that divergences from methods used widely in national CPIs should be kept to the minimum possible.

The very important question of whether the aim should be to change all the national CPIs so that they are compiled in a harmonized way, or whether each country should compile a new harmonized CPI, was raised at the TF1 meeting (see Chapter 3.3.1). It was not known at that time whether the HICP would ever become recognised as an established statistical series in its own right. The future is always uncertain! This feeling affected several countries who felt that the HICP should be merely a variant of the national CPI, using harmonized methodology. Others, perhaps more convinced about the future of the HICP, felt that the national CPIs should be allowed to continue and that the HICP should from the start be a separate and independent index. It was clearly a vital issue. Most countries' CPIs had a long history and had their own advisory/supervisory body, and were jealously protected. It was sometimes the case that the national CPI featured in government legislation, such as the indexation of tax thresholds or of pensions, and sometimes used in private or public contracts as escalation clauses. They didn't want any interference in this model. Significant changes to the national CPI methodology would almost certainly bring about discontinuities in the index, and, at worst, invalidate existing laws and contracts. Some experts (but not usually the NSIs themselves) favoured replacing the national CPIs with a harmonized index, despite the above problems, on the grounds that confusion would be sown by having two separate indices measuring more or less the same phenomenon. Others—including Eurostat itself—felt that the Commission did not have the authority to force member states to abandon their national indices, and a brand new harmonized CPI would therefore have to be created.

In the end, it was agreed that the HICP should from the start be a new index, separate from any of the national CPIs. This opinion was recommended to the SPC, which also accepted it. The Council Regulation[1] which was published later (October 1995) made it clear in Article 2 that the name of the harmonized index was to be the "Harmonized Index of Consumer Prices". In addition, one of the paragraphs in the preamble said "*Whereas comparable indices of consumer prices* [i.e. the HICP] *may be produced instead of or in addition to similar indices of consumer prices already produced or to be produced in future by Member States...*"

But there was still some argument about the method of constructing the harmonized index. One of the early thoughts seemed sensible: why not compile an inventory of the various features of national CPIs; see what they have in common, and make that the basis of the HICP? A counter-argument was that many of the national CPIs were of the "compensation index" type, whereas the new index would not be; it would be a macroeconomic index. So the inventory idea was dropped.

On the topic of "practicability", Eurostat said that the rules would need to take account of the likelihood that some required changes may take time for a country to implement. Equally, the cost to countries of each change which they were required to make must always be taken into account.

Concerning uses of the new index, it seemed likely (because of the Maastricht specification) that the main purpose of the HICP would be a tool for the measurement of inflation at the macroeconomic level, but other uses might emerge, such as a tool for indexation (taxes, social security benefits, contracts etc.) or for wage bargaining. In the latter context, it was mentioned that a recent Council Regulation[2] had referred to the plan for Eurostat to begin work on harmonizing CPIs in order to fulfil the needs for calculating the annual adjustments to the salaries of EU staff, which were (and still are) based on an average of the real (i.e. after taking account of inflation) salary changes of civil servants in member states.

The draft terms of reference referred to a "pan-European CPI", hereafter referred to as the EICP (European Index of Consumer Prices). At this stage, the future key use of the MUICP (Monetary Union Index of Consumer Prices) as the key indicator for determining the ECB's interest

[1] Council Regulation 2494/95, 23 October 1995.

[2] Council Regulation 3830/91,19 December1991.

rate policy was not clearly foreseen. But it did seem clear that the EICP would be a highly desirable tool for comparing inflation in the EU with that in other major countries or blocs, such as the USA (see Chapter 13), even if the various international indices were not harmonized.

2.3 Establishment of Task Forces

The meeting discussed the proposed creation of a number of specialist Task Forces (TFs) which would help to speed up progress on harmonization by studying particular topics and preparing draft regulations for consideration by the full WP. It was emphasised by Eurostat that the TF discussions would have to be monolingual, as it would be too costly to organise interpreted meetings. Monolingual meetings could also be held in member states, not necessarily in Luxembourg. After discussion, the following list of Task Forces was proposed:

- *TF1*: Purpose of the HICP.
- *TF2*: A wide-ranging TF charged with defining consumption (what it is and whose consumption is to be covered); and details concerning the specifications of the future HICP.
- *TF3*: Micro-Indices—i.e. the definition and computation of elementary aggregate indices.
- *TF4*: Quality adjustment.
- *TF5*: Sampling.
- *TF6*: Operational issues.
- *TF7*: Weights.
- *TF8*: Accuracy and bias.

Volunteers were requested from delegates to join these Task Forces, especially TF1 and TF2 which were regarded as the highest priority. It was expected that some, if not most, of the TF papers would be written by delegates rather than by Eurostat, and indeed this was the case.

Later, the WP agreed the following mandates for each of the TFs:

- *TF1*: *"To establish the primary purposes that harmonized indices will be required to serve, and explain how these are relevant to the definition of the index".*

TF2: *"To determine the scope and publication requirements of harmonized CPIs in the light of their primary purposes, and make proposals for the treatment of housing costs".*

In fact as time went on the mandate of TF2 was progressively widened, so that it eventually became effectively a pre-meeting of the main WP, especially for the task of drafting regulations.

TF3: *"To propose guidelines for the combination of prices into elementary aggregates".*
TF4: *"To review the problem of quality adjustment".*
TF5: *"To propose guidelines on sample size and design".*
TF6: *"To propose guidelines on aspects of operational design and practice".*
TF7: *"To consider what guidelines would be required with regard to weighting; identify issues, and discuss relations with plans for harmonizing Household Budget Surveys".*
TF8: *"To determine the potential for bias within "guidelines" and suggest criteria of requisite strictness, balancing cost with comparability necessary to limit bias to appropriate levels".*

In fact this TF was never created.

2.4 Topics of Work

The full list of topics for examination by the TFs and WP were agreed as follows. They were divided into three headings:

A. The scope of the index and the purposes it serves

1. Formulate the purposes of the index (and see below)
2. Define consumption:
    2.1. Acquisition, Payment or Use
    2.2. Factor cost or market value
    2.3. Include or exclude second-hand items?
    2.4. Treatment of insurance and other financial services
    2.5. Include or exclude benefits in kind and own consumption?
    2.6. Exclusion of items that are difficult or impossible to quantify

- 2.7. Include or exclude interest on consumer credit and housing finance?
- 2.8. Include or exclude holidays abroad?

3. Specify whose consumption:
   - 3.1. All income groups?
   - 3.2. Foreign tourists?
   - 3.3. Non-profit organisations and institutional households?
   - 3.4. Business purchases of consumer goods and services?
4. Propose the harmonized indices to be computed:
   - 4.1. What sub-indices for major expenditure groups will be required?
   - 4.2. Will a sub-index for tradeables be required?
   - 4.3. Will a European-wide weighted index (and sub-indices) be required?
   - 4.4. Will an aggregate European-wide index (and sub-indices) be required?
5. Period or point of time estimates (and does it matter?)
6. Revisability
7. Frequency of publication

B. Elementary Aggregates (price indices for basic headings):

1. Combining prices without weights
2. The treatment of seasonal items
3. The treatment of missing observations
4. Substitution of new products
   - 4.1. When and how to make explicit quality adjustments
   - 4.2. How to compute when no explicit quality adjustment is made: impute a previous price using price movements of other items or compute price relative to superseded item?
5. The treatment of sales, discounts, package-size changes, free delivery etc.
6. Sample size and frequency of price collection (i.e. sampling in commodity space, geographical space, outlet space and time)

C. Operational design and practice:

1. Methods of price collection
   - 1.1. By post, telephone, visit, or electronically
   - 1.2. Training and experience of price collectors

2. Precision of specifications versus the degree of collector discretion in item selection
3. Outlet selection and replacement criteria
4. Item selection and replacement criteria
5. Validation and correction of price reposts
6. Quality Assurance
7. Overall control
   7.1. EC/National Advisory Committee
   7.2. Updating guidelines or methods
   7.3. Audits

D. Weighting:

1. Frequency of re-weighting
2. Need re-weighting be synchronised between countries?
3. Might re-weighting of major groups be more frequent than re-weighting within them?
4. The quality and nature of the data used for weighting:
   4.1. Family Budget Survey data
   4.2. Other data

Regarding (A) above, the following categorization of users was listed:

European Commission DG2 (economics).
European Commission DG9 (staff remuneration).
International organisations.
Central Banks.
National governments (esp. EC).
National organisations.
Economic analysts.

TF1 was clearly going to have to be an urgent meeting, and indeed it met for the first and only time barely a month after the WP meeting, on 20 July 1993. Part of its report to the full WP is given in Chapter 3.3.1.

The representative of the Committee of Governors of Central Banks took the opportunity to set out the probable statistical requirements of the European Monetary Institute and its successor the European Central Bank. He said that the primary objective of harmonizing national CPIs was to measure inflation in the member states by a uniform yardstick.

This was not only for the purposes of convergence criteria as set out in the Maastricht Treaty, but also to allow the monetary authorities to assess the extent to which they were achieving their primary objective of maintaining price stability: the harmonization of CPIs was a prerequisite for this purpose. The Governors Committee's preference would be to have the new harmonized index replacing the national CPIs.

On technical issues, the representative said that it would be important to have harmonized definitions for the products included in the basket, and that the basket should not include interest, which was the cost of money. He also felt that the whole population should be covered by the new index, unlike some national CPIs which excluded certain elements of the population. Finally, he stressed that the new index should be produced monthly (as indeed were almost all existing national CPIs in the EC).

One of the participants at the meeting was responsible for Eurostat's work on Household Budget Surveys (HBS). She reported that considerable progress had been made in recent years in harmonizing the EU HBSs, which were now conducted every five years and were based on the consumption concept. All countries would conduct an HBS in 1993/94. These surveys were vital in providing weights for CPI expenditure baskets.

2.5 Summary of Meeting

A further topic discussed at the meeting concerned the possibility of establishing a permanent Advisory Board for the HICP, along the lines of similar CPI advisory boards which existed in many member states (see Chapter 15.4).

In summary, the chairman felt that the meeting had met its objectives as set out in the agenda, and in particular:

- Revised terms of reference for the WP would be provided for the next meeting of the SPC to approve;
- The TF approach had been endorsed, with priority being given to establishing the primary purposes of the harmonized CPIs;
- The list of technical topics had been amended and approved. It would form the basis of the programme of development.

It is worth noting that at this stage, as is apparent from the remarks made at the first WP meeting and before, no decision had been taken about whether national CPIs should be changed in such a way that they would become comparable, or whether a brand new harmonized CPI would be invented. Phrases such as "harmonizing national CPIs" implied the former, and the use of such phrases should have been avoided so as not to pre-judge the outcome of this vital decision.

The WP's draft terms of reference, proposed to the SPC at its meeting in December 1991, were duly amended. They were proposed to the SPC for approval at its meeting in November 1993, and approval was duly given. The re-drafted and expanded terms of reference were as follows:

> *The mandate of the Working Party is to draft guidelines for the construction of harmonised national consumer price indices suitable for inclusion in a legal instrument. It should also make proposals for the construction of a Community - wide index based on the harmonised CPIs. In seeking to meet its mandate the Working Party should have due regard to the primary purposes of the harmonised CPIs which are to provide comparisons of inflation in the macro-economic and international context. As required under the Treaty on European Union it should aim to provide comparable measures of inflation taking into account differences in national definitions. The Working Party should seek to base its recommendations on the best of current practices allowing for precedent and legal and institutional circumstances existing in member states. Proposals should be practicable for all member states and should involve minimum cost consistent with the required accuracy of the indices which the Working Party should attempt to establish on the basis of their many uses. The Working Party may delegate part of its work to sub-groups or task forces where this is likely to lead to a more rapid conclusion. The Working Party will report regularly to the Statistical Programme Committee and to the Committee on Monetary, Financial and Balance of Payments Statistics on the progress of the project and will consult with relevant Commission working parties and committees.*

(A minor point worth mentioning is the spelling of "harmonised" in the terms of reference. This contradicted an earlier decision that the word should be spelled with a "z" rather than "s"! The forthcoming Framework Regulation (Chapter 3) reverted to the "z"!).

The next chapter (Chapter 3) examines the early work of the Working Party and its Task Forces, leading up to the completion of the Framework Regulation, which was adopted by the Council in October 1995.

After the WP had begun to have 2-day meetings, we would have dinner together at a Luxembourg restaurant on the first evening. These were always pleasant social occasions when we could get to know each other better, and I am convinced this helped us to discuss technical issues at the official meetings with more understanding and rapport. I noted this coming together in the Preface.

CHAPTER 3

Guiding Principles: Framework Regulation

3.1 Introduction

CPIs are often used as multi-purpose indices. Very often, national CPIs began life as indicators of the change in the cost of living of working people. For example, the UK Retail Prices Index (RPI) was started in 1947 in order to provide a basis on which the wages of working people could be, if not indexed, then at least linked in some way. It was not therefore surprising that the RPI population coverage excluded those households at the upper end of the income range, and also pensioner households (who were assumed not to be wage-earners). This coverage still applies, with some relatively minor changes, at the time of writing (2020).

CPIs are often used by governments to automatically adjust levels of social benefits such as pensions, unemployment benefit and so on. They can also be used to update thresholds for income tax and other taxes.

In the private sector, CPIs are used not only as a point of reference for wage negotiations, but also in commercial contracts, particularly those covering a long period. CPIs used in these ways are sometimes referred to as "uprating indices" or "compensation indices".

The HICP falls into the category of a "pure price index", measuring average price change on the basis of the changed expenditure of maintaining the consumption pattern of households and the composition of the consumer population in the base or reference period. "Pure" means

J. Astin, *Measuring EU Inflation*,
https://doi.org/10.1007/978-3-030-68806-6_3

that, strictly speaking, only changes in prices are reflected in the measure between the current and the base or reference period. The HICP is not a "cost of living" index (COLI). That means that it is not a measure of the change in the minimum cost of achieving the same "standard of living" or "constant utility" (whatever that means in practice) from two different consumption patterns realised in the two periods compared, and where factors other than pure price changes may enter the index.

Most countries' national CPIs began clearly as household-based indices. Governments and economists needed to know how the household sector was behaving in response to persistent inflationary tendencies. This began in the early part of the twentieth century. As these CPIs developed, they became useful to trade unions and employers in relation to negotiating wage and salary increases.

It was only in the later years of the twentieth century that inflation measures took on a new role in managing the economy at the widest level. Inflation targets were being set in response to the needs of monetary policy management, and it became quickly apparent that the traditional "uprating" CPIs were not always appropriate. In economics, CPIs (often adjusted in various ways) are used to deflate monetary measures in the national accounts, in particular the major aggregates such as Gross Domestic Product (GDP). They are also increasingly used by central banks as a tool for monitoring the general level of inflation, in order to inform the process of setting interest rates and monitoring price stability. CPIs with this type of usage are often referred to as "macroeconomic" indices.

As outlined in Chapter 1, the HICP arose out of the requirement of the Maastricht Treaty. Its main aim lay clearly in the second of the uses mentioned above: its potential use as an indicator of the general level of inflation in the member states of the EC (for the convergence criteria) and of the future euro area (for the setting of the euro area interest rate by the future European Central Bank).

The main aims of the HICP were clearly macroeconomic: the mechanics for setting the interest rate for the euro area countries by the future European Central Bank should not include mortgage interest nor indeed any other form of interest payments.

Furthermore, the WP decided early on to exclude the value of own-account production from the HICP. This is a method used in some countries (particularly those with developing economies) where a significant amount of economic activity is carried on by and for the household.

Chief among these activities are of course agriculture, particularly the production of food for the farmer's household. It also covers the household production of clothing and certain other goods and services. In EU member states the value of "own production" was always likely to be a relatively small proportion of total production but it was nevertheless ruled out of the sphere of the HICP from the start.

One of the perennial and complex problems in defining the approach for a CPI is usually referred to as "acquisition, purpose or use". These somewhat arcane concepts were avoided in the draft versions of the Framework Regulation, but the phrase "goods and services available for purchase" perhaps implies that the underlying concept was to be "acquisition".

Let's look at the practical differences between "acquisition" and its two alternatives, "payment" and "use". "Acquisition" of a good relates to the transfer of legal ownership; physical acquisition upon payment for the good is not necessary (though this is what normally happens); it may be that a good is ordered and paid for but delivery is later. The acquisition of a service is not so clear; a simple service such as a haircut is usually "acquired" when the service is completed and payment is made. A ticket for a football match or concert is "acquired" usually on payment of the price, even though the service is not experienced until later.

The concept of "payment" is simpler, and payment and acquisition often occur simultaneously. Of course, one can argue that the timing of payments can differ substantially; cash is the most immediate form, but an online bank account can also be instant. Payment via a bank debit card is usually very fast but with a credit card the payers may be able to wait a month before having to pay it—and even longer if they don't pay each month's debt by the due date. Nevertheless, the payers know for sure that at some point they will have to effectively hand over the money, and one can reasonably define all of these methods as "payments"—and should enter the index in the month of the money transfer.

Finally, the concept of "use" is far more complex. I buy a car and pay the full price at a certain moment. Then I use the car for ten years. One can say that "consumption" takes place over a ten-year period. This would be a difficult concept to apply in a monthly CPI aimed at measuring current inflation, even though it is a concept much favoured by some economists.

The WP decided on the "acquisition" approach in general (but with some possible exceptions) and this underlies the wording in Article 4 of the Framework Regulation (see paragraph 3.3).

It should be remembered that at the early stages of the discussions, no final decision had yet been taken on whether the task was to harmonize existing national CPIs or to create a new harmonized index. In fact, this took place shortly before the Framework Regulation was finally adopted in October 1995. If the former, the changed national indices would still need to be able to serve the various purposes mentioned above, as well as satisfying the requirements of a macroeconomic tool for monitoring the general level of inflation. It was clear that some countries would find it difficult, if not impossible, to make significant changes to their national CPIs—as had been made clear in the 1974 Stadlbauer Report (see Chapter 1.2). On the other hand, some countries already published more than one CPI, such as regional CPIs or CPIs for different population groups such as pensioners. One country was about to start publishing its seventh CPI variant! But those countries which published only a single CPI were concerned that an additional index might create confusion and controversy in the minds of the public. If a new index were to be created, it would need to have a name that distinguished it very clearly from the national CPI. Other countries which had only one CPI would consider changing its CPI to the new harmonized index, provided, of course, that it was suitable.

3.2 Preparation for a Framework Regulation

Eurostat's original thoughts on the question of rules and regulations was that "guidelines" would be drafted on the various technical aspects of the HICP, and that these would probably be incorporated in a Council Regulation, to be adopted in good time before Stage 3 of EMU. But at quite an early stage of the discussions it became clear that this timetable was impracticable. Instead, the new strategy would be to move as fast as possible to a "framework" or "paving" regulation of the Council, which would set out the general aims and boundaries of the HICP. This would be followed by a series of technical implementing regulations, which would normally be regulations of the Commission rather than the Council.

However, in order to meet the timetable requirements for monetary union (see Chapter 4) it was realised that some form of harmonized CPIs would have to be available by early 1996: the first convergence report (see Chapter 4.4) had to be made in that year. So it was agreed that the first target would be to publish interim HICPs which would not be fully harmonized, but would be more comparable than the disparate national CPIs then available. These "Interim Indices of Consumer Prices" (IICPs) would be statutorily defined in the Framework Regulation.

The draft Framework Regulation was submitted to the Council in September 1995, and adopted the following month. The full name of the IICPs was defined as "Interim Indices of Consumer Prices for International Comparison". The IICPs were launched on 29 February 1996, and the first implementing regulation of the Commission (covering a range of technical topics) was adopted in September 1996. The first of a series of "convergence reports" was published—using the IICPs as the only source of relatively harmonized CPIs—in November 1996.

In a certain sense, the Framework Regulation was one of the easiest to draw up, since it contained relatively few controversial topics. Bear in mind that it contained little by way of detail, but simply outlined the broad approaches which the HICP would follow.

The first version of the draft Framework Regulation was discussed at the third meeting of the Working Party in February 1994. It bears little resemblance to the final version, and so is not discussed in detail here. It is worth mentioning, though, that the domestic concept for the scope of the HICP (Article 3—see below) was already proposed in the first draft. In addition, the first draft included an article on "sources" which is close to the wording of Article 7. Article 12, covering the matter of compliance, also found a place in the first draft.

The second version of the Framework Regulation was discussed by the Working Party at its fourth meeting in June 1994. Another vital article related to the frequency of the index: it was, of course, to be monthly. This affected only Ireland, which was at the time producing its national CPI only quarterly. The new draft also included an article on the abstruse subject of comitology—essentially, the legal procedures used for the process of adoption of EC legal acts. This topic is covered in some detail in Chapter 15.2.

By this time, the contents had been discussed on several occasions by TF2. This time, the word "imputed" was used explicitly in the article on Scope, saying "*The prices shall be actual prices and shall exclude imputed prices*". But this sentence was later dropped. And in fact, the concept of imputed rents was ruled out by the SPC much later, in 2000. A third draft also introduced a new and important wording on the matter of comparability, which was preserved in its essentials in Article 4 of the final version. Finally, and no doubt prompted by the approaching deadline for completion of the regulation, a new article was inserted, which eventually became Article 15 of the final version. This concerned the need for an official review of the operation of the regulation within two years of its entry into force. Though burdensome, this turned out to be a most effective tool for the management of the HICP.

Although the second draft was the final version discussed by the Working Party, a fourth version was prepared by Eurostat and sent to delegates in July 1994. Apart from some small details, this was the version that was submitted to the SPC for approval at its meeting in September 1994. The SPC approved the plan for a two-stage implementation of the HICPs but decided that some textual changes still needed to be made. These were subsequently passed on to Eurostat.

The draft regulation then had to pass through various stages of approval and adjustment by other bodies. These were:

The European Monetary Institute (March 1995);
The European Commission itself (effectively the Directorate-General for Economic and Financial Affairs) (April 1995);
The European Parliament (September 1995);
The Economic and Social Committee (September 1995).

This was followed by the final approval of the Council (October 1995), after which the text was published in the Official Journal as "Council Regulation (EC) No 2494/95 concerning harmonized indices of consumer prices".

The following sections explain the meanings of the various articles in the regulation. Later chapters discuss the individual technical topics for which rules were laid down in a number of technical implementing regulations.

3.3 Articles of the Framework Regulation

We now look at the Articles in the Framework Regulation, not in number order but in the categories of "Administrative" (Articles 5 and 10–15), "General Statistical" (Articles 1, 2 and 4) and "Technical" (Articles 3 and 6–9). The technical articles were all covered in more depth in the implementing regulations which followed the Framework Regulation and are dealt with in detail in Chapters 6–11.

3.3.1 "Administrative" Articles

Article 5. Timetable and Derogations

This is without doubt the most essential article, as without it there was no actual requirement to produce HICPs!

1. The measures necessary to achieve comparable indices of consumer prices shall be implemented in stages, as follows:

(a) Stage I:

By March 1996 at the latest, the Commission (Eurostat), shall, in collaboration with Member States, produce for the purposes of the report referred to in Article 109j of the Treaty ('convergence criteria') an interim set of indices of consumer prices for each Member State. These indices shall be based wholly on data underlying existing national consumer price indices, adjusted in particular as follows:

(i) to exclude owner-occupied housing;
(ii) to exclude health and educational services;
(iii) to exclude certain other items not covered or treated differently by a number of Member States.

(b) Stage II:

1. The HICP shall start with the index for January 1997. The common index reference period shall be the year 1996. The estimates of price changes for the twelve months prior to January 1997 and subsequent months shall be established on the basis of the indices for 1996.

2. Where necessary the Commission (Eurostat) may, at the request of a Member State and after consulting the EMI, grant derogations from the provisions of paragraph 1 not exceeding a period of one year where the Member State concerned has to make significant adjustments to its statistical system in order to fulfil its obligations under this Regulation.

3. The implementing measures for this Regulation which are necessary for ensuring the comparability of HICPs and for maintaining and improving their reliability and relevance shall be adopted, after consultation of the EMI, in accordance with the procedure laid down in Article 14.

Article 5 first sets out the principle of a staged introduction of the HICP, with the starting dates of each stage, and a hint of the name of the partially harmonized indices—the Interim Indices of Consumer Prices (IICP). It also refers to the groups of products which will be excluded from the IICPs: owner-occupied housing, health and education services, and certain other unspecified products.

Why were these particular exclusions selected? It was not an easy choice. The general argument was simple. We knew that there were very different approaches used in member states to deal with these major products in their national CPIs. It followed that if these products were excluded from the national CPIs, the resulting indices would be more comparable than not excluding them. We didn't know how much more comparable, but for sure more comparable. We did, however, know the weights which these products had in the national CPIs, so we were able to satisfy ourselves that the excluded products did not have such a large combined weight as to make the rump of the remaining indices so small as to be useless. In fact, on average, we found that the total weight of excluded products amounted to around 16% of the total weight when they were included. To put this another way round, we were able to say that the IICPs covered about 84% of all products in the national CPIs.

Of course, these exclusions were seen as only a temporary measure: the staging plan was due to bring them into the HICPs within a fairly short time. This was indeed achieved—with the exception of owner-occupied housing, which is still (2020) only "temporarily" excluded from the HICP—see Chapter 11.2.

Apart from the large product groups mentioned in this Article, which other products were temporarily excluded from the IICPs?

The national CPIs of some countries, at least in the early 1990s, had a tendency to exclude some items of "unhealthy" or "unwise" consumption. Examples of such exclusions are alcoholic drinks, tobacco products, narcotics, gambling, and prostitution. Sometimes the reasons for exclusion were not just that such products are "unhealthy" but also difficult to measure in practice. Another type of exclusion concerned products sold in the black-market ("hidden economy"), such as illegally imported cigarettes. These of course are also difficult to measure for CPI purposes.

It was felt from the start of discussion in the WP that, in principle at least, the HICP should include all products regardless of their nature. This was also the clear request of the CEIES—see Chapter 15.4. To have included all of the products referred to above right from the start would have clearly been challenging, and it was agreed that they should be introduced gradually into the HICP as resources and methods developed. But for the start of publication of the HICP, legal tobacco and alcohol consumption was covered. Narcotics, which are illegal in some or all countries, are still excluded as also is prostitution (partly at least from the practical point of view).

Paragraph 1(a) requires that the interim indices begin by March 1996 at the latest. This was a very tight timetable indeed, but it was managed. The first publication of the IICPs was on 29 February 1996—see Chapter 4 for more detail. Paragraph 1(b) requires that the HICPs be produced from January 1997—and this was also achieved: the first publication of the HICPs was in March 1997, and included the HICPs from January 1997. However, these first HICPs were still not fully harmonized. Paragraph 1(b) allowed for a full programme of progressive harmonization, which would be spread over a number of years. In fact during the period covered by this book (up to 2002) a total of 16 regulations and sets of guidelines had been adopted, and more were to follow in later years.

The phrase *"The estimates of price changes for the twelve months prior to January 1997 and subsequent months shall be established on the basis of the indices for 1996"* is not entirely clear. Which "indices" were intended? In fact, there was no choice: they had to be the IICPs, as there were no other relevant indices.

As mentioned in Chapter 2, it had been decided that most of the detailed technical topics would be handled in small "Task Forces" (TFs), comprising volunteer delegates from member states, meeting relatively frequently in monolingual (usually English) groups, either in Luxembourg or a host country. TF1 was charged with discussing the aim(s) of the HICP and making proposals to the Working Party. It was regarded as the top priority TF, and it met for the first and only time in Luxembourg just a month after the first WP meeting. It comprised six national delegates as well as participants from the EFTA secretariat, OECD, and the European Commission DG9 (Administration). A consultant for Eurostat, the late Professor Ralph Turvey (former Director of the Labour Information and Statistics Department at the International Labour Organisation (ILO) also attended and provided one of his first exceptional papers. He went on to do a great deal of fundamental clear thinking on many aspects of the HICP, and to whom I personally, and Eurostat generally, owe a great debt of gratitude.

TF1's remit (from the Working Party) was "*to establish the primary purposes that harmonized indices will be required to serve and explain how these are relevant to the definition of the index, particularly with regard to the choice between Acquisition, Payment or Use*".

The TF1 meeting discussed at some length the various uses of CPIs, grouping them into what they defined as "macroeconomic" and "microeconomic". The macroeconomic uses included:

- A general measure of inflation
- An indicator of economic performance
- A deflator of expenditure in the national accounts
- To provide international comparisons of inflation
- To measure the internal purchasing power of currencies.

Microeconomic uses included:

- Indexation of wages
- Indexation of state benefits
- As background to wage negotiations
- Indexation of tax levels or thresholds
- Indexation of rents
- Indexation of bonds
- Indexation of contracts.

TF1 considered that the harmonized index should be of the macroeconomic type, given that its main users were expected to be national governments, central banks and other institutions of the EC. The index should be designed primarily for the comparison of inflation between member states and between the EC as a whole and other countries or groups of countries.

The meeting was keen to make it clear that a CPI alone was insufficient to explain the entire inflationary situation in an economy. Other indicators, including producer price indices, the GDP deflator and price indices relating to tradeable goods and services were also necessary. Thus, a CPI could not even in principle be regarded as an overall indicator of inflation; it was a component indicator, and, as such, the harmonized CPI should attempt to cover only that aspect of inflation impacting directly on households.

Its underlying concept was later defined as "household final monetary consumption expenditure" (HFMCE). This decision was to become crucial in areas such as owner-occupied housing, where the concept would disallow the inclusion of imputed rents. It also allowed a useful link to the then new European System of Accounts (ESA 1995).[1]

TF1 felt that since inflation was essentially a monetary phenomenon, the index should be restricted to those goods and services where actual payments were involved, and exclude prices that were not directly paid by households. The TF agreed that the index should not include imputations of prices for such items as own account production and owner-occupied housing. This principle would not, however, rule out the "exceptional" use of proxy prices in transactions where an actual price was unavailable, for example where a retail outlet is temporarily closed.

A report from this sole meeting of TF1 was given to the full WP, which discussed it at its second meeting in November 1993. The report included the following:

> *The primary purposes of harmonized CPIs should be macro-economic as distinct from micro-economic. They should facilitate the comparison of inflation between Member States and between the EC as a whole and non-EC countries. However, it should be appreciated that inflation is not a simple concept captured by a single measure and the harmonized indices should be seen in a broader context. They should not attempt to capture the total*

[1] Council Regulation (EC) No. 2223/96, 1996.

picture but only that part of inflation which impacts on private households in the countries of the Community. The indices should be indices of consumer prices only and should relate to prices that are actually paid by households. These are prices which involve a transaction, that is a sale at an agreed price for a specific quantity of goods or services. The consequence of this requirement for the treatment of specific components of consumption has to be determined in another task force but the implication is that the imputation of prices for consumption that does not involve households in direct payments would be inappropriate. The index should measure changes in actual prices, not hypothetical ones.

The WP made the important decision that steps should be taken to create a new, harmonized CPI which would be named in such a way that it would be clearly distinguishable in all member states from their national CPI. It would also be vital to have public explanations available of the differences—and their implications for usage—between the harmonized and national indices. Member states would be free to choose whether the new index would be published in parallel to their national CPI(s) or to adopt it as their own national CPI. If the new index was not significantly different from the national index, a member state should not be required to produce it. (However, this possibility later came to be seen as impracticable, and was dropped.)

Some countries said that they felt that a new harmonized index would be likely to become the most important of their CPIs.

The Framework Regulation introduced the following names:

Firstly, and most importantly, the HICP itself (Harmonized Index of Consumer Prices). Following on from this, there are the EICP (European Index of Consumer Prices) and the MUICP (Monetary Union Index of Consumer Prices).

There is a story behind the choice of HICP for the new harmonized index. As we have seen, the WP insisted that its name should be easily distinguishable from any existing national CPIs. This gave rise to a surprisingly long list of candidate names. Leading contenders were:

Consumer Price Index—Harmonized
European Consumer Inflation Index
European Standard Inflation Index
European Standard Price Index
Harmonized Consumer Price Index

Harmonized Consumer Inflation Index
European Inflation Index.

The WP settled on "Harmonized Consumer Price Index", or HCPI for short. In fact, up to this point all the documents had the reference "HCPI/xx" in anticipation of this decision—it seemed rather obvious, after all.

But of course this was not the end of the story. The WP could only advise: decisions are taken higher in the command chain. And when the draft Framework Regulation reached the Council of Ministers (represented largely by senior staff from the National Statistical Institutes (NSIs)), the clinching argument came from one national head of statistics who maintained that since his country's national CPI was called "CPI" it would cause confusion in the minds of the public to have a second index called "HCPI". He proposed the alternative of "HICP" (Harmonized Index of Consumer Prices")—and this was rather grudgingly accepted by the other national delegates—some of whom thought (correctly, as it turned out) that it would be jokingly referred to in the press as the "HICCUP"! But the name soon became fairly well known, and a few years later, the compilers of the questions in the popular UK TV quiz "University Challenge" felt it reasonable to ask the question "What do the initials HICP stand for?". Sadly, not one of the eight students knew.

The HICP is thus the official name given to the harmonized CPI produced by each member state, and in this book I shall normally use the HICP name throughout, even though this name was not used in the discussions until late in 1995. But each country can, if it so wishes, choose a different name for the HICP to be used domestically. Thus, the UK in December 2003 changed the name of its HICP to CPI, which then became the official measure for the inflation target of 2%. Nevertheless, the UK CPI is known in the international context as the HICP.

Articles 10 and 11. Transmission and Publication of HICPs

(a) **Timing of Transmission and Publication**

An issue that caused some degree of controversy was not statistical but administrative. It centred on the timetable for publication of the monthly figures.

In developed countries, consumer price indices are one of the relatively few national statistics whose publication dates are noted in the financial markets and are eagerly awaited. They are often described as "market-moving" statistics. Consumer price inflation, employment and unemployment, GDP, international trade flows, oil prices: the financial markets are geared up to ensure that they are fully alert to such announcements, and the press who report them are keenly aware that even a few seconds' advantage can reap large benefits to certain markets.

For these reasons, considerable care had to be taken by NSIs when planning the timing and the manner of release of such statistics. This was of course appreciated by the WP from the start, and discussions took place to ensure that the dates of transmission of the national HICPs to Eurostat, and the dates of publication by both member states and Eurostat, were carefully planned and controlled.

(b) **Dates of Transmission from Member States to Eurostat**

Before the harmonization project began, there was no co-ordination on publication dates among the EC member states. Each country normally wished to publish its results as early as possible—consistent with the amount of time needed to carry out the checking of results and computation of the various indices, together with the appropriate commentary. As a result, there was considerable dispersion of publication dates, so that achieving a common transmission date from the member states to Eurostat was far from easy. Some arbitration was clearly going to be needed.

Moreover, it was clear that to have the acceptance of the European economists' community—the central banks in particular—there would have to be a high degree of certainty about the publication schedule. This in turn implied that the member states would have to provide Eurostat (who would be responsible for the monthly publication) with the monthly data on a pre-determined timetable. This carried important implications for the organisation of work within each national statistics institute, and hence became an important topic in the WP. Deadlines would have to be set, and they would need to take into account not only of the time taken in compiling the indices and checking them thoroughly, as well as allowing for the vagaries of the calendar (weekends and public holidays in particular). In the end, agreement was reached on these issues, and indeed over the years, gradual improvements in timeliness would be made.

The critical target was the number of days between the month of data collection and the date of transmission to Eurostat. This was agreed as being 30 days. This made it necessary for some countries to adjust their collection dates or shorten the time allowed for the checking and computation periods.

The initial transmission deadline was set out in Article 10 of the Framework Regulation:

> ***Article 10 Transmission of results***
> *Member States shall transmit the HICPs to the Commission (Eurostat) within a period which shall not exceed thirty days from the end of the calendar month to which the indices relate.*

An apparently simple Article, but one which was very slow in its birth.

The problem was essentially fear of the unknown. At this early stage of the HICP process, national experts were naturally wary of the detailed rules which might follow. According to EC rules, regulations had to be adopted by qualified majority voting, implying that changes strongly opposed by a weighted minority of countries could still be adopted. (Further details on the voting procedures are given in Chapter 15.2). Clearly, it would be difficult, if not impossible, to impose deadlines on member states which were shorter than those they already had for their national CPIs—and in fact, the range was quite wide, with some countries publishing their national CPI only a few days after the end of the index month, while others took much longer. In fact, one of the benefits of the harmonization process was the opportunity that delegate meetings offered for national CPI experts to compare their own methods with their colleagues in other countries. No doubt some countries were impressed by the relative speed of publication in other countries—and took steps to improve their own performance.

The 30 days (NB not working days!) was a compromise, but it was in fact not a difficult target for most countries.

Later discussions in the WP had to refine this requirement to some extent, bearing in mind the fact that weekend and public holidays may intervene in some months. Over the years, gradual changes were made to the deadline to speed up the process. By 2001 the average period between the end of the calendar month to which the HICP relates and the transmission of results from member states to Eurostat had been halved to slightly less than 15 days in all months except December and January when it was slightly longer. But 30 days remained the legal maximum until 2016[2] when it was reduced to 15 days (20 for the January index).

Individual member states were not required legally to publish their HICPs, but it was clearly going to be necessary to ensure that they did not publish their own national data before they were published in the complete set by Eurostat. Late each year Eurostat and the member states would agree on the planned transmission and release dates for the year ahead.

(c) **Dates of Publication by Eurostat**

There was no point in requiring member states to adhere to a transmission deadline unless Eurostat, on its part, made efforts to aggregate the data and publish the results with its own tight deadline. Once the transmission deadline had passed, and all the national data were in Eurostat's hands, Eurostat needed to allow time for uploading all the data into the complex suite of computer programs, carrying out final checks on consistency etc., performing all the necessary country aggregation tasks, checking once again the results, and writing a commentary for publication.

Again, there was a deadline set out in the Framework Regulation:

> ***Article 11 Publication***
> *The HICP, the EICP, the MUICP and corresponding subindices for a set of categories within those referred to in Article 9, selected by the procedure laid down in Article 14, shall be published by the Commission (Eurostat) within a period which shall not exceed five working days from the end of the period referred to in Article 10.*

Eurostat too had to take a deep breath on this, and agreement on five working days was reached. Note in this case it was "working days", unlike the 30 "days" in Article 10. This was because if the latest transmission date was a Friday, and only five days were allowed for Eurostat to carry out its checks, calculations and preparation of the News Release, this would mean only three working days, which would have been insufficient. With

[2] Council Regulation 2016/792, 11 May 2016.

five working days, this allowed Eurostat a full week to do whatever was necessary to prepare for publication.

By 2001 the five working days deadline had been more than halved: the average delay between receipt from the member states and publication by Eurostat had fallen to just two working days.

Eurostat also publishes a pre-announced schedule of future publication dates.

The ten EU "candidate" countries (see Chapter 14.1) began their monthly data transmissions to Eurostat at the start of 2002, initially with deadlines close to the 30-day schedule in the Framework Regulation. By the end of the year, the target was almost halved, so that they were virtually in line with existing member states.

(d) **Flash Estimates**

It was mentioned above that the HICP was from the start a "market-moving" statistic, eagerly awaited by financial agencies (especially the ECB), economic analysts and the media. It was a common practice for economic journalists to produce their own short-term forecasts of the latest inflation rates, and there was a certain amount of pressure on Eurostat to help make these forecasts more reliable. It didn't take long for demand to increase and to call for earlier estimates of the monthly data. The imminent commencement of the changeover to the euro currency (1 January 2002) added an additional impetus to the demand—especially for Eurozone countries. Nowhere was this greater than in Germany, where the National Statistical Institute (NSI) had begun in July 2000 to publish "nowcasts" or short-term forecasts of its own HICP some days in advance of its formal publication. At about the same time, some Italian regions began to publish similar types of nowcast for Italy.

These events of course came to the attention of Eurostat, which started to look at the possibilities of producing similar types of nowcast for the HICP aggregates, in particular the MUICP. It was clearly unsatisfactory to have a major element of the MUICP (i.e. the German and Italian elements) publicly estimating their HICPs a significant time before the publication of the official figures. After all, their combined weights were around one half of the total MUICP, and it would be relatively easy for analysts to calculate a fairly accurate forecast of the coming monthly

MUICP. The prospect of Eurostat itself publishing nowcasts for the entire MUICP was now being considered.

After many internal discussions, a plan was made to begin producing formal MUICP nowcasts on a trial basis, using the results of a model based on data from Germany and Italy, supplemented by up-to-date information on the important energy sector. (The latter data were collected under EC legislation and covered the prices of fuels for transport and domestic heating gas oil.) The test results were presented to the WP at its meeting in October 2000. Eurostat proposed to provide nowcasts to the ECB and DG2 (Commission Directorate for Economic and Financial Affairs), for a trial period before making a final decision to publish the data. These Eurostat nowcasts would in future be known as "flash estimates".

The trial period began in May 2001 and was regarded as successful enough to warrant regular publication by Eurostat. The first of the regular publications of the flash estimates was made on 5 November 2001. They related solely to the Euro area, i.e. estimates of the MUICP. The main text of that first publication ran as follows:

> *Eurostat publishes today, for the first time, flash estimates for the Monetary Union Index of Consumer Prices (MUICP). From this month onwards, these flash estimates will be published around the end of the reference month, i.e. between two and three weeks before the complete MUICP results are available. Eurostat seeks thereby to provide users with advance information about likely inflation movements.*
>
> *To compute the MUICP flash estimates, Eurostat uses early price information relating to the reference month issued at present by Germany, Italy, and if available, by other Member States, as well as early information about energy prices. The estimation procedure uses regression and time series modelling to combine historical information with information on recent price developments to a total index for the euro-zone. No detailed breakdown is available. The estimation model is flexible with respect to available data but requires some information about price developments in the reference month. In fact, early information accounts for more than 50% of the weight for the MUICP. Simulations done by Eurostat on real data show that the mean absolute error for the period between April 1999 and September 2001 is 0.04 percentage points for the annual rate for the euro-zone (18 times agreeing precisely, 11 times 0.1 index point deviation, and once 0.2). Changes in the trend of the*

inflation rate (turning points) are captured correctly except for August and September 1999, August 2000, and August 2001 where the flash estimate did not capture the turning point due to rounding effects. The differences are, with one exception, within the rounding margin of 0.1 percentage point and the estimated trend went in no single case in the opposite direction of the actual trend. This performance appears acceptable to Eurostat for a flash estimate. Nevertheless, structural changes may affect future performance. Such changes will become evident only when actual figures are available for all Member States. The model is, therefore, subject to regular maintenance and may be adjusted at any time to allow for changes identified in its underlying assumptions.

The flash estimates for the euro area are still published by Eurostat every month.

Compliance Monitoring
Article 12. Comparability of data

Member States shall provide the Commission (Eurostat) at its request with information, inter alia that collected pursuant to Article 6, at the level of detail necessary to evaluate compliance with the comparability requirements and the quality of the HICPs.

This is perhaps a rather strange title for an Article which is not so much about comparability—a technical issue—but about the powers given to Eurostat to monitor and indeed inspect the preparation of the HICPs in member states. This process later became known as "compliance monitoring"—in other words, checking to see to what extent member states are actually complying with the rules which they are expected to follow. This activity is in fact one of the main functions of the European Commission, and similar articles appear in many regulations.

The reference to Article 6 demonstrates that Eurostat intended to arm itself with strong teeth, by allowing the inspection of the basic data underlying the construction of the HICP, and not only its calculation procedures. Moreover, the reference to "quality" as well as to "comparability" suggested that Eurostat would not be content merely to achieve comparability at the expense of data accuracy and reliability.

Chapter 12 is concerned with the operation of this Article in the development of Eurostat's compliance monitoring methods.

Funding for the HICP

Article 13 Funding
The implementing measures for this Regulation shall be adopted taking the greatest account of the cost-effectiveness and on condition that no major additional resources are needed in a Member State, unless the Commission (Eurostat) bears two-thirds of the additional costs until the end of the second year of implementation of those measures.

At the stage of drafting the Framework Regulation, neither Eurostat nor the member states had the slightest idea of what extra costs might be faced by member states in creating and maintaining the HICP. Clearly, it was a worry to countries, none of which had any planned resources for this work. Hence this crucial Article. It should be appreciated that Eurostat also did not have any explicit advance budgeting for the HICP project, and therefore this Article was a real hostage to fortune. If the costs in member states were high, and Eurostat could not provide the bulk of the funding, the project would be slowed, if not halted. Chapter 15.5 gives more detail on how the funding arrangements worked. Suffice it to say here that Eurostat, during the first six years, provided funds to member states totalling around 6m euro. And the implementation of the HICP went ahead exactly on schedule.

Procedure (Article 14)

Article 14, which concerns the various procedures to be applied in the formal adoption of proposed Regulations, is administratively most important. Although the word usually used to describe these procedures ("comitology") is not used in the Article itself (it is an informal word) the topic is examined further in Chapter 15.2.

Review

Article 15
After consulting the Committee, the Commission (Eurostat) shall, within two years of the date of entry into force of this Regulation and again within two years thereafter, submit a report to the Council on the HICPs established pursuant to this Regulation and in particular on their reliability and compliance with the comparability requirements.

In those reports, the Commission shall state its views on the operation of the procedure described in Article 14 and shall propose any amendments it considers appropriate.

Article 15 follows another standard Commission practice. The Commission is responsible for proposing legislation and, after its adoption, ensuring that member states comply with it. Reports on compliance are not the property of Eurostat but must be provided to the Council which, after all, is the responsible authority for the legislation in the first place. Note that the Commission (normally this would be represented by Eurostat) must also provide its own comments on the administrative procedure outlined in Article 15 and, if it appears not to be working as intended, propose changes. (None were proposed).

Chapter 15.7 covers the regular reports from the Commission to the Council, which are publicly accessible in the 2001 Compendium (see Chapter 15.8).

3.3.2 General Statistical Articles

Article 1 Aim of the HICP
The aim of this Regulation is to establish the statistical bases necessary for arriving at the calculation of comparable indices of consumer prices at Community level.

This is perhaps the most important Article in the regulation. The keyword here is **"comparable"**. This first occurs in the Maastricht Treaty itself, which contains the phrase "*Inflation shall be measured by means of the consumer price index on a comparable basis*". We shall find this reference to comparability cropping up unceasingly in the course of the following chapters.

Article 2 Definitions
For the purposes of this Regulation, the following definitions shall apply:

(a) Harmonized index of consumer prices (HICP): the comparable index of consumer prices produced by each Member State;

(b) European index of consumer prices (EICP): the consumer price index produced for the Community by the Commission (Eurostat), based on the HICPs of Member States;

(c) Monetary Union index of consumer prices (MUICP): the consumer price index produced in the context of Economic and Monetary Union by the Commission (Eurostat) based on the HICPs of Member States without a derogation under Article 109k of the Treaty, as long as such derogations exist.

This is a particularly significant Article because for the first time the name of the harmonized index was given: the HICP. This was approved only shortly before adoption when the draft regulation was discussed by the Council (see Sect. 3.2).

Most legal acts need to have an article explaining some of the words or phrases used in the text. This is often not as easy as it may seem at first sight. Where does one draw the line? (see Chapter 15.3). Clearly, a word in common use, which is being used in its normal sense, should not need to be defined. For example, in the present context, the word "consumer" is used in its normal sense. Anyone in doubt as to its meaning need only look it up in a dictionary. At the other end of the scale there may be some words in the text which are highly specialised—indeed, they may have been invented specifically for that particular subject. Somewhere in between these two extremes are technical or semi-technical words for which a definition may help in understanding the legal act. In fact, there are no such technical words in the Framework Regulation, but just a few titles, as explained below. The word "derogation" occurs in Article 2, but it is assumed that the reader of an EC regulation will know what this means. If not, it is in most good dictionaries. It is an important word, however, and for those readers who do not know it, I will quote a dictionary definition:

> *In terms of EU legislation, a derogation can.. imply that a member state delays the implementation of an element of an EU Regulation into their legal system over a given timescale, such as five years...*

See Chapter 12 for information on derogation procedure.

Later, more technical regulations on the HICP do include definitions of technical terms, for example *"weighting reference period"*. Note that this book contains its own Glossary at the end.

The MUICP—Monetary Union Index of Consumer Prices—rapidly achieved prominence after the European Central Bank announced in 1998 that this would in future be the main index used by the Bank to monitor the level of inflation in the forthcoming Monetary Union. One could say that by this point the HICP had reached maturity.

Sharp-eyed readers may have already noted the spelling of "harmonization" and the other forms of this word used in this book. The use of the letter "z" rather than "s" was indeed controversial. The earliest documents tended to use "s", but in preparation for the Framework

Regulation it was necessary to make certain of the correct spelling. Dictionary research yielded the information that the "s" variant was American usage, while the "z" variant was English. Given that the UK, and not the USA, was a member of the European Communities, it was felt that the English version should be the one to be used in official documents, and it is indeed used in the Framework Regulation. However, this rule seems to have been forgotten over time, and the "s" variant is often to be found in later regulations and other EC/EU documents.

Article 4 Comparability
HICPs shall be considered to be comparable if they reflect only differences in price changes or consumption patterns between countries.

HICPs which differ on account of differences in the concepts, methods or practices used in their definition and compilation shall not be considered comparable.

The Commission (Eurostat), shall adopt rules to be followed to ensure the comparability of HICPs under the procedure laid down in Article 14.

This Article builds on the mention of the word "comparable" in Article 1. The concept of comparability lies at the heart of the HICP. The Maastricht Treaty requires that *"inflation shall be measured by means of the consumer price index on a* ***comparable*** *basis."*

How to interpret this requirement in a practicable and reasonably precise way was the subject of a great deal of discussion in the early WP meetings. The first of the three conditions in Article 4 implies that if a difference between the HICP results of different countries is due to a different approach to, say, quality adjustment, then the data are not comparable. This idea is put more concretely in the second condition. The aim was to ensure that differences in national HICPs could be due only to either (a) different price trends or (b) to different national weighting patterns. The methods of collecting prices and compiling them into HICPs must be similar in every member state—or, at any rate, as similar as makes no significant difference to the final results.

The third statement, which is found in several of the Articles, refers to the so-called "comitology" procedure which is described in Chapter 15.2, and which resulted in a series of technical implementing regulations.

In fact, this Article is the first example of Eurostat's general approach to the HICP regulatory process; the aim was not to specify in detail how countries should collect data and process them. Instead, the aim was to achieve **comparability of results** by ensuring that the various techniques used by different countries did not introduce significant variations in the overall results. How to judge what should be the acceptable level of "significance" was a matter dealt with in the first Implementing Regulation (1749/96)—see below. Eurostat would describe this approach as "output-based" rather than "input-based"—see Chapter 5.4. Thus, for example, in the case of pricing durables every quarter instead of every month, if a country could show that this technique made no significant difference to the HICP (and, incidentally, this would apply not only to the all-items HICP but also to the relevant published sub-indices) then such a procedure would be permitted by Eurostat. There was always considerable attention paid to the idea of "comparability". This wording in Article 4 turned out to be a hallowed phrase, and was constantly kept in mind during the drafting processes.

Later, the first Implementing Regulation (1749/96) defined the comparability requirement in an operational way: *"a change in the HICP by more than 0.1 percentage points on average over one year against the previous year"*. This too appeared many times in future discussions and rules.

3.3.3 Technical Articles

This section is still concerned with the contents of the Framework Regulation. That regulation did not go at all deeply into the technical aspects of HICP construction; the articles described in this section simply set out guiding principles, leaving it to the later Implementing regulations to flesh out the detail. These later regulations are described in some detail in Chapters 6–11 of this book.

A highly important concept was introduced into the draft Framework Regulation, namely that imputed prices should be excluded. In fact the word "imputed" is not used in any of the regulations. Instead, the concept of "monetary expenditure" is used—we will come to this in the context of the regulation on the coverage of goods and services (Chapter 7.5). In fact one draft of the Framework Regulation contained the phrase: *"The prices shall be actual prices and shall exclude imputed prices"*. But this sentence was later dropped. The most important use of imputed prices was the use of imputed rents as a measure of the costs of owner-occupied housing. Since there is no monetary transaction involved, this could hardly be included in a central bank's index of inflation—by definition a monetary issue. The EMI (the predecessor of the ECB) had a permanent presence at the WP meetings, and made clear always that these two aspects were critical from the point of view of European monetary policy. They suggested that rather than excluding owner-occupied housing from the harmonized index the implementation should be phased, with OOH excluded at the start, but included later.

This is covered more fully in Chapter 11.2.

Article 3 Scope

The HICP shall be based on the prices of goods and services ***available for purchase in the economic territory of the Member State*** *for the* ***purposes of directly satisfying consumer needs****. Questions concerning weighting shall be decided on by the Commission under the procedure laid down in Article 14.*

The term "CPI scope" has a number of dimensions. It may describe the coverage of the different goods and services whose prices and weights are included in the index (these may be limited in various ways); it may describe geographic coverage, which relates mainly to the regions of the country concerned; but this term can also refer to foreign countries where residents of the "home" country make purchases; and it may refer also to the coverage of the population whose expenditure underlies the index—which may also be limited in various ways, such as the inclusion or not of institutional residents.

For Article 3, "scope" in fact refers only to one aspect of geographical coverage—but a vital aspect, especially considering the international role of the HICP. The important phrases in this article are those highlighted in bold. What do these phrases mean, and what was their origin?

The phrase ***"available for purchase in the economic territory of the member state"*** also has enormous significance for the boundaries of the HICP. It means in effect that the coverage of weights and prices should relate to all sales taking place within a country, regardless of the nationality or residence status of the consumer. Visiting tourists would be covered, for example. So also would cross-border shoppers, who visit a neighbouring country purely to make purchases (such as alcohol or petrol) at lower prices than they would have to pay in their home country.

The phrase also implies that any purchases made by the residents of a country when abroad would not be covered in the HICP of their home country.

This concept of coverage is known in national accounts terminology as the "domestic" concept. The alternative, known as the "national" concept, requires that the CPI should measure all prices faced by the national (i.e. resident) population of a country, regardless of the country in which the expenditure was made. Obviously, this causes tremendous difficulties of measurement, as it would be necessary, for example, to monitor on a monthly basis the prices of hotels and restaurants used by the national population while they are on holiday in foreign countries. (Note that business travel is excluded from the HICP.)

Many countries do in fact use the national concept for their national CPI. There was a particular reason for choosing the domestic concept for the HICP. This arose from its unique use as an aggregate CPI for the EU and for the euro area. If—as the WP mandate made clear—it was going to be necessary to compare the average inflation rate for the euro area or for the entire EU with other countries, we had to be sure that (a) we were covering the whole of consumer price inflation within the EU or MU, and that (b) we were not double-counting any of it. See further discussion of this in Chapter 7.3.

Again, different arguments apply to indices for a single country or for a group of countries.

Articles 6 and 7. Data Sources; Prices, Weights, Burdens

The Framework Regulation has two related Articles on these topics. Article 6 is headed "Basic Information" while Article 7 is "Sources". This section deals with the subject matter of both Articles.

Article 6 Basic information

The basic information shall be those prices and weightings of goods and services which it is necessary to take into account in order to achieve comparability of indices as defined in Article 4.

That information shall be obtained from statistical units as defined in Council Regulation (EEC) No 696/93 of 15 March 1993 on the statistical units for the observation and analysis, of the production system in the Community or from other sources, provided that the comparability requirements for indices referred to in Article 4 of this Regulation are met.

Most statistical regulations at that time included an article about "basic information". This is an acknowledgement of the need to ensure that a regulation does not, without warning, impose important responsibilities, including the provision of data, on external organisations or individuals. In the case of consumer price indices, the vast bulk of basic data comprises prices and weights (referred to in the regulation as "weightings").

[A small diversion here on wording. In English, there are two words "Weights" and "Weightings". The shorter word is used to describe the actual values as in "Food has a weight of 17%". "Weighting" refers more to the method involved in setting weights. In French, there is a single word "pondération" which has both of these meanings, depending on the context.]

What will be the source of these data, and whose responsibility will it be to provide them? As statisticians like to remind others, prices do not grow on trees. Quite the opposite: collecting prices for a CPI is a large and expensive process, but the greater part of the cost is borne by the NSIs whose job it is to collect prices according to the sample design. It was always the intention that the HICP should make as full a use as possible of prices collected by NSIs for their national CPIs. As a general rule, it would only be in cases where the sample in a national CPI was inadequate either as to the products covered or as to the geographical or outlet coverage that additional price collection would be needed for the HICP. Meanwhile, NSIs had already started to ask Eurostat about the possible reimbursement of extra costs associated with the HICP, and this was an important matter which is taken up in Chapter 15.5.

As far as weights are concerned, the primary source is the Household Budget Survey (HBS),[3] often supplemented by data from the national accounts. The weights of the HICP may not always be the same as those used in the national CPI—indeed usually not. But the HICP weights would normally be expected to be obtained by some re-arrangement of the weights of the national CPI, which should be relatively easy to do by computer. There may also be some major exceptions, similar to those mentioned above for prices, namely those product groups which some countries may cover in their CPI in a different way from those in the HICP, or maybe not at all, such as hospital operations. Of course, it was always likely that the frequencies of the HBS and their classification

[3] Sometimes referred to as the Family Budget Survey or the Household Expenditure Survey.

systems would need to be altered; and indeed these aspects were also involved in the question of funding.

Article 6 is especially concerned with the burden on respondents in reporting data. For prices, to some extent, those would be retailers and other providers of goods or services. These are the "statistical units" mentioned in Article 6. The origin of this expression lies in the 1993 Council Regulation quoted, which is a very lengthy and complex document. For HICP purposes we can define them as being those organisations (whether shopkeeper, shop owner, government department etc.) which provide, or allow officials to gather information on prices and sales volumes to the NSIs.

For weights, this would mainly be the householders themselves, in the HBS. As we have seen, it was not expected that harmonization in itself would impose any significant burden on these types of respondent. All regulations had to have attached notes regarding various aspects of the consequences of the regulation, including the burden on respondents as well as the cost implications.

> **Article 7 Sources**
> *The statistical units called upon by the Member States to cooperate in the collection or provision of price data shall be obliged to allow observation of the prices actually charged and to give honest and complete information at the time it is requested.*

In this article there is again a reference made to "statistical units"—see above re Article 6.

The bulk of retail prices collected each month by NSIs for their CPIs are obtained by a large team of price collectors (sometimes contracted out to a private sector agency) who visit each sampled retail outlet to observe and note the prices of the various items on their list. (Nowadays, of course, there is much more use of such sources as barcode scanner data and "web scraping".) It will usually be the case that on a first visit to a particular outlet, collectors will announce themselves to the manager or proprietor and explain the purpose of the visit. But, once established, there is usually no objection to regular visits by price collectors. The purpose of this Article is to give the requisite authority to NSIs to make it compulsory for retailers to permit price observation on their premises—even though, as mentioned, permission is in practice almost always given.

The reference to giving "honest and complete information" is required because price collection is not always a simple matter of noting the marked price of an item in a shop. As we shall see later, there are problems relating to "missing price observations", such as when an item is temporarily out of stock. The collector may need to ask the shop management about the likely period of the item's absence and when it is likely to return. (This is needed because of the rules on the treatment of missing price observations—see Chapter 9.2). There may be questions to be asked about item specifications when these change, and a quality adjustment may need to be made. Sometimes the retailer may need to be asked for their advice on the value relating to a changed specification. In other cases, commercially confidential information may be requested concerning the breakdown of tariff prices. These matters are dealt with in detail in later chapters.

The bottom line for this Article is to make it clear that when prices are being obtained for inclusion in the HICP, no retailer or other provider of price data may legally refuse to cooperate. For sure, some retailers were suspicious about collectors, believing that they were either government inspectors or representatives of competitors seeking more information on the products being sold and their prices. This led to the provision of appropriate IDs for many price collectors in the EU. However, in practice it occasionally happens that a retailer does refuse. The outlet will then be replaced with another which fulfils the sample requirements.

Article 8 Frequency: Prices and Weights

1. The HICP, EICP and MUICP shall be compiled each month.

2. The required frequency of price collection shall be compiled once a month. Where less frequent collection does not preclude production of an HICP which meets the comparability requirements referred to in Article 4, the Commission (Eurostat) may allow exceptions to monthly collection. This paragraph shall not preclude more frequent price collection.

3. The weightings of the HICP shall be updated with a frequency sufficient to meet the comparability requirement laid down in Article 4. This paragraph shall not require family budget surveys to be carried out more frequently than once every five years, except in Member States which, under the procedure in Article 14, are acknowledged as experiencing changes in consumption patterns such as to make more frequent surveys necessary.

The first paragraph of this Article, not surprisingly, requires a monthly frequency of the HICP and its aggregates. In fact at this time all member states except Ireland published monthly national CPIs. Ireland published its CPI quarterly, but realising it was out of line readily conceded that the HICP should be monthly, and changed its national CPI to monthly. All central banks which had been consulted, as also the European Monetary Institute (forerunner of the European Central Bank) had advised Eurostat that a monthly harmonized inflation index was essential.

The second paragraph is somewhat more technical. The requirement to produce (and of course publish) a monthly HICP does not necessarily require monthly price collection, at least not for every item. Some items tend to change price only occasionally, for example, electricity prices, rail fares, educational fees, and rents. Several member states were aware of this and collected prices for these and other such items at less frequent intervals than monthly. At least one country did the same for large durables such as washing machines and refrigerators, where prices were collected quarterly. This was perhaps a more debatable practice.

There is, however, a subtle distinction that needs to be made between physical price collection and the assumption of unchanged prices when there is no physical "collection". If, for example, it is known for certain that a university changes its fees only at the start of each academic year, then it would be a waste of time to contact the university every month simply to obtain confirmation of this fact. The new fees need to be collected only annually. But this can be regarded quite reasonably as "monthly collection"—since the fees in eleven months of the year are in fact known. The same cannot be said about the price of durables. Even though the price of a specific model may remain unchanged for many months, the prices of models generally may rise much more frequently—and this is a contribution to the inflation rate.

Finally, the paragraph states that the usual monthly price collection requirement does not prevent a member state from collecting prices more frequently, and indeed several countries, especially in southern Europe, collect(ed) food prices on a weekly basis.

The third paragraph is concerned with the frequency of updating weights rather than prices. We shall come later (Chapter 10) to the question of weights in more detail. Suffice it to say here that the basis of a price index is to measure the changes in prices of groups of relatively homogeneous products, and then to calculate an overall average by multiplying the group averages with the weight of each group relative to the total weight. From time to time, the weights need to be reviewed and updated if the index is to be kept up-to-date and relevant.

This paragraph requires, in rather vague terms, that weights should be updated sufficiently frequently as not to jeopardise the HICP comparability requirement. Put bluntly, it would be difficult to maintain that the HICPs were "comparable" if one country was using ten-year-old weights and all the other countries five.

During the discussions, many delegates were worried that Eurostat might try to impose more frequent HBS's—the ultimate source of most CPI weights. That is why the paragraph states clearly that the HBS would not be required more often than five-yearly, unless exceptional changes in expenditure patterns were thought to be being made. At the same time that this regulation was being drafted, discussions were going on between member states and Eurostat on the possible harmonization of Household Budget Surveys.

Eurostat produced in 1993[4] and 1997[5] two methodological manuals on HBS giving some specific recommendations on many technical issues. These exercises have allowed considerable improvements to be made in the comparability of HBS data, and consequently their usefulness for European purposes.

In 2003 a fresh manual[6] was published by Eurostat, updating the former recommendations.

Article 9 Production of Results; Formula for Aggregating Higher-Level Indices; Product Classification

Member States shall process the data collected in order to produce the HICP, which shall be a Laspeyres-type index, covering the categories of the COICOP international classification (classification of individual consumption by purpose), which shall be adapted under the procedure in Article 15 to establish comparable HICPs. The methods, procedures and formulae to ensure that the comparability requirements are met shall be determined by the same procedure.

[4] 'Family Budget Surveys in the EC: Methodology and Recommendations for Harmonisation', Eurostat, Luxembourg 1993.

[5] 'Household Budget Surveys in the EC: Methodology and Recommendations for Harmonisation', Eurostat, Luxembourg 1997.

[6] 'Household Budget Surveys in the EU. Methodology and recommendations for harmonisation', Eurostat, Luxembourg 2003. ISBN 92-894-5435-0.

Another slightly oddly worded Article! This paragraph contains two important principles. First, it says that the HICP will be a "*Laspeyres-type*" index. It may seem surprising to twenty-first-century readers that this reference to the higher-level index type is the only one contained in the HICP regulations up to 2002 at least. By contrast, the formula for the calculation of elementary aggregate indices is dealt with in some detail in the first implementing regulation—see Chapter 8. Since the HICP was launched, there have been many academic studies regarding the most appropriate formulation of CPIs. (See, for example, Chapter 8 of the latest version of the ILO International Manual[7]). Moreover, there was at the time little or no discussion of the concept of a Cost of Living Index (COLI), a concept that would occupy the minds of many price statisticians in the years to come.

In defence of this Article, it should be pointed out that then—as now—the national CPI of every member state was of a Laspeyres type, though sometimes differing in the detail. A true Laspeyres index is one in which the base or reference period is the same for both initial prices and weights. A true Laspeyres index is very difficult in practice to compile since it would not be possible to compile a timely index if the same base period applies to both prices and weights. It takes a long time to establish weights for a particular month or year. There are other tricky practical and theoretical issues, including the question of how long a "period" should be (one year, five years, ten years..), and what should be done about calculating the indices for the elementary aggregates if there are no weights attached to the items within them? Using this rather vague concept ensured that the HICP would be of a general type familiar to member states, and thereby reducing the time needed to make progress on other details of the new index. In practice, the usual index is a variant of the Laspeyres index, known as the Lowe index, in which the price reference period is normally later than the weights reference period. (In fact, technically speaking, the Laspeyres index is a variant of the Lowe index and not the other way round) (see Chapter 8.2).

Product Classification

The second part of Article 9 is concerned with the classification system used for the products included in the HICP. This matters more for an international index than for a purely national one, since if comparisons

[7] ILO and others, "Consumer Price Index Manual: Concepts and Methods", Draft Jan 2020.

are being made for a sub-index for, say, transport services, it is important that what one country includes in this heading is the same as what other countries include. We were fortunate in this, because at the same time that the HICP Framework Regulation was being discussed, progress on a new UN-sponsored classification of household expenditure was nearing finality. This was the Classification of Individual Consumption According to Purpose (not quite exactly what was written in the regulation!)—or COICOP for short. This was not finally adopted by the UN until 1999—but in any case, as this Article shows, it was decided in Regulation 1749/99 to make some adaptations to the official UN version (which was written perhaps more with national accounts rather than CPI compilers in mind) so as to make it more relevant for the HICP. The difference between the official UN COICOP and the version used for the HICP (later known officially as "COICOP/HICP[8]) were in any case not great. They were mainly in the COICOP 09 range (Recreation and Culture).

The detailed COICOP/HICP classification was included as an Annex to a later regulation—see Chapter 6.

[8] Now re-named "ECOICOP".

CHAPTER 4

The Interim Indices of Consumer Prices (IICP); First Convergence Report

4.1 Administrative Aspects

The publication of the Interim Indices of Consumer Prices (IICP) was a significant step in the harmonization process, fulfilling the requirement—with one month to spare—set out as Stage I of the harmonization timetable in Article 5 of the Framework Regulation (see Chapter 3.3.2). Because of this requirement, there was no need for any separate legislation to cover the production of the IICP.

The question had been raised earlier as to what the interim indices should be called. The Framework Regulation simply called for "an interim set of consumer price indices". For several months the Working Party had been referring to the new indices simply as the "Stage I indices". Names suggested by delegates included "Partly harmonized indices of consumer prices" and "Preliminary indices of consumer prices". But a proposal made to the SPC at its meeting in September 1995 was that the indices should be known as "Interim Indices of Consumer Prices for International Comparisons", or "Interim Indices" for short. The abbreviated title was slightly different: "IICP", or "Interim Indices of Consumer Prices".

A decision needed to be made on the starting date of the IICPs. In order for the Commission to make judgements on price stability, it would be necessary to have a sufficiently long series of IICPs available before the first full convergence report was drafted. The report was due by the end of

J. Astin, *Measuring EU Inflation*,
https://doi.org/10.1007/978-3-030-68806-6_4

1996. It was decided, in agreement with DG2, that the IICPs would start from January 1994, with the launch in February 1996. The last month for which the IICPs were published was January 1997, the month for which the HICPs were first published.

All countries except Ireland were publishing their national CPIs on a monthly basis—Ireland was quarterly. By mid-1996, when the first Commission convergence report would begin to be drafted, there would be 2½ years of monthly IICP data available. Eurostat hoped that the first IICPs would be ready by December 1995 rather than the achieved date of February 1996, though that was clearly an ambitious target; to meet the convergence report timetable, the final deadline would require publication by March 1996 at the latest. Some member states were concerned that the deadline may be too short to allow them to extend the national CPI coverage where this was necessary. Most of the changes, however, comprised exclusions from the national CPI, which would not be a particularly onerous task for the member states.

Separate from the matter of the starting date for the IICPs was the question of which index reference period to use. The index reference period is a purely arithmetical device which more or less arbitrarily gives a starting point when the index is set to 100. Some countries used a particular month, such as January 1994 = 100, while others used a full year, such as 1994 = 100. There are technical reasons for choosing between these two main options. For the IICP it was decided to take 1994 = 100. That meant that to start the index off, it was necessary to have the index numbers for each month of 1994 and take the average for the year. This index number would then be set at 100. Thus the IICPs for the early months of 1994 would generally be below 100 and those of later months would be likely to be above 100.

The question of which organisation should produce—and also disseminate—the IICPs was discussed by TF2 and the full WP. It was felt that each member state must have the responsibility for producing its own IICP, but that the dissemination of the complete national range of IICPs, and the aggregated results, would be the task of Eurostat. This allocation of tasks was carried over into the HICPs. Nevertheless, there were concerns that the presentation of the IICPs would need to be coordinated between Eurostat and the member states. Even though the prime responsibility for dissemination would rest with Eurostat, no doubt each member state would wish to publish at least its own IICP, in its own language, and it was important to ensure that the messages conveyed to the public did not conflict in any way. Since the IICPs would generally differ from the national CPIs it was important to avoid any confusion or misapprehensions. The draft Eurostat News Release would therefore be agreed with the member states in advance of publication. It was realised early on by TF2 that the published IICP News Releases would have to stress that the indices were merely "stripped" CPIs and would not be suitable for national purposes. And indeed the first IICP News Release specifically remarked that "*neither the interim indices nor the Harmonised Indices of Consumer Prices replace existing national Consumer Price Indices; they are not designed for domestic purposes such as indexation or wage bargaining*".

The question of the precise timing of the monthly News Release was also discussed. The EU has two time zones: UTC (or GMT) and UTC + 1 (both increased simultaneously by one hour during summer months). Brussels used UTC + 1, so that if the Commission issued a News Release at 12 noon, for example, the time in the UK, Ireland and Portugal would be only 11 a.m. After some discussion within the Commission, it was agreed that the Commission News Releases would not be published before that of the "slowest" member state. The IICP data would, naturally, be treated as confidential before official release.

During the period of the discussions on the IICP, Eurostat continued to publish the national CPIs of member states each month. This would cease when the HICPs were published as they were considered to be the responsibility of the member states themselves rather than Eurostat. But what to do during the lifetime of the IICPs? Since the IICPs were regarded as only the first step towards harmonized CPIs, it was agreed that the national CPIs would continue to be published by Eurostat, and that this would be done in the same News Release as the IICP.

It was also proposed that there should be some regular analysis of the differences between the IICPs and the national CPIs. But this was not done, no doubt because of the foreseeably short life of the IICPs. In any case, publishing the IICPs alongside the national CPIs at least allowed users to see for themselves what the differences were, and given that the categories of expenditure which were excluded or included in the IICPs were also published, it would not be too difficult a task for users to carry out their own analysis, despite the fact that the published IICPs were restricted to the all-items indices; no component indices were published. Table 4.4 below was a one-off analysis showing the differences between national CPIs and the IICPs as at September 1996.

The long-standing Eurostat publication of national CPIs had a relatively relaxed monthly timetable, as the indices were already published by each country. The only "value added" was the inclusion of a weighted average of the national CPIs for the EC as a whole. So the timing of publication depended only on the date of arrival in Eurostat of the last-published national CPI. There had been no regular August news releases, on the grounds that most users were likely to be away on holiday!

With the imminent arrival of Stage 3 of the EMU—the start of the Monetary Union, 1 January 1999—the political temperature was beginning to rise, and it was appreciated that a stricter timetable regime would be necessary, especially when the HICPs themselves were published a year later. Accordingly, an agreement was reached with member states on the deadlines for submitting national CPIs to Eurostat. For the first publication (indices for January 1994 to January 1996, to be published at the end of February 1996), data up to October 1995 had to be in Eurostat's hands by 3 November 1995. In subsequent months, the rule was that the data should be transmitted to Eurostat immediately after the national CPI was published, and no later than the 20th of the month following the index month; publication by Eurostat would follow after about a week. For a few countries, this timetable was rather demanding. (After the HICPs themselves were published, the timetable became much stricter, with advance notice being given of future publication dates and times—but that is another story—see Chapter 3.3.1.)

4.2 Technical Issues

On 29 February 1996—just four months after the Council had adopted the Framework Regulation—the Interim Index of Consumer Prices (IICP) was launched in the form of a Eurostat News Release. The IICP series as first published covered the period January 1994 to January 1996. This is what the first page looked like:

No 15/96
29 February 1996

Interim step towards harmonised measurement of consumer prices
NEW WAY OF COMPARING EU INFLATION
Required for the assessment of convergence for
Economic and Monetary Union

An important step is about to be taken towards fully harmonised inflation figures which will be used for decisions on which Member States meet the price stability convergence criterion for participation in Economic and Monetary Union. National measures of inflation will not be affected - Member States will continue to calculate and publish their own Consumer Price Indices according to national needs and definitions.

The introduction of the new system will take place in two steps: Interim indices are being published for the first time this month by **Eurostat - the Statistical Office of the European Communities in Luxembourg** - and the national statistical institutes (NSIs) of Member States. **Harmonised Indices of Consumer Prices (HICPs) will start in January 1997.**

The interim indices are based largely on existing national Consumer Prices Indices (CPIs). However, in order to improve comparability certain categories of spending have been excluded. In particular owner-occupied housing costs, expenditure on health, education and insurances are left out. They are **designed expressly for international comparisons of consumer price inflation**, particularly by the Commission and European Monetary Institute in their EMU convergence reports under article 109j of the Treaty. Neither the interim indices nor the Harmonised Indices of Consumer Prices replace existing national Consumer Price Indices; they are not designed for domestic purposes such as indexation or wage bargaining.

M. Yves-Thibault de Silguy, the member of the European Commission responsible for EMU and Eurostat, has especially welcomed this development which will enable the European Council to take its decisions on countries participating in Monetary Union on the basis of comparable data.

Eurostat - in close collaboration with NSIs - has been working for over two years on harmonising the different methods used by Member States to compile such indices. The interim indices announced today result from this. They will be produced by each Member State in co-operation with **Eurostat**.

Note in the above sub-headline the reference to “assessment of convergence”. This was indeed the first and vital use of the HICP and the IICP. This was about the convergence for price stability in the member states of the EU, in the context of preparations for Stage 3 of Economic and Monetary Union (EMU), scheduled for 1 January 1999.

The IICPs were in themselves not especially difficult to produce, as they were simply the national CPIs, adjusted solely so as to make the coverage of goods and services as similar as possible. National CPIs were thus coincident with the corresponding IICPs regarding methods, concepts and definitions. The difference was that certain sub-indices were excluded. The exclusions were:

- Owner-occupied housing (including the imputed rents of owner-occupied dwellings and mortgage payments)
- Healthcare products (goods and services)
- Educational services
- Certain other items not covered, or treated differently, by a number of member states. In this group were included package holidays; expenditure abroad; water supply and disposal when paid as a tax and not by the amount consumed; taxes related to the use of cars including road tax, tolls and driving licences; financial services including insurance; social services; other miscellaneous services.

As regards health and education services, the problem was twofold. Firstly, there were no existing international standards on how to measure prices in these complex areas. And secondly, the institutional arrangements for delivery of these services differed considerably between member states. For example, in the UK consultations with general medical practitioners ("family doctors") were free within the National Health Service. But in many other countries, there was a fee, usually heavily subsidised by the state. To have included such services without any special adjustment in a harmonized CPI, albeit "interim", would have introduced serious inconsistencies.

Although most of the differences between national CPIs and the IICPs comprised items which were often included in national CPIs and excluded from the IICPs, two important items of consumption, alcohol and tobacco products, were included in the IICPs although they were excluded from the CPIs of Italy and Luxembourg. However, an important safeguard for member states was an assurance by Eurostat that the IICP would not require any additional price collection. Italy and Luxembourg did in fact collect prices and weights for these categories, though they were not incorporated into their national CPIs.

Full details of the products which were removed from or added to the CPIs of member states in order to compute the IICPs are given in Tables 4.1 and 4.2.

One of the difficulties foreseen in presenting the IICPs was that their total coverage, after excluding the above items, was well below the full coverage. But Eurostat considered that by removing the major non-comparable items from the index, what remained would by definition be more comparable than the unadjusted national CPIs, and hence more suitable for international comparisons. In any case, most of the excluded items, with the major exception of owner-occupied housing (which is still [2020] "temporarily" excluded) were incorporated in the HICPs less than a year later, when they were launched in March 1997. Nevertheless, calculations were made for each member state as to what proportion of the total national CPI was being excluded in the IICPs. It turned out that the combined net weight of the exclusions and inclusions was about 16% of total consumption expenditure ranging between 8 and 25%, as shown in Table 4.3.

Table 4.1 National CPI product categories excluded from the IICPs

	B	*DK*	*D*	*GR*	*E*	*F*	*IRL*	*I*	*L*	*NL*	*A*	*P*	*FIN*	*S*	*UK*
Imputed rents of owner occupiers		out	out							out		out		out	
Mortgage interest payments	out						out						out	out	out
Refuse disposal and sanitation services (payment as tax regardless of consumption)				out						out					out
Insurance in respect of the dwelling	out		out		out		out				out	out	out	out	out
Water supply (payment as tax regardless of consumption)				out											out
Health	out	out	out	out	out	out	out	out	out	out	out	out	out	out	out
Package holidays and expenditure abroad	out		out		out	out	out	out	out	out	out	out	out	out	out
Travel insurance			out							out		out	out		out
Taxes related to the use of a car, road taxes and tolls	out		out	out	out	out	out		out	out	out	out	out		out
Car insurance	out		out	out	out		out	out	out	out	out	out	out	out	out
Drivers licence fee			out				out		out	out	out	out	out	out	
Education	out	out	out	out	out	out	out	out	out	out	out	out	out		out
Social services	out										out	out			
Financial services n.e.c.	out	out	out		out	out		out		out		out	out	out	out
Other services n.e.c.	out	out	out		out		out	out	out	out	out	out	out	out	out

Source "Compendium of HICP Reference Documents" 2/2001/8/5, Table 5, Luxembourg, 2001

Table 4.2 Categories excluded from national CPIs but included in the IICPs

	B	*DK*	*D*	*GR*	*E*	*F*	*IRL*	*I*	*L*	*NL*	*A*	*P*	*FIN*	*S*	*UK*
Alcoholic beverages									in						
Tobacco								in	in						
Services for the routine, maintenance and repair of dwellings				in											

Source "Compendium of HICP Reference Documents" 2/2001/8/5, Table 4, Luxembourg, 2001

Table 4.3 Approximate weights per thousand of major product group differences between the IICPs and national CPIs

	B	*DK*	*D*	*GR*	*E*	*F*	*IRL*	*I*
IICPs total	822	821	826	916	913	875	846	900
+ Housing	40	126	92	–	17	–	40	–
+ Health and Education	56	36	45	76	44	112	43	78
± Others	82	17	37	8	26	13	71	22
= National CPIs	1000	1000	1000	1000	1000	1000	1000	1000
	L	*NL*	*A*	*P*	*FIN*	*S*	*UK*	
Interim Index	883	749	871	876	774	793	796	
+ Housing	–	118	9	62	100	160	120	
+ Health and Education	85	12	46	39	41	25	[a]	
± Others	33	121	74	24	85	22	84	
= CPI	1000	1000	1000	1000	1000	1000	1000	

[a] *The UK weight for Health and Education is included in Others*

Source "Compendium of HICP reference documents", 2/2001/8/5, Table 3, Luxembourg, 2001

4.3 Differences between IICPs and CPIs

The differences between IICPs and CPIs depended very much on the existing structure of national CPIs.

For countries where the CPIs incorporate items like health care or imputed rents in owner-occupied housing, the IICPs tended to be lower than the CPIs, because the prices of these items tend to rise faster than those of internationally traded goods. On the other hand, for the two countries where alcohol and tobacco prices were excluded from the CPIs, the differences with the IICPs were positive, since price increases on these goods were typically greater than average. Countries where mortgages were included in the national CPIs displayed erratic differentials. At the Community level and for a number of countries, differences between the CPI and the IICP were minor—in the range of ± 0.1 percentage point to ± 0.3 percentage point. Table 4.4 shows the complete set of national CPIs and IICPs for the 12-month period September 1995 to September 1996.

It can be seen in Table 4.4 that overall there was little difference between the EU average CPI and IICP—just 0.1 percentage point. But there was quite a wide variation between countries, ranging from −0.6 to +0.8 percentage points.

Table 4.4 National differences between CPIs and IICPs

	IICP	*CPI*	*Sep 96/Sep 95 DIFFERENCE IICP-CPI*
B	2.1	1.9	0.2
DK	2.5	2.3	0.2
D	1.3	1.4	−0.1
EL	8.1	8.5	−0.4
E	3.6	3.6	0.0
F	1.6	1.6	0.0
IRL	2.2	1.4	0.8
I	3.5	3.4	0.1
L	1.5	1.4	0.1
NL	1.4	2.0	−0.6
A	2.2	2.0	0.2
P	3.2	3.4	−0.2
FIN	1.2	0.6	0.6
S	0.6	−0.1	0.7
UK	2.9	2.1	0.8
EUR	**2.4**	**2.3**	**0.1**

Source "Report on Convergence in the European Union in 1996", COM(96) 560 final, Brussels, 1996

4.4 Convergence Reports

There was an exacting timetable laid down in the Maastricht Treaty for the progress towards monetary union. Briefly, the timetable called for reports to be made to the Council by both the Commission and the EMI (European Monetary Institute—the future European Central Bank). These became known as "convergence reports". The EMI had already embarked on its own convergence reports, the first being published in November 1995.

The Council was required to make a decision by the end of 1996 on:

(a) whether a majority of the member states fulfilled the necessary conditions for the adoption of a single currency;
(b) whether it was appropriate for the Community to enter the third stage of monetary union (i.e. the establishment of the euro currency), and if so
(c) set the date for the beginning of the third stage.

The Commission's first Convergence Report following the Maastricht Treaty was published on 6 November 1996.[1] It reported, among other things, progress towards price stability, measured according to the IICPs which had by then been published monthly since February of that year. The report included a commentary on the statistical aspects of the IICP results compared with the national CPIs. But most significantly this was the first occasion on which a decision had to be made about the detailed interpretation of the Maastricht text regarding price convergence. The English version of the Maastricht text is as follows:

> *The criterion on price stability referred to in the first indent of Article 109j(1) of this Treaty shall mean that a Member State has a price performance that is sustainable and an average rate of inflation, observed over a period of one year before the examination, that does not exceed by more than 1½ percentage points that of, at most, the three best performing Member States in terms of price stability. Inflation shall be measured by means of the consumer price index on a comparable basis, taking into account differences in national definitions.*

It may be noted that the French version omits the word "points", referring to "1.5%". One can also argue that "1½" is not necessarily the same as "1.5". The latter could be a rounded decimal lying somewhere between 1.45 and 1.54. The Italian version differs again with "1.5 percentage points". The French and Italian versions were (surely correctly) ignored by the Commission.

The first Commission convergence report identified six different interpretations of this seemingly straightforward text.

Firstly, what type of "average"? Arithmetic, geometric, median or another type? The Commission chose the arithmetic mean on the grounds that it is the most commonly used method. They might also have said that it was the most easily understood method. But they made a comparison test and found that the difference between the arithmetic and the geometric averages were very small—especially when inflation is low, as it was at the time (typically around 2% per annum).

Secondly, how to interpret "*observed over a period of one year*"? The Commission said that two main approaches were possible:

[1] European Commission, report on convergence in the European Union in 1996 (COM96 [560]).

(a) using the year-on-year change of a monthly indicator (for instance, September 1996/September 1995), or
(b) using the average change of the latest twelve months over the preceding twelve months.

The advantage of (a) was that it was straightforward and easily understandable. But, the Commission felt, the disadvantages outweighed this advantage. Indeed, results may vary importantly from month to month, because of possible base month effects, due for instance to changes in indirect taxes.

Furthermore, and more importantly, as the criterion should assess the sustainability of price stability and of inflation convergence, taking into account a longer period seemed more appropriate. So (b) was the chosen option.

Thirdly, concerning the number of countries to be included in the calculation of the reference value, different approaches were conceivable. One approach would be to take just a single country to calculate the reference value.

Three options were possible:

- Option 1: the best performing country plus 1.5 percentage points.
- Option 2: the second best performing country plus 1.5 percentage points.
- Option 3: the third best performing country plus 1.5 percentage points.

A second approach would take an average of two or three countries:-

- Option 4: the unweighted average of the two best performing countries plus 1.5 percentage points.
- Option 5: the unweighted average of the three best performing countries plus 1.5 percentage points.
- Option 6: the weighted average of the three best performing countries plus 1.5 percentage points (and, if so, the question of what to use as weights).

Reference values were calculated according to each of the six options for December 1995 and for September 1996. The Commission chose to use option 5. (I am unaware of any published report explaining this choice). Using the chosen method, comparing the 12-month period to September 1996 with the previous 12-month period, the three best-performing countries were: Finland (0.9%), Netherlands (1.2%) and Germany (1.3%). The unweighted arithmetic average was 1.1%. Adding 1.5% to this yields the reference figure of 2.6%. 10 member states had rates of inflation under this value in the period concerned, while 5 were higher: Portugal (3.0%), UK (3.0%), Spain (3.8%), Italy (4.7%) and Greece (8.4%).

As mentioned above, the EMI had produced a convergence report in November 1995, although at that time the IICPs were not available, and the calculations were made using unadjusted national CPIs. Using these data, the EMI calculated that 4 (rather than 5) out of the 15 member states would fail to reach the Maastricht criterion threshold on inflation. In its November 1996 convergence report, the EMI, alongside the Commission, was able to use the IICPs, and naturally arrived at the same figures as those quoted above.

Based on the 1996 Commission convergence report, covering all criteria, not only that relating to price stability, the Council in December 1996 decided that a majority (12 out of 15) of the member states did not yet fulfil the necessary conditions for the adoption of a single currency. Only Denmark, Luxembourg and Ireland qualified on all criteria (though in fact the Danish government decided against joining the EMU). Allowing time for greater convergence, the Council set the date for the start of Stage 3 of EMU—the introduction of the euro to replace the ecu (European currency unit)—for 1st January 1999. (If a relatively large number of member states had fulfilled the convergence criteria in December 1996, Stage 3 of EMU could have started in January 1997). The delay was generally welcomed from the technical point of view, since the HICPs were due to be launched at the beginning of 1997, and work was well advanced to achieve this.

It is clear that all of the issues described in this chapter generated a great deal of work, both at Eurostat and in the member states. But this period was by no means devoted solely to the preparation of the IICPs; in fact this was a relatively small part of the ongoing work preparing the HICPs themselves. During 1995 there was a total of 11 meetings of TFs and the WP. As a result, by the end of 1995 no less than eight HICP regulations were in various stages of drafting. And, as we shall see in later chapters, 1995 was by no means the busiest year for HICP development.

The SPC meeting on 28 September 1995 approved the proposals for the launch of the IICPs. They were also presented with a draft regulation on the formula to be used for calculating elementary aggregate indices (see Chapter 8.3). However, there was a problem! The final draft of the regulation was on the agenda for discussion at the WP meeting on 26 June 1995. But the meeting was disrupted by a bomb alert (a hoax it seems). So there was no chance of obtaining the WP's immediate approval of the draft. Given that it contained no significant changes compared with the draft from TF3 which had been in the hands of WP delegates since February, Eurostat decided it would be safe to present the draft to the forthcoming SPC, despite the fact that the "rule" requiring WP majority vote had not been taken.

As a result, the SPC felt that the rule should be followed and they returned the draft to Eurostat. It was duly approved (though by the skin of its teeth!) at the next WP meeting (25 October), and agreed by the following SPC on 1 December 1995.

Meanwhile, the Council adopted the all-important Framework Regulation[2] in October 1995.

In retrospect, the development of the IICPs can be seen as an excellent "rehearsal" for the much more important preparation of the launch of the HICPs a year later. Issues such as transmission timetables, coordinated release, embargoes, as well as many technical issues, had already been successfully addressed for the IICPs and the transition to the HICPs was eased as a result. And the good work done by Eurostat and the CPI staff of member states paid dividends: the official launch of the IICPs on 29 February 1996 was widely regarded as successful. Given that the IICPs were, technically speaking, not a major step forward in statistical terms, the launch method was kept to a low profile, being restricted to a News Release without an accompanying press conference.

The next chapter takes us on to the launch of the HICPs in March 1997.

[2] Council Regulation 2494/95; OJ No L 257, 27.10.1995.

CHAPTER 5

Launch of the HICP

5.1 Preparation for the Launch

The HICPs were designed as a tool for the Maastricht criterion on entering the Economic and Monetary Union (EMU). So at the start of the harmonization project the most important use of the HICPs was in the application of the criterion of convergence for price stability in the context of the preparations for Stage 3 of EMU (the launch of the euro in electronic form). In line with this, the harmonization work during this early period focussed on measures to remove or reduce significant long-term effects ("non-comparabilities"), as these were most likely to distort the assessments of sustainable price stability.

The date of the launch of the HICP was 7 March 1997 (with a start day of data for January 1997 compared with January 1996, as required by the Framework Regulation (see below)). Additionally, Eurostat provided a table showing a comparison of 1996 with 1995. However, member states were not required by the Framework Regulation to provide harmonized data for 1995. This was done on a voluntary basis.

The countries included in this first release of HICPs were all EU member states plus two European Economic Area (EEA) countries, Iceland and Norway.

What exactly needed to be done before the launch date? Firstly, the completion of the Framework Regulation, which was adopted by the Council in October 1995. This was the first ever Council Regulation on

J. Astin, *Measuring EU Inflation*,
https://doi.org/10.1007/978-3-030-68806-6_5

statistical harmonization to set out compulsory rules for member states to follow.

The development of the Framework Regulation was described in Chapter 3. It must be stressed that on its own this regulation provided insufficient technical detail to permit the production of fully harmonized CPIs. It covered only the essential aspects of the HICP, specifically, its general scope, the frequency and timing of production, the frequency of the updating of weights, the initial product coverage, the basic formula ("Laspeyres-type") and the basic product classification (COICOP/HICP). This regulation remained the foundation of the entire HICP opus, until it was repealed and replaced by Council Regulation 2016/792 which took effect in January 2017. It was thus in force for a little over 21 years.

Just as several other macroeconomic measures are subject to revision in the light of later or better data, it was decided that the HICP should similarly be potentially subject to revision following publication. This was in contrast to some national CPIs (such as the UK's Retail Prices Index) which had been developed especially for uprating wages, pensions or benefits, where revision would bring confusion if not chaos, as well as uncertainty, to the public. This (unwritten) rule would not apply, however, during the crucial period for the decision on Stage 3 of Monetary Union. Retrospective revisions were allowed, in principle, following Regulation No. 1921 in 2001—see Chapter 15.9.

This chapter does not cover technical issues: Chapters 6–11 cover the various technical topics individually. This chapter focuses on the details of the actual launch of the HICP, including its reception in the professional world and the widespread press commentary. It also describes the following preparatory work done for implementing regulations.

5.2 Launch Day

On 7 March 1997, I went with the Director-General of Eurostat, Yves Franchet, to Brussels to present the new HICPs to the press in a briefing room in the Berlaymont building, the Commission HQ. There was a large attendance by journalists and a lively range of questions asked. Media comment afterwards was supportive of the new index.

The presentation had been preceded on 5 March by a published document preparing for the launch and explaining in some detail the special nature of the HICP and how it differed from national CPIs. These two news releases (English version) are reproduced below.

news release
eurostat

No 21/97
5 March 1997

Big step on consumer price indices
HARMONIZING THE WAY EU MEASURES INFLATION
Important component of EMU convergence assessment

Harmonized Indices of Consumer Prices (HICPs) for **EU** Member States—designed specifically with EMU convergence in mind—will be published for the first time at noon on 7 March by **Eurostat, the Statistical Office of the European Communities in Luxembourg**.

These harmonized inflation figures will be used for the assessment of inflation convergence. They are not intended to replace existing national Consumer Price Indices (CPIs) which may still be published according to national need and definitions.

HICPs are designed for **international comparisons** of consumer price inflation. They will be used in particular by the European Commission and European Monetary Institute in their EMU convergence reports under Article 109j of the Treaty on European Union.

Joint Effort with Member States

The HICPs are the result of three years' collaboration between Eurostat and National Statistical Institutes (NSIs) of member states on harmonizing the different methods used to compile price indices. The harmonization process has also resulted in generally improved quality of the indices.

The following will be available:

- All-items HICPs for all member states plus Norway and Iceland
- A European Index of Consumer Prices (EICP)
- A European Economic Area (EEA) index

- About 100 sub-indices for all member states plus Norway and Iceland with weighted averages for both the EU and the EEA.

The monthly index level, monthly and annual rates of change, annual average index and annual average rate of change will be produced every month by each Member State in cooperation with Eurostat.

The News Release continued with several pages of Background Notes. Three of the headings are reproduced here as examples:

Common classification *While the assessment of price stability under the convergence criterion primarily concerns the 'all-items' HICPs, the analysis of sources of inflationary pressure requires a sub-division of the HICP into component parts relating to different product groups. International comparability of these sub-indices thus requires a common classification. The HICPs are compiled using a relatively new international classification of consumers' expenditure known as COICOP (Classification Of Individual COnsumption by Purpose). A version of this classification has been specially adopted for the HICPs, known as COICOP/HICP. The sub-indices which will be published by Eurostat will be based on this classification: a list of the sub-index headings is given in the Annex. The weights assigned to each sub-index vary from country to country depending on the relative importance of consumers' expenditure on each sub-category in each country. That means that there is* ***no*** *'uniform basket' applying to all Member States, but comparability will be ensured.*

Extended coverage *Particularly in the fields of health and education many prices are heavily subsidised by the state. It is not always clear which prices should be included in an index of consumer prices, and the ways of treating this problem differ between Member States. The main options are the net prices actually paid by consumers or the total cost of providing the good or service. A decision on these matters is expected to be made soon.*

Compliance monitoring *Council Regulation 2494/95 requires Eurostat to adopt rules to be followed to ensure the comparability of HICPs. Plans are currently being drawn up to set in place a monitoring system designed to ensure that Member States are following the various Regulations on HICPs, so that users can be assured that the results are achieving what was intended.*

In line with the practice existing in many Member States, Eurostat also plans to establish an independent advisory body for HICPs which will help to guarantee the quality and independence of this important new economic indicator.

Below is the News Release issued with the HICPs on 7 March 1997.

---

eurostat news release

No 22/97
7 March 1997

First results of new harmonized system
EU ANNUAL INFLATION: 2.2% IN JANUARY

EU* annual inflation in January was 2.2%. This is as measured by the new Harmonized Indices of Consumer Prices (HICPs), published today for the first time by **Eurostat, the Statistical Office of the European Communities in Luxembourg.**

A year earlier the corresponding **EU** rate was 2.7%. However, this January it was higher than last January in eight Member States. Biggest rises over the year were in **Denmark** (from 1.2 to 2.6%) and **Belgium** (1.3–2.2%).

In five **Member States,** January's inflation rate under the new system was lower than a year before. There was a big fall in **Italy**—from an estimated 5.7 to 2.6%.

Lowest rates this latest month were in **Finland** (0.9%), **Luxembourg** (1.3%), and **Sweden** (1.3%); highest in **Greece** (6.6%), **Portugal** and **Spain** (both 2.8%).

Annual inflation in the whole **European Economic Area** was also 2.2% in January. And in January last year it was also 2.7%. In **Iceland** the rate was 2.0% compared with 1.6% last January. In **Norway** it was up to 3.2% from 0.5% a year before.

The EU average figure is the European Index of Consumer Prices (EICP), calculated from the 15 Member States' HICPs.

Designed for International Comparison

HICPs will be used for the decision on which member states meet the criterion on price stability for European Economic and Monetary Union (EMU) and will be used by the Commission and the European Monetary Institute (EMI) in their convergence reports. HICPs are harmonized inflation figures required under *Article 109j* of *the Treaty on European Union* (Maastricht Treaty).

HICPs are designed for international comparison of consumer price inflation, although member states are free to apply them for domestic uses such as indexation or wage bargaining. The focus is on comparability among the indices of different countries as well as on their relative movements. They are not intended to replace national consumer price indices (CPIs)—many member states are likely to continue using their CPIs for domestic purposes.

Eurostat—collaborating closely with national statistical institutes and drawing on expert advice of academics working in the field of price indices—has been working for over three years to harmonize the different methods used by member states to compile national CPIs. The methodological details of how HICPs are constructed are given in news release *21/97*, *Harmonizing the way the EU measures inflation.*

A news release will be published each month by Eurostat with information on the overall HICP. More detailed information can be obtained from the publication: *Statistics in focus*, Economy and finance, *Harmonized indices of consumer prices*. About 100 HICPs sub-indices with corresponding weights are available on Eurostat's database *Newcronos* through Eurostat's Data Shop network.

Harmonized Indices of Consumer Prices (HICPs) in ascending order of inflation (percentage change)
Table 1

eurostat	*Jan 97 / Jan 96*		*Jan 97 / Jan 96*
EU15*	**2.2p**	**Belgium**	2.2
Finland	0.9	**Denmark**	2.6
Luxembourg	1.3	**Italy**	2.6
Sweden	1.3	**Spain**	2.8p
Austria	1.6p	**Portugal**	2.8
Germany	1.7	**Greece**	6.6

(continued)

(continued)

eurostat	*Jan 97 / Jan 96*		*Jan 97 / Jan 96*
France	1.8		
Netherlands	1.8	Iceland	2.0
Ireland	1.9p	Norway	3.2
United Kingdom	2.1	EEA	**2.2p**

Harmonized Indices of Consumer Prices (HICPs) in ascending order of inflation (percentage change)
Table 2**

eurostat	*Dec 96 / Dec 95*	*Nov 96 / Nov 95*	*Oct 96 / Oct 95*	*Jan 96 / Jan 95*
EU15**	**2.1e**	**2.2e**	**2.3e**	**2.7e**
Finland	1.7	1.6	1.6	1.4
Luxembourg	1.3p	1.4p	1.2p	1.0p
Sweden	0.5	0.2	0.4	1.2
Austria	2.2p	2.2p	2.1p	1.3p
Germany	1.2	1.3	1.2	1.2
France	1.7	1.6	1.8	2.0
Netherlands	2.0	1.7	1.8	1.3
Ireland	:	2.3	:	:
United Kingdom	:	:	:	:
Belgium	2.1	2.1	2.2	1.3
Denmark	2.1	2.1	2.3	1.2
Italy	2.9e	2.9e	3.1e	5.7e
Spain	3.3p	3.3p	3.6p	3.8p
Portugal	2.9	2.9	2.8	2.5
Greece	6.9	7.4	7.7	7.8
Iceland	1.9	2.1	1.9	1.6
Norway	1.4	1.3	1.3	0.5
EEA	**2.1e**	**2.2e**	**2.3e**	**2.7e**

e = estimated; p = provisional; : = not available
*The new European Index of Consumer Prices (EICP).
**Member states are not required by Council Regulation (EC) no. 2494/95 to provide harmonized data for 1995, it is done on a voluntary basis. Therefore, the EU average is not strictly speaking an EICP.

In line with Article 5(1)(b) of the Framework Regulation, the HICP started with the index for January 1997. The common index reference period was the year 1996. That is to say, the indices with the starting value of 100 represented price levels for the average of the calendar year 1996. The rates of change for 1997 were established on the basis of the indices for 1996. The HICP concepts thus applied as from the index for January 1996.

Although the indices for 1995 cannot be considered as a legal requirement, all member states agreed to provide them.

The 1995 indices for the UK are the interim indices for 1995 adjusted for the geometric mean effect. The indices for 1995 and the rates of change for 1996 based on 1995 do not fulfil the HICP standards, but they are considered to be superior to national CPIs and the interim indices as regards comparability. They are, therefore, considered as the harmonized measures of inflation for the months of 1996.

Ireland estimated monthly HICPs and monthly sub-indices for 1995 and 1996 based on its quarterly national CPI data. The monthly figures are adjusted linear interpolations of the quarterly indices, making allowances for several sales effects. The estimation of these sales effects was based on seasonal patterns identified from UK data.

Finland discovered a mistake in its HICP calculation just after the launch of the first set of indices. This mistake was corrected, and the Finnish HICP series was revised with the publication of the February indices on 7 April 1997. The German and Austrian HICP series were also corrected for mistakes; revised figures for both member states were disseminated with the publication of the August HICPs on 7 October 1997.

5.3 Media Reaction

The launch was well received in the media. The following day the main national newspapers of the member states all had a mention—often a lengthy detailed report and comment on the new index. Typical headlines on 8 March included: "New Inflation data ease EMU path"; "Majority pass EU inflation test"; "Inflation down sharply on new measure"; "Italy and Spain fail EMU inflation test"—and so on.

Most attention was focussed on the fact that for recent months the HICP was significantly lower than the national CPIs. This was ascribed—correctly—to the wide use of the Jevons formula (see Chapter 8) in the sub-aggregate averages. This frequently gave a figure around 0.5–0.9 percentage points lower than the national figures. For example, the UK annual increase for January 1997 was 2.8% using the Retail Prices Index but only 2.1% with the HICP. [UK readers should note that the UK CPI is the official British name for the HICP. It is still being produced following the UK's withdrawal from the EU in 2020, though no longer required by EU law.]

The maximum permitted annual inflation rate for entry to the Monetary Union had been set at a level of no more than 1½ percentage points of the average of three best-performing countries (see Chapter 4.4). Several member states were well above this before the HICP was launched, but afterwards, all but four (Spain, Italy, Portugal and Greece) were below the new threshold. The average annual inflation rate for January 1997 with the HICP was 2.2%, compared with 2.7% using national indices. (Finland and Sweden, however, had an increase in their rates compared with the previous year—though they remained the countries with the lowest rates.) A related point that was noted in the press was that the spread between the best and worst performers was much less pronounced with the HICPs than with the national indices. This should be expected since the HICP was intended to result in a greater degree of comparability. Incidentally, the difference in the indices calculated with the geometric means or with the arithmetic means is still (at the time of writing, 2020) a bone of contention in the UK, where the RPI has been de-classified as a "national statistic" and the HICP (CPI) has become the most prominent measure of inflation.

The monthly publication thereafter also worked to the satisfaction of users. The European Commission, which had been represented throughout in the WP, was naturally pleased that the timetable for the launch of the HICP had been kept, though there was some disappointment at the initial lack of historical data for some member states.

By the year 2001, out of the 4000 or so European press cuttings relating to Eurostat news releases, the HICP accounted for nearly a quarter.

Two years after the launch of the HICP, the first of January 1999 became a historic date in the process of European economic integration. Stage 3 of Economic and Monetary Union began with 11 countries participating in the single currency—the euro. From that date, there is a single central bank interest rate applied in the euro area, fixed by the European Central Bank (ECB). As required by the Maastricht Treaty, the maintenance of price stability is the primary objective of the European System of Central Banks (ESCB). The main tool of this policy was the MUICP—the weighted average inflation rate of the members of the euro area, based on their national HICPs. The term "price stability" was defined precisely by the ECB in 1998: *a year-on-year increase of below 2% in the MUICP, to be maintained over the medium-term.*

5.4 Criteria for Setting Rules of the Implementing Regulations

The plan was to flesh out the Framework Regulation with a series of Commission Regulations aimed at implementing the various technical issues required for fully comparable HICPs—whether or not these issues were explicitly mentioned in the Framework Regulation. It was not known at any stage how many implementing regulations would be required; nevertheless, it was necessary to make early decisions concerning the general approach to the detailed rules which would be applied. Perhaps the most important of these general approaches was the concept of "minimum standards". Minimum standards in the sense that banning acknowledged bad practices has the effect of not only achieving convergence of good practices, but also raising the general level of standards.

"Minimum standards" also imply that outputs rather than inputs should be specified. In other words, the regulations should state what the required outputs should be, rather than how to achieve those outputs, the detail of which could generally be left to the member states, sometimes with the agreement of Eurostat. This principle became known as the "output-based" method of specification, as opposed to a more specific and detailed "input-based" method.

Below are some of the criteria which were applied for setting the rules in the implementing regulations:-

(a) Necessity. Rules should be made only where there is evidence that non-comparability may arise in the absence of such rules.
(b) Practicability. Rules should be made only when NSIs are able to follow what is required.
(c) Specificity. Rules should be clear, unambiguous and suitably restrictive in order to promote comparability, while at the same time

being sufficiently general as to allow a degree of variation in practice consistent with national circumstances.

(d) Coherence. Rules should not conflict with other rules or guidelines.

(e) Completeness. Taken together, rules and guidelines should cover all that has to be done in constructing HICPs.

(f) Best practice. Where possible, rules should follow the best of existing practices as long as they can be applied to all Member States.

(g) Efficiency. The costs of following the rules should not exceed what is necessary to achieve comparable HICPs.

5.5 Specific Topics for the Implementing Regulations

Before the launch of the HICP it was agreed that certain topics would need to be addressed for the first HICPs. These were (with the Task Forces leading the discussions):

- Initial product coverage (TF2)
- Quality adjustment (TF4, then TF2)
- Sampling of prices (TF5, then TF2)
- Formula for elementary aggregate indices (TF3, TF2)
- Treatment of new products (TF2)
- Transmission and dissemination of sub-indices (TF2)
- Revisability of the HICP (TF2).

Most of these topics were addressed in their own implementing regulations. And several more topics were later identified as candidates for specification. Some of these topics had to be returned to during the following years since in the rush to get the legislation through the system, and also, with the benefit of hindsight, some changes and additions were needed.

The first topic, Initial Product Coverage, was from its very title clearly going to have to be amended sooner or later, and this was done in a Commission Regulation in July 1998.[1] Quality Adjustment—one of the

[1] Commission Regulation 1687/98.

most difficult topics facing price statisticians—was dealt with in a relatively superficial way in the first implementing regulation. However, it was many years before the topic was covered in a new regulation[2]—see Chapter 9.5.

Sampling is a very wide and fundamental issue in a CPI, and again the first implementing regulation was rather superficial:

> **Article 8:**
> *HICPs constructed from target samples which, for each category of COICOP/HICP and taking into account the weight of the category, have sufficient elementary aggregates to represent the diversity of items within the category and sufficient prices within each elementary aggregate to take account of the variation of price movements in the population shall be deemed reliable and comparable.*

The regulation articles concerning the formula for elementary aggregates proved durable (though recent academic work has cast some doubt on its theoretical foundations).

The section on the treatment of newly significant products and on the transmission and dissemination of sub-indices has also stood the test of time.

Finally, the question of whether or not the HICP should, in principle, be a revisable statistic, was considered important—see Chapter 15.9.

5.6 Allocation of Regulation Topics to Task Forces

The Task Forces (TF), as described in Chapter 2, were small groups of up to about 10 members, taken mainly from the Working Party. They met not only in Luxembourg but also in other EC capitals. They were monolingual and mainly conducted in English.

A full list of the TFs and their titles and remits is given in Chapter 2.3.

The TFs were a vital part of the process of reaching consensus on the regulations. It was the TFs that began the discussions on each topic, and spent many hours and days in preparing recommendations for the Working Party to discuss. Some statistics on the TF meetings are:

Total number of meetings between 1993 and 2001: 33

[2] Commission Regulation 1334/2007.

Total number of official TF papers: 227 (of which 168 were for or from TF2)

From 1998, the TF meetings were supplemented by separate meetings of the candidate countries—see Chapter 14.1. The latter meetings, chaired by Eurostat, started in April 1998 and continued through to 2002. By February 2002 there had been 11 candidate country meetings and 40 papers.

Combining all the WP, TF and candidate country papers, a total of over 700 papers over a 9-year period were written on the various aspects of HICP production! Well over one a week. We were indeed kept very busy!

The following six chapters are devoted to the details of each of the topics which were discussed by the TFs and were included in subsequent Regulations. They cover the following topics:

Chapter 6 Classifications and sub-indices.
Chapter 7 Coverage: geographic, population and products.
Chapter 8 Index formulae.
Chapter 9 Price collection issues.
Chapter 10 Weights.
Chapter 11 Special products.

PART II

Technical Aspects of HICP

CHAPTER 6

Classification of Household Consumption Expenditure; HICP Sub-indices

6.1 Types of Product Classification

The classification of products is the backbone of any CPI. Products (the term covering both goods and services) could be classified in many different ways. Goods could be classified according to their main component: glass, metal, wood, cloth, plastic, etc.—this could be fairly closely matched to the types of outlet which sell them. They could be classified by price, with cheaper products at one end and expensive ones at the other. That could form a useful basis for sampling. They could be classified by type of product: grouping together food items, clothing items, transport services and so on. And they could be classified according to the purpose they serve. In most cases, this would be very similar to a classification by type of item. Food, for example is definable as a type of product, and is also definable according to its use: food is for eating!

Why are CPI classifications important? The reason is that the prices collected for a CPI are based on a very small sample of products—very small, that is, compared with the total number of products whose prices could potentially be collected. Amazon UK (with its associates) has more than 350 million! The UK HICP product list, at its most detailed level, has about 720 items. If you are taking a sample, it must be representative of actual consumer purchases, and the only way to ensure this in practice is to group products together in such a way that sufficiently accurate weights can be assigned to the various groups. And what is the usual source of

J. Astin, *Measuring EU Inflation*,
https://doi.org/10.1007/978-3-030-68806-6_6

CPI weights? Mostly, they come directly or indirectly from Household Budget Surveys (HBS). If I am asked to record my detailed purchases over a period of time, I will need to have some form of classification. I go to a supermarket or grocer to buy food, a clothing store to buy clothing, a railway station to buy a train ticket and so on. Consumer behaviour thus dictates the general structural form of the classification of a CPI. To have a single weight covering train tickets, ladies' clothing and groceries would be economically meaningless as well as difficult to measure. So it makes very good sense to group products related in some way to type of product.

Many national CPIs were (and some still are) using the "type of product" classification. But COICOP/HICP (the UN-based standard classification used for the HICP) is a classification for grouping consumer expenditures on goods and services by "type of purpose". However, the units of classification are the expenditures on specific goods and services and not expenditures on purposes as such. This becomes evident when looking at the hierarchical structure of COICOP/HICP: only the first two hierarchical levels (divisions and groups) can be viewed as levels depicting "purposes", the third level (classes) is an arrangement of products which are assumed to serve the same purpose shown at the respective group and division level. For example, 02.1.1 (Spirits)—part of the Alcoholic Beverages and Tobacco Division 02—might have as items: whisky, gin, brandy, rum and so on.

It was mentioned above that the P of COICOP refers to "purpose". What is the difference between such a classification and one based solely on the nature of the product? The UN publication of the various expenditure classifications[1] has this to say about the subject (page 20):

> *The important point to note is that the units of classification are expenditures on specific goods and services – they are not expenditures on purposes as such. Divisions 01 to 12 of COICOP convert these basic statistics into purposes, such as nourishing the body [i.e. Divisions 01 and 02, Food and alcohol* etc.*], protecting it against inclement weather [i.e. Division 03, clothing and footwear], preventing and curing illness [i.e. Division 06, health], acquiring knowledge [i.e. Division 10, education], travelling from one place*

[1] «Classifications of Expenditure According to Purpose» (UN Statistical Papers, Series M No. 84, 2000).

> *to another [i.e. Division 07, transport], etc.* [Note that the references in square brackets are the author's].

The passage goes on to say:

> *The majority of goods and services can be unambiguously to a single purpose, but some goods and services could plausibly be assigned to more than one purpose. Examples include motor fuel which may be used to power vehicles classified as transport, as well as vehicles classified as recreational".*

My own view on all of this is that the differences in practice between a type-of-product classification and a purpose-of-product classification are largely illusory, since the choice of the division into which a product is assigned is, sometimes, arbitrary. And it needs to be said that if I drive in my car the short journey to a food shop to buy food, the expenditure on petrol is not classified to food in COICOP, even though a consumer might think of it as the cost of buying food, certainly when comparing the cost of driving to an out-of-town supermarket to the cost of walking to the local corner shop. So in practice the definition of "purpose" usually closely matches the associated product.

It is interesting to note that the classification of the UK Retail Prices Index (RPI), which has scarcely changed for many years, is not described as a type-of-purpose index, yet in some cases it more resembles such an index than does COICOP. For example, it has a main heading "Personal Goods and Services" which includes "Chemists' goods". In COICOP such goods are all classified as "Health". Again, the RPI has a main heading "Household Services", which includes postage and telephone, which in COICOP are assigned to "Communication". Which of these allocations most closely describes "purpose" seems to me a theological issue.

So we need not concern ourselves any longer with the theoretical difference between these two types of classification, but simply accept that the HICP is based on COICOP. Its main advantage was the fact that when the HICP was being designed, COICOP was about to become the standard global classification. There would have had to be a very good reason to depart from it.

6.2 Development of COICOP/HICP

An "International Classification of Household Goods and Services" was first developed for use in the UN System of National Accounts (SNA) in 1968. It went through several versions over the years, and when the HICP was being developed in the 1990s a new version of it—known as COICOP (Classification of Individual Consumption According to Purpose)—was being developed. However, at about the same time that the early work on the HICP was starting, a new version of COICOP was being developed by the OECD (Organization for Economic Co-operation and Development). A draft version was adopted at a joint UNECE-OECD-Eurostat meeting on National Accounts held in Geneva in 1996. It was finally published by the United Nations in 2000.[2]

For the HICP it was particularly important to have an agreed classification, as this would enable international comparisons to be made not only at the all-items level of the HICP but at more disaggregated levels too. When comparing inflation between EU member states, it is important not only to look at the overall inflation figures; analysts need to know where the inflation is lower and higher: goods versus services, for example, or, at a more detailed level, durables versus non-durables. To make such comparisons possible, it was necessary to ensure that similar products were being included in all the various categories of expenditure.

COICOP was therefore already earmarked as the future official international classification for household consumption expenditure, and it did not take long for agreement by the HICP Working Party that it should also be the classification to be used for the HICP. COICOP provides a worldwide classification, common across several statistical domains, not only CPIs but also Purchasing Power Parities, Household Budget Surveys and National Accounts.

The connection with National Accounts was important for the HICP, particularly because of the common use of HFMCE (Household Final Monetary Consumption Expenditure), a concept also used in national accounting. The HICP at first followed ESA95 (European System of Acounts) insofar as the latter is consistent with the purposes of the HICP. The most important departures from the ESA95 definitions are:

[2] Classifications of expenditure according to purpose: COFOG, COICOP, COPNI, COPP, Series M: Miscellaneous Statistical Papers, No. 84, New York: United Nations. ST/ESA/STAT/SER.M/84. ISBN: 92-1-161420-1.

HICP follows only that part of HFCE (Household Final Consumption Expenditure whether or not monetary) which is relevant to inflation measurement. So imputed rents for owner-occupiers were excluded from the HICP. The HICP also excludes life insurance, narcotics, gambling, prostitution and financial intermediation services indirectly measured (FISIM).

In both the HICP and the ESA95, volumes are generally valued at purchaser prices, following the acquisition principle. However, there are some differences between HICP and ESA95 in the timing of recording transactions.

6.3 COICOP/HICP

COICOP/HICP closely followed the official COICOP, but there were a few differences. This was always likely to be the case, since the official COICOP was designed to be used by all countries and is probably not ideal for many.

The main structure of COICOP/HICP follows exactly the main structure of the official UN version of COICOP, except that it omits the two last divisions: COICOP Division 13 relates to the individual consumption expenditure of non-profit institutions serving households (NPISHs); COICOP Division 14 covers the individual consumption expenditure of general government. Both of these two areas fall outside the scope of the HICP. Division 13 covers such items as expenditure by old people's homes on accommodation, food and medicines for the benefit of the residents, while Division 14 covers such items as the expenditure by national health services on medicines and other services destined for household consumption.[3]

COICOP/HICP thus contains 12 basic Divisions, such as Food and Non-alcoholic beverages (Div. 01), Furnishings, household equipment and routine maintenance of the house (Div. 05), and Communications (Div. 08). Each division is subdivided into Groups, and most groups are

[3]The COICOP-1999 version has been revised and now contains 15 Divisions (COICOP-2018).

further divided into Classes. Every EU member state will normally classify its own products as separate elements of COICOP/HICP classes, enabling them to aggregate data up to the level of Class and above.[4]

Just to illustrate how the multi-level classification works in practice, here is an example from Commission Regulation 1749/96:

> ***Division**: 05. Furnishings, Household Equipment and Routine Maintenance of the House*
> ***Group**: 05.3 Heating and cooking appliance, refrigerators, washing machines and similar major household appliances, including fittings and repairs.*
> ***Class**: 05.3.2 Small electric household appliances.*

The HICP regulations specified not only the overall classification, but how it was to be divided up as far as reporting of sub-indices was concerned. At levels below the lowest COICOP/HICP level (such as 05.3.2 above), member states were free to select the products most typical in their country; there was no specified "basket" of goods and services at this lowest level.

An important factor in the choice of sub-aggregate products is the classification used in the main source of data for the weights: the national Household Budget Surveys (HBS). Ideally, the classification of products in the HBS would match the classification of products in the HICP. However, this was not necessarily the case for all member states. COICOP was still in a development stage in the early 1990s, and most national HBS surveys would have had their own independent classification. The UK Retail Prices Index, for example, did not (and still (2020) does not) use the COICOP classification.

It was shown earlier in this chapter that there are some differences between the official UN version of COICOP and COICOP/HICP. There are, incidentally, other variants of the official COICOP, for example for calculating purchasing power parities in the EU and linked countries, household consumption expenditure uses a version of COICOP called COICOP-PPP. The Household Budget Survey has a version COICOP-HBS. These versions are close to COICOP, but have some

[4] Eurostat has since changed the name of COICOP/HICP to ECOICOP, the E referring to Europe.

small differences which are not always the same as the differences between COICOP/HICP and COICOP.

As far as COICOP/HICP is concerned, just what are the differences between it and the official COICOP? Apart from the absence of the two Divisions referred to above, there are about 20 smaller parts of the COICOP/HICP classification where differences are to be found from the official UN version of COICOP. The great majority concern groupings where COICOP/HICP headings are formed of aggregations of COICOP headings. For example, COICOP headings 5.5.1 (Major tools and equipment) and 5.5.2 (small tools and miscellaneous accessories) are combined into 5.5.1/2 for COICOP/HICP.

As mentioned before, the early work on the HICP took place in parallel with the development of the UN COICOP, which was entrusted to the OECD. For that reason, several versions of COICOP/HICP were produced, with the final version being published as late as 1999, in Commission Regulation 1749/99. Article 9 of the 1995 Framework Regulation simply referred to the requirement for the HICP to *cover "the categories of the COICOP international classification .... which shall be adapted under the procedure in Article 15 to establish comparable HICPs"*. (Article 15 concerns the procedures to be used leading up to the adoption of regulations). A footnote provided a reference for the version of COICOP to be used: *"United Nations, series F No 2, revision 3, table 6.1, amended by the OECD (DES/NI/86.9), Paris 1986"*. The final version of COICOP/HICP was based on a draft of the final version of COICOP, which was approved by the UN Statistical Commission in 1999 (see 6.2 above).

6.4 Changes Made to COICOP/HICP

A number of changes in the various versions of COICOP/HICP were made over the period 1996–1999. In several instances, it is awkward to make comparisons between the various versions because of changes in the code numbers. For example, Social Protection was not included in the first version, and needed to be slotted in at category 12, requiring the existing category 12 (Insurance) to be re-numbered to 13.

It should also be noted that in fact that—up to 2002—there were only two listings of COICOP/HICP coverage in the HICP regulations. The first one was published as an Annex to the early Regulation 1749/96. The second, published in Regulation 1687/98 in July 1998, was in the form of a list of headings showing, for each heading, whether that heading was included in the initial HICP coverage (January 1997), or to be included in December 1999. (For those interested in these differences, the above Regulation included an Annex showing the original items covered in 1997 along with the revised list from January 1999, plus the few excluded items such as life insurance and games of chance.) There were two other regulations containing COICOP headings, but these related not to coverage as such but to the list of sub-indices which member states were required to provide to Eurostat each month. These were not always identical to the coverage lists. For example, heading 05.3.1 (major household appliances whether electric or not) and 05.3.2 (small electric household appliances) are listed separately in Regulation 1687/98, but Regulations 2214/96 and 1749/99 required member states to provide a sub-index only for the combined products 05.3.1 and 05.3.2. The reason for this was that the weights of each separate index would have been, for some countries, below the 0.1% threshold (see 6.5 below) and thus would have absolved the countries from the need to provide indices at that level. Rather than risk losing data for both categories, it was decided to merge the two headings, which, at the combined level, would have had a significantly larger weight.

All of the above-mentioned regulations except 1687/98 also provide detailed lists showing examples of the types of products covered (and also not covered) by each heading. As an example, heading 05.4.0 (glassware, tableware and household utensils) includes the following more detailed products:

- *Glassware, crystal-ware, ceramic ware and chinaware of the kind used for table, kitchen, bathroom, toilet, office* [sic!] *and indoor decoration,*
- *Cutlery, flatware and silverware,*
- *Non-electric kitchen utensils of all materials such as saucepans, stew-pots, pressure cookers, frying pans, coffee mills, puree-makers, mincers, hotplates, household scales and other such mechanical devices,*
- *Non-electric household articles of all materials such as containers for bread, coffee, spices, etc, waste bins, waste-paper baskets, laundry baskets, portable money-boxes, towel rails, bottle racks, irons and ironing boards, letter boxes, feeding bottles, thermos flasks and ice boxes,*
- *Repair of such articles.*

– *Excludes: lighting equipment (05.1.1); electric household appliances (05.3.1 or 05.3.2); cardboard tableware (05.6.1); personal weighing machines and baby scales (12.1.3).*

6.5 Specification and Production of HICP Sub-indices

The issue of which sub-indices were to be produced and published has already been mentioned in this chapter. Clearly, this issue could not be settled until the precise structure and content of the HICP classification had been decided. In fact the first regulation specifying the list of required sub-indices (Regulation 2214/96) followed only two months after the first implementing regulation which set out the initial coverage of products in the HICP (Regulation 1749/96). The timetable was indeed an early example of "just-in-time" management, as the publication of the latter regulation came only two months before the launch of the HICPs in February 1997. Regulation 1749/96 contained a crucial article on initial coverage—Article 3—which reads as follows:

> *HICPs which include price indices and weights for each category given in Annex 1 accounting for more than one part in a thousand of the total expenditure covered by all these categories, shall be deemed comparable.*

This reference to a threshold of one part per thousand (i.e. 0.1%) set an important precedent for other aspects of HICP production. It followed a decision to publish the HICPs to the level of one decimal place. The wording is slightly misleading, since the 0.1% threshold only has any meaning for the size of the weights; it cannot refer to the index itself. But if the weight of a sub-index is less than 0.1% of total weights, neither the weight nor the index would be published. Thus it became important to be able to measure weights to a fairly precise degree. If a particular sub-index weight was below the 0.1% threshold, a member state would not be required to report the index. That rule, of course, did not prevent the member state from reporting the index if it so wished, and indeed it is likely that this happened from time to time. But the initial selection of sub-indices to be produced did pay due regard to the probable level of the weights, and, as already mentioned, it was decided to merge some COICOP headings for the production of some of the sub-indices for precisely this reason. The last regulation on sub-indices

(Regulation 1749/99) contained twelve combined sub-indices, ten of which were combinations of two COICOP classes and two of which were combinations of three COICOP classes.

CHAPTER 7

Coverage of the HICP: What, Where, Who?

In this chapter we will be looking at one of the fundamental questions faced during the creation of a new CPI. **What, where and who** should be within the scope of the index? This covers the choice of products, matters of geographic and population coverage as well as outlet types. Questions concerning "how?", which are mainly technical, are dealt with in Chapters 9–11, for example how should insurance premiums be dealt with?

7.1 Product Coverage: Specific Issues

Let's first be clear about what exactly a "product" is. Many people, if asked the meaning, tend to assume that a product is tangible—what are commonly called "goods". In the HICP, "products" cover both goods and services. This not only saves on printing costs, but is also a useful concept, since in many respects there is little economic difference between a good and a service. We can buy food (a good) and eat it at home, or we can buy a meal in a restaurant (a service). Both fulfil the same primary purpose of satisfying (or preventing) hunger. But there is a big statistical difference between the two, as well as a difference in the experience itself.

Some member states, at the time that we were developing the HICP, included or omitted certain products in their national CPI. This, of

J. Astin, *Measuring EU Inflation*,
https://doi.org/10.1007/978-3-030-68806-6_7

course, was one of the many reasons why CPIs were not directly comparable. In the early discussions, as noted in Chapter 1, Eurostat was steered strongly in the direction of the maximum coverage of all possible products. Italy and Luxembourg excluded tobacco products and most alcoholic beverages from their national CPIs, for their own reasons, mainly to do with health. In Eurostat we were concerned to ensure that no products were excluded for reasons which had nothing to do with economic theory. Tobacco may be bad for your health, but it is an important item of consumer expenditure and it forms part of GDP. There was no reason to exclude it. The same goes for alcohol.

Other types of product were more problematic. One of the most difficult areas concerned health and education products. If these important items of consumption were all consumed within the private sector there would be little argument about whether or not they should be within the scope of any CPI—even though there would still be problems of price measurement. But in most member states these products were divided between the private and public sectors. A patient could be treated in a private clinic and pay the full market price. Or, more commonly, the patient could be treated in a clinic run by the state or local authority, and would receive free or discounted treatment. Should both types of transaction be included in the HICP, and to what extent? Chapter 11.1 deals specifically with these sectors; suffice it to say here that it was decided that the entirety of actual health and education expenditure by households should be covered.

Owner-occupied housing (OOH) was another problematic sector—and remains so at the time of writing in 2020. There is a strong argument that since OOH is considered as capital expenditure in the United Nations System of National Accounts (SNA), and also in the EU version, the European System of Accounts (ESA), then it should not be included in a CPI, because it is simply not regarded as consumer expenditure. The OOH problem is dealt with in some detail in Chapter 11.2. Briefly, it was felt by a special Task Force (TF12) that OOH should in principle form part of the product coverage of the HICP. The main problem was how it should be measured, and that is a topic which is still hotly debated. The SPC in September 2000 was presented with a long Eurostat paper offering three options. One was to include OOH in the HICP on the "net acquisitions" basis (housing new to the private market); one was to compile a separate OOH index on the same basis; and the third was effectively to do nothing. In any event, OOH was "temporarily" excluded from coverage pending further debate. Much later, in 2013, a regulation was adopted[1] requiring member states to produce a quarterly OOH price index on the net acquisitions basis (option 2 above), and this has been produced and published[2] as the Owner-Occupied Housing Price Index (OOH-HPI), beginning with 2005 data for almost all member states, and on an annual basis from 2010 for all member states. Not being monthly (though some member states are able to provide this) it cannot (yet?) be included in the HICP. In addition, the same regulation introduced a simpler measure, the House Price Index (HPI) which measures all transaction prices by households on housing, whether or not new to the household sector.

Special attention was paid at later stages of the HICP project to other products displaying unusual or unique characteristics. These were dealt with in separate regulations, or dealt with more informally, and some are addressed in Chapter 11. These products include:

- Insurance (except life insurance, which is permanently excluded, being regarded as a form of investment rather than consumption)
- Service charges which are proportional to transaction values (such as foreign currency exchange charges)
- Social protection services
- Books, CDs and games
- Motor vehicles
- Data processing equipment
- Package holidays
- Clothing
- Financial services
- Delivery charges
- Products with income-related prices.

A different category of products was also carefully considered for inclusion, and in these cases rejected.

[1] Commission Regulation 93/2003.

[2] https://www.ons.gov.uk/economy/inflationandpriceindices/bulletins/housepriceindex/previousReleases.

7.1.1 Narcotics

A narcotic drug has a chemical or medical classification which defines it as a narcotic. Whether or not a narcotic is illegal depends on the member state where it is used or purchased. Some are illegal in most or all countries, while others are legal in some countries and illegal in others. Should illegality automatically require exclusion of the product from the HICP? Aside from the serious problems of price and weight measurement, the general view was that such products should be excluded. If the HICP were to be used as a compensation index (though not designed for that purpose), why should wages rise when the price of illegal drugs rises? That being so, what to do about legal narcotics, whose prices and weights can be measured in the countries where they are legal? But to include some products in one country's HICP and not another's would lead to the very incomparability we were trying to reduce. So the solution adopted was to exclude all narcotics, regardless of their legal status.

7.1.2 Prostitution

A slightly similar problem—at least as far as the HICP was concerned—was prostitution. As with narcotics, prostitution was included in the UN classification of consumer expenditure (COICOP 12.2), but few, if any, member states included it in their national CPI, regardless of its potential weight in total consumer expenditure. Again, there are problems of measurement, as well as the question of legality. Doubtless, moral stances affected the argument too. However, decisions regarding the coverage of the HICP should not be based on moral grounds, but rather on economic and practical considerations. The upshot was that it was decided that prostitution should also be excluded from the HICP.

7.1.3 Gambling

A third category of expenditure which was specifically excluded from the HICP is gambling, or "games of chance", in all its forms. This activity may sometimes be illegal but usually is not. It is covered in the UN COICOP classification, and it includes (under heading 9.4.3: Games of chance) the following: "service charges for lotteries, book makers, totalizators, casinos and other gambling establishments, gaming machines, bingo halls, scratch cards, sweepstakes, etc".

Why just “service charges”? This is because the act of gambling is where an individual makes a wager which may result in all or part of the wager being returned to the individual, but some part of which is retained by the organisation which manages the gambling situation. That part of a wager which is effectively paid out to other winners, is regarded as a transfer between households, and not a payment for a consumer item. Only the service charge is regarded as the payment of a consumer item. So by excluding gambling entirely from the HICP does not exclude the major part of bets and winnings, but simply the (usually relatively small) percentage retained by the organiser.

But why not include the service charge of gambling, given that it is within COICOP? The answer was simply that to measure it for the purpose of including it in a price index was felt to be impracticable. It would be difficult, if not impossible, to draw up a list of individual “items” to be priced and equally difficult to measure the prices of such items. In addition, gamblers may well know the gross or net amount of their stakes but are unlikely to know what the service charge is. So it would be impossible to obtain the weights from a standard HBS. In any case it seems quite likely that gamblers in general will spend more or less the same proportion of their disposable income on gambling (after deducting the cost of essential items like food, shelter and clothing)—and the result may be that the “price” of gambling tracks the overall consumer price index fairly closely.

7.1.4 *Black-Market Products*

In fact, the first three products, narcotics, gambling and prostitution, were the only specific “products” to have been excluded from HICP coverage. However, there is one other class of products which is also excluded from the HICP (and probably most other CPIs): the black-market (sometimes referred to as the “hidden economy”). The black-market may be defined as the sales of goods or services which are not officially recorded, usually because the circumstances surrounding the sale are illegal. An obvious example is the sale of illegally imported cigarettes. The main reason for exclusion from the HICP is the difficulty of measuring prices. Clearly, the sellers of black-market goods are not going to give their prices to official surveyors—and equally it would be regarded as improper or even dangerous for price surveyors to seek out illicit sellers. But perhaps this is not such a big problem from the point of view of accuracy of the HICP.

It seems likely that the price trends of black-market products will follow fairly closely the price trends of similar products sold legally, even though the price levels may differ significantly. If the weights can be estimated with reasonable accuracy, there will be little degradation of the index.

These exclusions were of course discussed in the HICP WP during the preparation of the regulation on coverage,[3] but the proposal to exclude them did not cause much controversy.

7.2 Initial and Extended Product Coverage

Readers will recall that the product coverage for the Interim Indices of Consumer Prices (IICP)—see Chapter 4—was based on a reduced set of COICOP headings, removing those headings where it was known that comparability between member states would be poor. Chief among these exclusions were health and education products and costs associated with owner-occupied housing. But many other products—averaging about 5% of the total possible coverage in terms of weight—were also excluded. Among this group of excluded products were:

- Package holidays;
- Expenditure abroad;
- Water supply and disposal when paid as a tax and not by the amount consumed;
- Taxes related to the use of cars, including road tax, tolls and driving licences;
- Financial services including insurance; social services;
- Other miscellaneous services.

The first task before the launch of the HICP was to bring into coverage as many as possible of the excluded products, without putting at risk the comparability requirement. A great deal of work was done by the member states in preparation for the extended coverage. At the launch of the HICP in March 1997, the following additions (compared with the IICPs) were made to product coverage, as provided for in Regulation 1749/96:

[3] Council Regulation 1687/98.

- Insurance for cars and dwelling contents
- Package holidays
- Banking services
- Various administrative fees and charges
- Educational products (including evening classes)
- Non-prescription medicines
- Toll charges, driving licences, road taxes.

Later, further additions were made. Regulation 1687/98 amended Regulation 1749/96 by adding further categories for full inclusion by December 1999. These were:

(a) **New additions to coverage:**

- Medical services
- Dental services
- Paramedical services
- Primary, pre-primary, secondary and tertiary education
- Education not definable by level (e.g. language courses)
- Social protection services (partial)
- Transport insurance (full)
- Health insurance
- Other insurance.

(b) **Previously only partial coverage:**

- Housing rentals
- Refuse collection
- Sewerage services
- Water supply
- Medical products, appliances, equipment
- Books
- Stationery and drawing materials
- Canteens
- Accommodation services
- Dwelling insurance
- Other financial services.

Regulation 2166/99 amplified the coverage details of some of the earlier regulations in the fields of health, education and social protection, following evidence that not all member states were interpreting the previous descriptions in similar ways. For example, Article 3.2 of this Regulation says:

> *All providers of goods and services in the health, education and social protection sectors . . shall be covered in the HICP independently of their status. This excludes individuals or groups of individuals as producers of goods and non-financial services for exclusively their own private use.*

This Article perhaps demonstrates the enormously detailed attention that the designers of the HICP were paying to the precise construction of the evolving index. Regulation 2166/99 extended the coverage of the HICP in these sectors from January 2000 as follows:

- Social protection services within the home
- Hospital services (partial)
- Retirement homes
- Residences for the disabled.

It may perhaps be noted that a later Commission Regulation—1749/99—is concerned not with product coverage per se, but its classification, in particular for the decisions on which sub-indices should be computed. This Regulation was needed because in 1999 the UN agreed on a new version of COICOP, requiring a revised version of COICOP/HICP. This is dealt with in more detail in Chapter 6.3.

7.3 Geographic Coverage

The broad question of geographic coverage was addressed in Chapter 3.3.3. This section goes into further detail.

The heading covers two rather separate issues. The first is perhaps the more important, at least as far as economic concept goes. It concerns the question of consumption abroad and consumption in the home country by foreigners. This is a fundamental issue because it poses the question: "Whose inflation are we trying to measure?"

Two distinct approaches are possible. The first, known as the "national" approach, considers the experience of the residents of the home country, whether their expenditure is actually in the home country or abroad, for instance when they are on holiday (all business-related expenditure is in any case out of the scope of the HICP). The second, known as the "domestic" approach, considers inflation in the home country, whether the expenditure is incurred by domestic residents or by foreign visitors, such as cross-border shoppers or holidaymakers.

Both approaches carry some difficult practical measurement problems: the national approach requires a survey of prices faced by home country residents when visiting foreign countries, while the domestic approach requires estimates of the weights of the various types of expenditure made in the home country by foreign visitors. But, regardless of these difficulties, it was felt that a macroeconomic index such as the HICP should in principle be measuring total consumer inflation within a country, rather than inflation faced by the households of a country, regardless of the country where the expenditure takes place.

The Monetary Union Index of Consumer Prices (MUICP) was to provide a measure of price stability in the euro area. The objective was to measure price change in the euro area as a whole by aggregating price changes within each of the national territories of the euro area Member States, regardless of the nationality of the consumers facing such price changes.

It was necessary to have a rule requiring all member states to use the same approach, otherwise there would be inconsistencies when aggregating the national HICPs to the EMU (or indeed EU) total. For example, if country A, using the domestic approach, included the expenditure of visitors from country B in its HICP, and country B, using the national approach, included the same expenditure, that expenditure would be double-counted in the HICP for the EU as a whole. Moreover, the expenditure of country A residents in country B would not be covered at all.

This situation may be seen better in a diagram (Fig. 7.1).

Box A shows the situation in country A. The letter "a" represents the national residents of country A, while b′ represents foreign visitors from country B.

Box B shows a similar situation in country B. The letter "b" represents the national residents of country B, while a′ represents foreign visitors from country A.

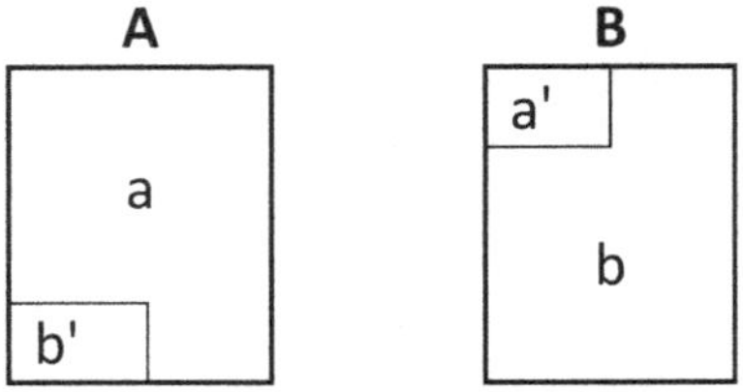

Fig. 7.1 Domestic and National approaches to coverage

If country A uses the domestic approach, it will include the expenditures of a and of b′. If country B uses the national approach, it will include the expenditures of b and b' but exclude the expenditure of a′.

Mixed approach:

Expenditure of country A (domestic approach) = a + b′

Expenditure of country B (national approach) = b + b′−a′

Domestic approach:

Expenditure of country A = a + b′

Expenditure of country B = b + a′

Accordingly, the rule adopted for the HICP was that all countries must use the domestic approach.

Some countries did not support this view. One country with a high level of inward tourism did not, in its national CPI, include expenditure on hotels, restaurants, etc. at its popular seaside resorts because they were used mainly by foreign holidaymakers—and at that time those prices were rising relatively fast. For the HICP these prices would have to be included, and HICP inflation would (other things being equal) appear higher than inflation as measured by the national CPI. Moreover, there would be significant extra expenses incurred in covering new price collection in the tourist districts.

A second issue concerning geographic coverage is a purely national one: the geographic coverage of prices within a country. A CPI should, in principle, be representative of the average changes in prices across an entire country. Prices can, of course, be collected only in a relatively small selection of places, because prices are (or were at that time) mainly collected in person by individual price collectors—an expensive resource. So in practice price collection is restricted to particular towns and cities and (rarely) villages.

It must always be remembered that a CPI is a measure of price changes, not price levels. If it is believed (preferably with some evidence) that the price changes in a certain district can be measured effectively by reference to price changes in specific towns in that district, then a sample of such towns should be sufficient for compiling the index. We look at sampling in more detail in Chapter 9.1. The main point here is that it would be highly unusual—and indeed probably wrong—for a country simply to assume that prices collected only in, say, the capital city and two other cities would yield price changes representative of price changes across the whole country.

Article 8 of Regulation 1749/96 refers to ". . *sufficient prices within each elementary aggregate to take account of the variation of price movements in the population shall be deemed reliable and comparable.*"

This is a good example of the general approach to the harmonization process. Rather than having Eurostat specify in detail how the national HICP is to be calculated, the technique is to specify the required outputs of the HICP process. So in this instance, the regulation does not specify that there must be *x* urban centres and *y* rural centres in the price collection sample. It leaves the choice of *x* and *y* to each member state, depending on its economic and geographic circumstances. A large country with many large cities, where a large majority of the population lives in cities, may be able to produce a representative sample by restricting price collection to the cities, ignoring completely the rural areas. Other countries may have large rural populations where it may be essential to include a sample of rural towns and even villages in the price collection.

How are these requirements to be applied in practice? It is generally believed that a sample which includes several (or even most) regions is likely to be more representative than one which does not. Also that the sample should include a fair representation of rural districts, where price changes may be different from urban districts (possibly linked to the types of retail outlet found in small places compared with cities). An NSI should be able to demonstrate that its geographic sample is a good representation of the entire country as far as price change is concerned. (The topic of quality control and compliance monitoring is dealt with in Chapter 12.)

On-line shopping in the earlier days of the HICP was growing in importance, but had not nearly reached the levels of today. Serious discussion of the problems began only after I had left Eurostat in 2002. There were a number of issues to be considered. For example, should the transaction be allocated to the place of residence of the purchaser, or to the place where the good was shipped from? Or the place where the company supplying the good was situated? Some of these places could well be in a different country from the person ordering the goods. In the end, there was no regulation but an official Recommendation, published in 2014. The address where the goods were to be delivered was the main criterion for the allocation of the place of transaction. Other matters covered issues of sampling, weights, etc.

7.4 Population Coverage

This chapter began by saying that it would be concerned with "what, where and who" should be covered by the HICP. So far, we have discussed the first two of these—the products and the geography. Now we turn to the domestic population to be covered. Isn't this obvious? Everybody should be covered! Even prisoners? Maybe not. But if not, why not? These are the type of question that had to be addressed in this context. And national CPIs were quite varied in their population coverage. Many countries did not include any type of institutional households at all. (By this, I mean not just prisons but care homes, hospitals, boarding schools and so on.) Some countries excluded parts of the ordinary population depending on their income level. For example, the UK Retail Prices Index (RPI) excluded (and still does at the time of writing in 2020) households where the main income earner has an income within the top 4% of all households, and also pensioner households which derive at least three quarters of their total income from state pensions and benefits. This type of exclusion had its origin in the early uses of the index, which were aimed particularly at wage negotiation, and, later, wage indexation. So it was felt that an index including coverage of the wealthiest part of the population and many of those who were both retired and badly off would not be appropriate for a so-called "compensation index".

But the HICP was never intended as a compensation index. It was intended as a macroeconomic indicator of general inflation, and thus it should cover as wide a segment of the domestic population as possible.

In principle, no resident household should be excluded from the sample. Of course, the contribution of households to the construction of a CPI is limited to information concerning their patterns of expenditure, in order to provide accurate weights for the index. But this fact makes it necessary to ensure that different types of institution are covered in the HBS. Many institutions, such as care homes and boarding schools, provide food for their residents; the cost of providing food is paid for by the residents themselves (or their families), sometimes assisted by a state subsidy. The payment of fees to such institutions is itself part of consumer expenditure (e.g. COICOP 12.4)—but the actual purchase of food is made by the institutions and not by the residents. Many other items of ordinary consumers' expenditure may also be provided by the institution, leaving relatively little for individual residents to buy. So their patterns of expenditure are likely to be very different from those of non-institutional households.

Extending the coverage of the HBS to institutional residents was a major task for several countries and involved some considerable expense. (The question of financial assistance to member states towards the extra costs of the HICP are discussed in Chapter 15.5.)

Another problem faced when a price index covers the whole nation is ensuring that the coverage of expenditure by the wealthiest households is adequate. It has been known for many years that the wealthiest households tend to give a relatively low response to HBS surveys, the result being an underestimation of the weights of certain types of product bought mainly by the wealthy—top-range cars, expensive jewellery, high-end clothing, and so on. This is relevant to the often-mentioned question of whether the HICP should be weighted by households (so-called "democratic" weighting) or by expenditure (so-called "plutocratic " weighting). The HICP has from the start been computed with expenditure weights, as befits a macroeconomic index.

The household weighting method (which is more appropriate for an uprating index) gives more difficulties of compilation. However, the expenditure weighting method tends to result in an index which relates to the better-off households, while the household-based index effectively results in an index which is more relevant to typical households, towards the centre of the expenditure distribution, i.e. the median level. (The Household Costs Index, currently being developed in the UK, is an example of a household weighted index).

7.5 Household Final Monetary Consumption Expenditure (HFMCE)

Before concluding this chapter, I turn to an extremely important aspect of the HICP which fits quite conveniently into the subject matter of the chapter. Household Final Monetary Consumption Expenditure (HFMCE) is a sub-category of total household expenditure which was originally defined for the UN System of National Accounts (SNA) and later adopted also for the European System of Accounts (ESA).

What exactly is HFMCE and why is it important for the HICP? Perhaps the best way of answering these questions is to look at why it was originally proposed—and thanks are due to the late Professor Peter Hill, an international expert in the field of national accounts, who acted as a consultant to Eurostat in the early years of the HICP.

There was never much doubt about the H and C parts of HFMCE. H is for households, whose expenditure is clearly the subject of the HICP. C is for consumption—also rather obvious: the HICP is not aiming to measure capital expenditure or government expenditure. Slightly more difficult is the F, which stands for Final (as opposed to Intermediate) consumption. If a rural household, especially in a developing country, purchases agricultural tools to enable it to grow its own food for consumption within the household, this is in a certain sense intermediate consumption: the tools simply enable the production of food, they are not directly "consumed" themselves. But, by convention, such tools are treated as final consumption, and would be included in the HICP in principle. But if a private household happens to be running a business from home, and spending money on a computer or on filing systems, these items are classed as business expenditure, and are not covered in the HICP. So Final Consumption is normally what households themselves consume, sometimes immediately, like food and drink, sometimes over a longer period of time, like clothing or household durables.

Perhaps the most critical word of HFMCE is the M: Monetary. This means that to qualify as HFMCE the expenditure by the household must be in actual money. This does not mean it must be in cash; any form of money is included, whether a bank transfer, a credit or debit card, a cheque, and so on.

The concept of HFMCE, which already existed in the NSA and ESA, was used in the HICP in the first place to formalise a decision concerning the treatment of subsidised expenditure in health and education. This issue raised some protracted arguments in the WP. For example, some countries argued that the price of a medicine prescribed by a doctor should be the full market price and not the reduced price actually paid by the consumer after deducting the government subsidy—regardless of whether the subsidy is given at the moment of purchase or reimbursed later. This topic is dealt with in greater length in Chapter 11.1. The same issue arises in respect of other medical services and also many educational services such as subsidised university fees.

The use of HFMCE specifies rather precisely that the amount to be covered in the HICP is the monetary expenditure paid by the consumer, i.e. the subsidised price in the case of health or education. (The subsidy itself would form part of government expenditure, and fall within a price index of government expenditure, if such an index existed.)

It also helps to resolve the problem of how to measure the price of owner-occupied housing—an eternal problem for the CPI compiler! One popular method is to assume that an owner-occupied house is rented, and to impute the estimated rent to the owner, as if the house were rented rather than owned. The HFMCE concept in effect forbids this, as the "expenditure"—and indeed the transaction itself—is merely imputed and not "monetary".

The HFMCE principle caused a good deal of controversy in the WP, both on conceptual and practical grounds. The ESA has another category, "household actual final consumption", which includes social transfers in kind, such as the provision to households of free or subsidised health and education services. Some countries felt that this would be more relevant for the HICP than HFMCE. However, others argued that HFMCE was the appropriate operational implication of the wording in the Framework Regulation concerning the scope of the HICP: *"the prices of goods and services available for purchase in the economic territory of the Member State for the purpose of directly satisfying consumer needs"*; and was felt to be consistent with the view that inflation is a monetary phenomenon, manifested only in actual monetary transactions.

In fact most of the arguments against HFMCE were based on the practical issues involved, for example that it would be easier to measure gross prices (i.e. gross of any reimbursements) than net prices.

It was also argued that for reasons of comparability, the government sector, and consequently most of social protection, health and education services, should be excluded entirely, given the widely varying institutional arrangements in different member states. Eurostat's view was that for the purposes of a consumer inflation index there was no danger of introducing non-comparability by such services, as long as prices are taken "net", i.e. the index measuring changes in the prices actually paid by consumers in exchange for the services concerned.

A further argument against the HFMCE concept was that changes in social protection policy and particularly in reimbursements financed, for instance, through changes in direct taxation and vice versa could distort the picture of inflation provided by an HICP which included health, education and social protection services. But on the other hand, if the aim of the HICP was to measure changes in prices actually faced by consumers—whatever the reason—such changes should be included. So that, for example, if a government decided to reduce a percentage rebate on prescription charges, which in effect would require the consumer to pay more, the HICP should reflect this as a price increase.

Implementing the HFMCE concept in practice did, for sure, involve significant costs for some countries. For example, the UK had to switch to using the National Accounts as a data source for certain weights, but as the national accounts data were not classified to the necessary COICOP 4-digit level the task was a heavy one. In France, estimates had to be made of "net" weights for health products and social protection services.

CHAPTER 8

Index Formulae

8.1 Introduction

The issue of index formula has in recent years become a major topic of discussion among producers and users of consumer price indices. But in the early days of the HICP it did not rank quite so high in the discussions, though it was always regarded as an important issue. Most of the controversies surrounding this topic focus on the formula used at the level of the elementary aggregate.

This book is not a textbook, but the issue of elementary aggregate formulae can have resounding consequences, as can be seen by the UK's problems with the conflict between the RPI and other price indices in recent years. This conflict mainly concerned the choice for formula and in the end led to the RPI losing its "National Statistic" status in 2013.

The chapter begins with a short glossary of terms related to index formulae. This supplements the main glossary at the end of the book, but it may be more convenient for readers to have these technical terms to hand while reading this particular chapter.

J. Astin, *Measuring EU Inflation*,
https://doi.org/10.1007/978-3-030-68806-6_8

8.2 Short Glossary of Formulae Terms

The following definitions are given in alphabetical order.

Aggregation	The process by which price indices for elementary aggregate indices are combined to obtain indices for higher-level aggregates.
Carli Price Index	An elementary price index covering two periods to be compared, being the arithmetic mean of the price relatives (i.e. ratios) between the two periods.
Chain Index	An index number series for a long sequence of periods obtained by linking together index numbers spanning shorter sequences of periods.
Dutot Price Index	An elementary price index covering two periods to be compared, being the ratio of the arithmetic mean prices in each of the two periods.
Elementary Aggregate	The smallest grouping of products for which expenditure data (and hence weights) are normally available. The term "products" in this definition may refer to a product (including both goods and services) with the added dimensions of the region of a transaction and the type of outlet. For example, an elementary aggregate may comprise the set of "razor blades" sold in supermarkets in the capital city region.[1]
Elementary (Aggregate) Price Index	a price index for an elementary aggregate.
Higher-Level Price Index	A price index for a grouping above the level of elementary aggregate.

[1] See "Practical Guide to Producing Consumer Price Indices", United Nations, 2009, Table 10.2.

Jevons Price Index	An elementary price index covering two periods to be compared, being the ratio of the geometric mean of the price relatives for each element between the two periods, or the ratio of the geometric means of the prices in each of the two periods. (These give identical results).
Laspeyres Price Index	A higher-level weighted price index covering two periods to be compared, in which the basket of products comprises the quantities of goods and services in the earlier of the two periods.
Lowe Price Index	A higher-level weighted price index that measures the change in the value of a basket of products between two periods, where the basket does not necessarily have to consist of the actual quantities in the same periods.
Paasche Price Index	A higher-level price index covering two periods to be compared, in which the basket of products comprises the quantities of goods and services in the later of the two periods.
Price Updating	A procedure whereby the quantities in an earlier period are revalued at the prices of a later period, using the components of the price index.
Quantities	Strictly speaking, quantities of products are the physical weights, numbers, etc. of the products. Given that these are not directly additive, expenditures on the quantities are used instead, in particular for the purpose of calculating weights.

8.3 Development Plans for Formulae Regulation

The question of index formulae was included in the first of the HICP implementing regulations, 1749/96, and was indeed the first implementing regulation to go before the SPC. Its preparation and drafting was thus a pilot exercise in the HICP technical development, and for that reason this chapter goes into perhaps more technical detail than most of the subsequent technical chapters.

The Task Forces (TF) were described in Chapter 2.3. The topic of index formulae was given to a specialist TF (TF3) which was given the sole task of preparing the text of the implementing regulation. It may be noted that the TFs had no decision-making powers. They were there to allow experts from several countries to discuss the various issues and prepare the text of a regulation.

TF3 met for the first time for a single day in September 1993. Its remit was simply:

> *To propose guidelines for the combination of prices into elementary aggregates.*

(Note that at this stage the term "guidelines" was used for what later became regulations).

This was followed by a second meeting which resulted in a proposal for the WP in 1995. It proposed to carry out its remit in the following ways:

(a) *define the term "elementary aggregates";*
(b) *determine the formulae to be used in combining prices;*
(c) *propose treatments for missing observations and for seasonal items;*
(d) *identify the implications of its proposals for other Task Forces;*
(e) *test the sensitivity of CPIs to different guidelines;*
(f) *identify the potential costs of implementation.*

We turn next to the technical development of the ideas which led up to the rules on the elementary index formula. It needs to be recalled that at this period—the early 1990s—rather few countries used the Jevons formula in their national CPIs. One important reason for this can be clearly linked to the development of computer power. The calculation of *n*th roots, where *n* may be quite large, while simple on a computer, is far less easy or time-consuming using manual logarithm calculations or even with the early electronic calculators. An additional concern was what to do with a missing price, where consequently one of the values in a set of prices will be zero. The calculation of an arithmetic mean of such a dataset poses no difficulty, but it is impossible to calculate a geometric mean. Multiply anything by zero and the answer is always zero!

After a total of four meetings, TF3 arrived at the following conclusions relating to the elementary index formula and also to the method of aggregating elementary indices to the all-items index. It is interesting to see that they were already using quasi-legal phrasing, in anticipation of the forthcoming regulation.

(1) The meaning of the term "elementary aggregate"

TF3 produced the following set of definitions relating to elementary aggregate indices:

The harmonised consumer price index shall comprise a weighted average of price indices for elementary aggregates. An elementary aggregate shall refer to the expenditure (or consumption) covered by the most detailed level of stratification classified according to such criteria as commodity group, geographic location and outlet type. The elementary aggregate relates to the level of stratification down to which satisfactory expenditure information is available for weighting together price indices. Below that level, equal weights are taken. Thus, the price indices for elementary aggregates (elementary indices) comprise only price data. An elementary price index where the number of prices or price changes is proportional to volume or value of consumption covered is termed a self-weighted elementary index. An elementary index where equal weights are used is termed a simple elementary index. A price index where both price and weighting data are used is termed a composite price index.

TF3 added a short commentary or explanation as follows:

This definition is designed to identify unambiguously the level at which there is an issue of how to combine price data when no weighting information is available and to set a common terminology for the purposes of discussion.

(2) The required number of elementary aggregates

The number of elementary aggregates comprising the harmonised consumer price index shall be such that:

(a) *all commodity groups at the 3-digit classification of the CPA*[2] *are distinguished;*
(b) *geographic locations where price levels differ by more than 5 per cent from the national average are distinguished;*
(c) *outlet types offering different levels of prices and services are distinguished;*
(d) *no simple elementary aggregate shall represent more than 0.5 percent of total expenditure unless prices are standardised or uniform within the aggregate.*

The commentary on the above was:

It is necessary to set a minimum level of disaggregation in order to ensure comparability of price indices. The commodity breakdown will allow components of the community-wide index to be computed. Geographic disaggregation does not necessarily improve the accuracy of the CPI but is currently practised by most countries. Disaggregation by outlet type may present problems for some countries in establishing weights but will generally improve the estimate of price movements.

Rough weights are better than equal weights.

TF3 followed up these basic ideas with a set of draft "guidelines".

In later years, it seems to have become widely believed that the HICP regulation required the use of the geometric mean formula (i.e. the Jevons formula), but this was most certainly not the case. The basic choice was between the Dutot or Jevons formulae, as serious issues with the Carli formula had been identified (see next-but-one page). But member states could use an alternative formula if it provided similar (but not necessarily identical) results. The one formula that was "normally" ruled out was the Carli formula, though even this was allowable if it could be shown that its results did not fail the comparability test.

Of course, it is possible (and in fact frequently done) to use more than one formula in compiling elementary aggregate indices. Given that particular formulae are more suitable in certain circumstances than others, this

[2] Classification of Products by Activity [highly detailed]. Council Regulation 451/2008.

is perfectly acceptable, and may indeed sometimes be considered necessary. For example, the Dutot formula can be more appropriate than the Jevons formula in some situations. And when there are cases of zero prices, such as where an item is missing, the Jevons formula cannot be used, at least not without some modification. More is said about the choice of formula below.

The TF3 recommendations on the formula for the elementary aggregate induces were particularly important, as they later became the subject of the very first Implementing Regulation to appear before the SPC, and indeed to be approved by that important body. The role and composition of the SPC will be examined later (see Chapter 15.2). For the moment, we will trace the history of the elementary aggregate index regulation through the Working Party.

A first draft Commission Regulation was discussed at a meeting of the WP in June 1995. Being the first of what was to be a long line of implementing regulations, it is worth recording part of the covering paper:

> *The attached draft Commission Regulation ... is presented to the Working Party in order to:*
>
> (a) ***Provide a model****for the series of Commission Regulations which will be required to produce harmonized CPIs;*
> (b) ***Test the procedure****for setting down (Comitology) and implementation "rules";*
> (c) ***Set down the rules****which must be followed by member states in order to ensure comparability between member states in the methods of compiling elementary indices.*

Most readers will perhaps not be overly concerned with the administrative aspects of the regulation, the general layout of which is broadly similar to that described in Chapter 3 concerning the Framework Regulation.

The comitology procedure follows a different path for a regulation of the Commission rather than the Council, and aficionados of these procedures should consult Chapter 15.2.

The rules concerning index formulae formed just a part of the first implementing regulation (1749/96). The other topics covered in that regulation were: Initial Coverage, New Products, Quality Adjustment and

Sampling. Each of these important topics was being dealt with in parallel in the same manner as that used for the formulae, and are dealt with in Chapters 6–11.

Apart from the definition of elementary aggregates, the main element of the regulation was the appropriate formula to be used in calculating the elementary aggregate indices. This has always been a bone of contention among statisticians and economists and remains so to this day (and probably for evermore—there is no sign of any formula which makes a CPI suitable for all of its several purposes).

This book is most definitely not the place to delve deeply into the pros and cons of the various formulae that have been used and proposed for calculating elementary aggregate indices. Here I shall just recapitulate the main issues.

In the early 1990s, many countries used either the Carli or the Dutot formula (sometimes both), but, with increased computer power, Jevons was gradually becoming more popular. Contemporary academic work showed clearly that the Carli formula had some important disadvantages, and was being viewed with some suspicion by a number of price statisticians. In particular, use of the chained Carli formula exhibits an upward bias as well as intransitivity, i.e. if prices return to the level of an earlier month, the Carli index does not necessarily return to its previous level. The decision to rule out the Carli formula in the regulation was not taken on the grounds that that it was generally accepted as "wrong" but rather that it fails to give results which are "comparable" to those given by other formulae.

It had also been shown that the Jevons formula displayed several theoretical advantages over most other formulae, but the Dutot formula was regarded as at least as good—especially in certain circumstances, such as a zero price, where Jevons simply doesn't work. In recent years, Jevons has also been criticised on the grounds that it implicitly assumes a degree of item substitution when relative prices change.

Fighting a way through this thicket in 1995 was not easy, to say the least. Some sort of compromise seemed inevitable. TF3 proposed Dutot as the preferred formula, while permitting the use of Jevons or another formula as long as the results did not show any systematic differences from one or other of the allowed formulae—at least to the extent of failing to meet the overall comparability test, which allowed differences provided they were less than 0.1%. This wording meant that if a country wanted to use Jevons, it would have to demonstrate that the results were similar to Dutot (which in many cases would not have succeeded.) This was first discussed at the WP in June 1995, but the discussion was inconclusive. There was no clear view articulated which would amend this draft, which consequently was sent to the SPC for a decision. The SPC didn't approve it, and sent it back to the Working Party with an instruction to propose a formula which had the clear support of a qualified majority of countries. A further discussion took place in the WP in October 1995.

A compromise was presented by Eurostat under which Jevons was promoted to sit alongside Dutot as equal "winners" in the game of choice. Only Carli was relegated to the class of "other formulae" which could be used only if it could be shown that the results were comparable. (It was not said which of the two allowed formula would serve as the comparator in such a comparison!).

The proposal was fiercely fought over in the WP, and it was decided to take a vote. Indeed, the remit from the SPC required a vote, since it demanded a clear majority. It was felt that the majority should be calculated according to the normal Commission voting rules, under which the larger countries had more votes than the smaller ones. The total number of votes possible was 87, and a "qualified majority" required 62 votes. The WP voted—and precisely 62 votes were in favour!

So the draft, duly amended, was sent back to the SPC, who decided at their meeting in December 1995 to approve it by a large majority.

There were of course other amendments to the text along the way, but these were all relatively minor in comparison with the formula issue.

8.4 The Regulation on Index Formulae

The Framework Regulation (2494/95) had laid down that the HICP was to be a "Laspeyres-type" index (Article 9). No later regulation elaborated on this, which left the precise formulation of the higher-level indices open to differentiation in the member states. In practice, however, the higher-level indices are calculated in exactly the same way in all member states—and this follows the usual treatment in most national CPIs. I will return to this topic later in the chapter.

So the Implementing Regulation 1749/96 dealt only with how the elementary indices were to be calculated. The preamble includes the following:

> *Whereas the coverage of the existing consumer price indices produced by the Member States, practices followed for … the methods of combining prices to form price indices for elementary aggregates … differ between Member States to the extent that the resulting consumer price indices produced by the Member States fail to meet the comparability requirement necessary for the production of the HICP …*

In other words, as with most of the other aspects of harmonization, the aim was to increase comparability of the HICPs, as laid down in the Maastricht Treaty. The aim was not to harmonize the precise methods of producing HICPs. This is an important point of principle for HICP construction, and it became known as the principle of "output-based" rather than "input-based" methodologies (see Chapter 5.4). The principle is well illustrated in the part of this regulation which relates to the elementary index formulae.

There is just one Article of the Regulation which deals with index formulae, supplemented by Annex II.

> ***Article 7***
>
> ***Price indices for elementary aggregates***
>
> *HICPs shall be compiled using either of the two formulae given in paragraph 1 of Annex II to this Regulation or an alternative comparable formula which does not result in an index which differs systematically from an index compiled by either of the given formulae by more than one tenth of one percentage point on average over one year against the previous year.*

> ***ANNEX II***
>
> ***Formulae to be used in compiling elementary aggregates***
>
> 1. *When compiling price indices for elementary aggregates either the ratio of arithmetic mean prices* $\frac{\frac{1}{n}\sum p^t}{\frac{1}{n}\sum p^b}$ *or the ratio of geometric mean prices* $\frac{[\prod p^t]^{\frac{1}{n}}}{[\prod p^b]^{\frac{1}{n}}}$*, where p is the current price, p the reference price and the number of such prices in the elementary aggregate, shall be used. An alternative formula may be used provided that it fulfils the comparability requirement laid down in Article 7.*
> 2. *The arithmetic mean of prices relatives* $\frac{1}{n}\sum \frac{p^t}{p^b}$ *should not normally be used, as it will in many circumstances result in failure to meet the comparability requirement. It may be used exceptionally where it can be shown not to fail the comparability requirement.*

3. *The price index for an elementary aggregate may be calculated as a chain index using one of the above two preferred formulae. For example using the ratio of arithmetic means:*

$$I^{tb} = \frac{\sum_{i \in s_b} P_i^1}{\sum_{i \in s_b} P_i^b} \cdot \frac{\sum_{i \in s_I} P_i^2}{\sum_{i \in s_I} P_i^1} \cdots\cdots \frac{\sum_{i \in s_{t-1}} P_i^t}{\sum_{i \in s_{t-1}} P_i^{t-1}},$$

where P_i^t *denotes the* ith*price quotation for a given elementary aggregate in period* t*and* s_t, *denotes the sample of prices obtained for the elementary aggregate in period* t. *This sample may in practice be updated monthly or, more usually, when prices cannot be obtained, over longer periods. If between base period* b *and period* t *there is no replenishing at all,* I^{tb} *becomes* $I^{\text{tb}} = \frac{\sum_{i \in S_b} P_i^t}{\sum_{i \in S_b} P_i^b}$, *the simple ratio of arithmetic means (or similarly with the geometric formula described above). The arithmetic mean of price relatives must not be used where chaining is more frequent than annual.*

The meat is of course in Annex 2 rather than in Article 7.

Annex 2 also provides (paragraph 3) for the use of a chain index, that is to say, the construction of a continuous price series by multiplying together price indices using different weight reference periods, using either the Dutot or Jevons formula. Chaining of the Carli index is not allowed where chaining is more frequent than annual, due to its overestimation.

Given the controversy over the elementary index formula which is still raging at the time of writing (2020), readers will not be surprised to learn that that the rules in Annex II were not agreed overnight—although in the light of the current arguments, the decision did not take all that long. The early date of the Regulation (September 1996) demonstrates that the committee procedure was surprisingly quick. In the end, eight Member States were required to change their elementary aggregate formula. All but one changed to the geometric mean (Jevons). Another changed to the Dutot formula. Almost all countries also changed the formula in their national CPIs to the geometric mean. Some countries also changed to the geometric formula retrospectively, to 1995 or 1996, in order to improve comparability.

This was the first HICP implementing regulation to go before the SPC, and it was a great relief to the statisticians in Eurostat and the member states that it had cleared this most important hurdle. The subsequent stages were more or less out of the hands of Eurostat; it involved formal consultations with the European Parliament, the European Monetary Institute (later to become the European Central Bank), the Economic and Social Committee, and of course the Commission itself, in particular the Economic and Financial Directorate-General (DG2). This procedure had to be followed for all the HICP Regulations, and it naturally acted as a brake on the timetable (see further detail in Chapter 15.2).

Returning to the matter of the formula to be used for aggregating the elementary aggregate indices to the higher-level indices, readers may be surprised to know that there was no regulation on this important subject! TF3 did in fact make a proposal on this topic. It was simply a formulation of a "Laspeyres-type" formula as required by Article 9 of the Framework Regulation: "*Member States shall process the data collected in order to produce the HICP, which shall be a Laspeyres-type index …*".

Since all member states were calculating their national CPI using a "Laspeyres-type" index, more or less as formulated in the TF3 proposal, this caused no controversy at all. Nevertheless, in retrospect, it does seem surprising that no specific formulation was given in any subsequent regulation.

In fact, the formula quoted by TF3 corresponds to a Lowe index, which is used almost invariably as a method of calculating CPIs. It is different from a true Laspeyres, but it undoubtedly qualifies as a "Laspeyres-type". The Lowe formulation is in general broad enough to cover a number of specific variants depending on the specification of the quantity term, *q*. The Laspeyres, Paasche, and Walsh indices, for example, all fall within the Lowe family of indices.

The generic Lowe formula for the overall HICP is:

$$I^{\mathrm{tb}} = \sum W_e^r I_e^{\mathrm{tb}}$$

where W_e^r is the expenditure share of the *e*th elementary aggregate in the reference period r and
I_e^{tb} is the price index for the *e*th elementary aggregate for the current month, taking the base period $t = b$ as 100.

The crucial aspect of the Lowe index concerns the reference periods for weights and prices, and the methods of updating these to the current period. Most member states used a fixed base index, while several others, including the UK, computed a chain index, with annual updating of weights. To obtain a set of national HICPs with sub-indices allowing for consistent aggregation, it was necessary to present the HICPs as if they were all computed with the same formula. So it was necessary to apply common index reference periods for both prices and weights. The Framework Regulation defined the common index period as 1996 = 100. In order to obtain a common weight reference period, Eurostat "price-updated" the weights delivered by member states to each December. What exactly is meant by "price-updating"? Weights can be updated basically in two ways. The first is by using fresh estimates of weights obtained from one or another source. If the two periods concerned are fairly close, one would expect the updated weights to be fairly similar to the earlier ones. But if this is impossible or impractical, a more common method is by "price updating". This is simply taking each weight in turn and applying the appropriate HICP index or sub-index so as to re-value the original weight according to the HICP price increase since then. Of course, the updated weights are unlikely to add to 1000, and they must be rescaled so that they do. The result is a set of price-updated weights.

CHAPTER 9

Price Collection Issues

9.1 Sampling

For a national statistic of such importance as the HICP, it is self-evident that the underlying data must be based on a well-designed sample. Billions of consumer transactions take place every year and until we reach a level of electronic sophistication beyond our current imagination, transaction prices and indeed weights must be based on relatively tiny samples.

The Framework Regulation (2494/95) made no reference to sampling. But the first Implementing Regulation (1749/96) had plenty to say. Even the preamble mentioned it:

> *Whereas the coverage of the existing consumer price indices produced by the Member States, practices followed for the inclusion of newly significant goods and services, procedures for adjusting prices for quality changes of the items priced, methods of combining prices to form price indices for elementary aggregates, or sampling methods and practices for obtaining prices differ between Member States to the extent that the resulting consumer price indices produced by the Member States fail to meet the comparability requirement necessary for the production of the HICP.*

Article 1 (Aim) said:

J. Astin, *Measuring EU Inflation*,
https://doi.org/10.1007/978-3-030-68806-6_9

> *The aim is also to ensure that the sampling of prices is such that the HICPs are sufficiently reliable for the purpose of international comparisons and to provide information from which to set minimum standards for sampling.*

Other articles of this Regulation provided a definition of the term "target sample":

> *the set of prices of goods and services which the Member State plans to obtain for the production of the HICP from January 1997 or plans at some subsequent date in order to meet the Member States' own or any European standard for reliability or comparability.*

It referred to minimum standards for sampling and to provide Eurostat with a formal statement of the target sample, with all relevant detail.

Thereafter, there were no mentions of sampling in any of the regulations produced during my time in Eurostat. That had to wait until 2007, when Regulation 1334/2007 was adopted. This was a general regulation which repealed 1749/96 and replaced it with more up-to-date phrases and terminology. But it didn't add anything about technical methods of sampling.

The heart of the problem of technical detail is that the design of a good sample depends on many parameters which usually differ considerably between countries. A good sample for a small country like Luxembourg would be entirely inappropriate for a large country like Germany. We need to remember that HICP samples need to refer not only to the number of prices collected, but outlet types, products, geographic regions, types of urban/rural districts and other variables. Each country must make its own design according to sound statistical principles.

Nevertheless, it was clear that countries could learn from each other about aspects of sample design, and there were many papers discussed at TF and WP level over the years. In addition, special Study Groups were formed to investigate a number of specific products in depth—see Chapter 15.6.

The sample designs in member states are of course subject to inspections and general compliance monitoring by Eurostat—see Chapter 12. In any case, the usual approach of Eurostat to all of such technical matters is that the regulations state the desired outputs, and not the detailed inputs.

9.2 Missing Price Observations

All CPI price collectors frequently experience being unable to record the price of a product during their monthly price surveys. There are a number of possible reasons for this, including the following:

(a) The outlet is closed. This may be a permanent closure or a temporary one (e.g. for a holiday);
(b) The outlet is open but the product is not available on display. This may be the result of a number of possibilities:

- The product is temporarily out of stock;
- The product is no longer stocked by that specific outlet;
- The product has been temporarily withdrawn from the market generally—possibly because it is a seasonal product;
- The product has been permanently removed from the market generally.

This is not the place to delve deeply into these problems, but the first Implementing Regulation (1749/96) addressed the issue, albeit briefly. Article 6 (Minimum standards for prices) says:

1. *Member States shall produce HICPs using the observed prices of the target sample.*
   (a) *Where the target sample requires monthly observation, but observation fails due to non-availability of an item or for any other reason, estimated prices may be used for the first or second month but replacement prices shall be used from the third month.*
   (b) *Where, exceptionally, the target sample requires observations less frequently than monthly, estimated prices shall be used for those months where observed prices are not required. Estimated prices may also be used on the first occasion on which price observation fails. Where observation fails for a second consecutive occasion, replacement prices shall be used.*
2. *Where, in the circumstances referred to in this Article, replacement prices are not available, estimated prices may continue to be used, provided that the extent of their use is limited to a level appropriate for achieving comparability.*

It is a little difficult to imagine how para. (2) may be put into practice. The paragraph contains no specific time limit for the continued use of estimated prices so how should a decision to continue be justified? Only, it seems, by reference to the comparability question, i.e. is the use of an estimated price likely to give the resulting index an error of more than 0.1%? If a test on this criterion were to be made, the difference between the estimated price of one specific product and a possibly more "realistic" price would probably have to be very large and hence unlikely.

This paragraph most definitely came into play during the COVID-19 periods of lockdown in 2020 where some outlets were closed for long spells and price observation of many items was impossible.

An important issue arises in the context of this regulation. The regulation uses the word "estimated". What is the difference between "estimation" and "imputation"—the latter word referring to the fact that imputed prices are not allowed in the HICP? The difference is subtle. In practice "imputation" is used when not merely a price but in fact the very transaction is not observable. The most common usage is in the field of owner-occupied housing, where "imputed rents" are frequently used in place of actual values. The major difference in such cases is that has been no actual transaction; it is not just the rent which is "imputed" but the very fact of renting. In fact the rent in such a case is purely hypothetical; it does not exist in reality and its value has to be "estimated" by using the rent of a similar—but actually rented—property.

A second issue also arises in connection with this Article. For some types of product—often in the field of services such as education—prices are normally changed annually; an example being school or university fees being changed at the beginning of each academic year. When this is the usual practice in a Member State it would clearly be wasteful to organise actual price collection every month. Instead, collection can be limited to once a year (at the usual start of the academic year). The institution concerned should be required to inform the NSI if, exceptionally, there is a change in the fees during the academic year. The price for the HICP can then be changed.

This procedure can fairly be described as being monthly rather than annual collection, since it is known that the monthly fees are unchanged unless otherwise informed.

9.3 Seasonal Products

Seasonal products—especially items of food and clothing—can be difficult to deal with in a CPI.

Seasonal products can be defined as:-

- Products showing a strong seasonal variation in prices;
- Products showing a strong seasonal variation in quantities sold;
- Products showing a strong seasonal variation in monthly expenditure (price × quantity);
- Products showing a strong seasonal variation in quality (e.g. potatoes);
- Products showing a strong seasonal variation in demand (e.g. Christmas trees) and
- Products showing a strong seasonal variation in supply (e.g. melons, cherries, etc.).

There was no mention of seasonal products in the early HICP regulations. But from the early discussions in the WP it became apparent that, even though most, if not all, member states were including seasonal products in their HICP, they were dealing with them in different ways. On the other hand, it would probably be reasonable to assume that countries with similar climates would show similar annual patterns of seasonality, certainly as far as many food items are concerned.

Following the January 1999 WP meeting, a questionnaire concerning the treatment of seasonal products in the HICP was distributed.

The aim of the exercise was to reach an overview of the methods used, and to what extent different methods resulted in non-comparable indices.

Replies were received from 13 countries representing sufficiently colder and warmer climatic zones of the EEA. There was clear evidence that, as far as fresh food was concerned, the earlier supposition mentioned above was not in fact correct: seasonal patterns ranged from zero to as much as 0.5 percentage points on the HICP for countries in the same climate zone.

Fresh fruit and vegetables were partially or fully treated as seasonal products in 12 of the 13 respondent countries. The exception was a country which treated fresh fruit and vegetables in the same way as they treated bread and fish. In that country, these products were available throughout the year in most outlets, and if a product was not available in a particular outlet, it was treated simply as a missing observation.

Clothing items were partly or fully treated as seasonal products in 8 out of the 13 countries. Other products were also mentioned. These included energy products, gardening products, winter and summer sports equipment, package holidays and accommodation services.

The responses showed that it was always assumed that seasonal products would become available again in the following year.

We now look briefly at some of the technical aspects of treating seasonal products in the HICP.

Two of the basic elements used in index calculations are weights and base prices. Normally, for non-seasonal products these parameters remain fixed at the same level for the full year. This is unrealistic for seasonal products, where there are four possible combinations for the index calculations.

Where the same or similar product is expected to become available again the following year, the following options are available:

1. Index calculation method	Varying monthly weights and fixed base prices
2. Base price	Weighted average over the (base) year (re-referenced to base period using an appropriate index
3. Monthly weights	Monthly weights determined before the beginning of the actual year
4. Imputed prices in months with positive weights and no actual price observations	Carry forward (if needed) of last regular price

For fresh fruit and vegetables, most countries used varying weights with fixed base prices (option 1).

Non-observed prices are usually not a problem for indices using varying weights. They may, however, be a problem in some special cases:

(a) If the season starts later or ends earlier than expected and (b) chaining countries require (normally) a December price. In this case, it is possible either to carry forward the last observed price, or to impute the December price by uprating the last observation using the price change in the outlet stratum.

In the Eurostat survey mentioned above, the results showed that.

- 7 countries carried forward the last regular price;
- 4 countries carried forward the observed (sales) price;
- 1 country excluded the product from the sample;
- 1 country used a different method (Rothwell type).

Following this survey of national methodologies, there were later discussions of the importance of the variations in methods in the context of comparability of the resulting HICPs. Some tests were made: it seemed that at the standard test level of 0.1 percentage points there was little evidence of any need to harmonize the methods. As a result, the subject of harmonized seasonal methods was put on the back burner for some time. It was last discussed at the WP which met on the eve of my departure from Eurostat in July 2002. However, the subject was not entirely forgotten, and finally in April 2009 a Regulation (330–09) was adopted.

9.4 Newly Significant Products

Items in a CPI "basket" are carefully specified so that price collectors know exactly what products they should be pricing. In many sectors of the market, small changes may be made over the course of time to these specifications, and prices may be adjusted using "quality adjustment" methods (see Chapter 9.5). But sometimes a product comes to the market whose characteristics do not fit comfortably within any existing product group. Some such products may have a short life on the market, others become popular. In practice, price statisticians cannot know in advance which products will become popular or rapidly disappear. Another factor is the volume and value of sales. Again, statisticians do not have early information on this. It can (and does) happen that a new product's popularity (and sales) accelerate quite quickly, reaching a point where it may well pass the 0.1% threshold of significance.

Unfortunately, there is rarely a sharp dividing line separating a new product from an existing one whose quality has been improved. As with many aspects of CPIs, qualitative rather than quantitative judgments must be made.

Until the discussions on this important topic began in the WP, the phrase in common use was "new products", and it was generally accepted that some items were genuinely new to the market: items such as mobile phones, laptops in the 1990s. One delegate pointed out that in his country sheep meat had become increasingly popular in recent years; earlier, it had not been included in the product list as it was a very low-weight item. Another delegate said that after decades of widespread use, candles had been dropped from their country's national CPI. But more recently sales had increased dramatically as candles had become an important part of household decoration, especially in the dining room. They had decided to re-introduce it into the national CPI.

After a discussion of such items it became apparent that the statistical problem should be discussed in terms of "newly significant" instead of merely "new" products, and this concept was rapidly accepted. It applied not only to goods but also to services. In this context, "significant" means that a product must have sufficient weight (value of sales) that it passes the critical 0.1% test. Lack of sales data may often make this a difficult test to perform, and there will usually be a lag until the relevant data have been identified.

In the 1990s, delays in the introduction of newly significant products became a well-publicised deficiency in the US CPI, following a report by the Boskin Commission[1] This famous report identified several products whose sales had reached a point where they were for sure qualified to enter the CPI basket, but had so far failed to be included.

It said *"An extreme example involves room air conditioners, which were widely sold in 1951, but not introduced into the CPI until 1964"*, and *"In an even more contemporaneous example, there are .. currently more than 40 million cellular phone* [mobile phone in British parlance] *subscribers in the United States, but the cellular phone has yet to be introduced into the CPI"*.

The WP was impressed by the Boskin report. The report addressed in some detail the matter of the effect on the CPI of any failure to include new products in the CPI basket, especially considering that new products tend to rise rather quickly in price in the period after their introduction, and their omission could cause a negative bias in the CPI.

The Boskin Report was published at an opportune moment for the HICP WP, and there was much discussion about the need for clear rules on dealing with newly significant products. In fact there was already a

[1] Final Report of the Advisory Commission to study the Consumer Price Index, US Senate Committee on Finance, 1996.

general rule in the first Implementing Regulation (1749/96), which has the following:

Article 2 (Definitions)

…(b) "Newly significant goods and services" are defined as those goods and services the price changes of which are not explicitly included in a Member State's HICP and the estimated consumers' expenditure on which has become at least one part per thousand of the expenditure covered by that HICP.

Article 4 (Newly significant goods and services)

Member States shall:

(a) *systematically seek to identify newly significant goods and services and*
(b) *check the significance of goods and services reported to be newly significant in other Member States.*

The HICP shall be compiled to include the price changes of a newly significant good or service, where the good or service has been estimated as falling within the definition in Article 2 (b). This shall be accomplished within 12 months of their identification either by adjusting the weights of or within the relevant category of COICOP/HICP classification given in Annex I to this Regulation or by assigning part of the weight specifically to the newly significant good or service.

It may be noted that Article 4 does not specifically refer to the (obvious) point of collecting prices of the newly significant products, referring instead to the need for adjusting weights to include it appropriately in the HICP.

In 2000, the WP, after a number of discussions, decided to accept some informal rules concerning the treatment of newly significant products. It felt that rather than leaving it to each country to identify and introduce its own newly significant products to its HICP, Eurostat should compile a list of such products supplied by each country; the list would be accessible to all countries. Of course, such a product may reach a market threshold qualifying it for inclusion in the HICP of a particular country, but it may not necessarily do so in other countries. These rules were simply advisory, with no legal backing. The WP felt that the principle given in Regulation 1749/96 was sufficient, and the detail could safely be left to the NSIs, with guidance from Eurostat.

Table 9.1 illustrates a technical products list at this time:

Table 9.1 Example of EEA-wide list of newly significant products in the technology field

PC work place (incl. accessories and games)	
(a) hardware	
Zip-drive	9.1.3
DVD-drive	9.1.3
Disk writer	9.1.3
Scanner	9.1.3
Joystick/gamepad/racing wheel for computers	9.1.3
Personal digital assistant	9.1.3
Internet video camera	9.1.3
(b) software	
Computer game software, e.g. Tomb Raider III, Age of empires	9.1.3
Language course software	9.1.3
Voice recognition software	9.1.3
Encyclopedia software	9.1.3
Video games	
(a) hardware	
Joystick/gamepad/racing wheel for video consoles	9.3.1
Video consoles	9.3.1
(b) software for e.g. Dreamcast/Game Boy/Nintendo 64/Playstation	9.3.1
Other accessories for the house	
Battery recharger	05.3.1/2
Rechargeable batteries	05.5
Telephone equipment	
ISDN telephone, cordless	8.2./3.0
ISDN telephone/fax combination	8.2./3.0
Handsfree facility for mobile phone (in the car)	8.2./3.0

9.5 Quality Adjustment

To price statisticians, the term "quality adjustment" trips off the tongue as easily as "open the book"! Unfortunately, the reality is rather more complex.

We have described the basics of product definition and price collection: to measure price change accurately it is important to note the price of a certain product in consecutive time periods and calculate the percentage change. But "a certain product" means just that: the product price in each of the time periods must be the same product. We have to compare like with like. This is often impossible, as the detailed product descriptions are prone to changes over time. Obvious examples are PCs; where the various aspects of disk memory, speed, screen size and so on are likely to change very frequently. But even simpler products, such as a box of washing powder, do have changes over time, whether it be the chemical composition or merely the weight of the box.

Instead of replacing the product, which is not always helpful in a price index as it damages the continuity, the usual procedure is to make a so-called "quality adjustment" (QA hereafter) to the observed price. In principle this is a simple procedure. Rather than recording the new price of the product, the new price is changed, upwards or downwards, to reflect the value of the change in specification.

Note that here I used the word "specification". This is important for me, as I have long felt that the word "quality" is unhelpful. Quality is a subjective evaluation, and may (and does) vary from person to person. Specifications, on the other hand, are physical measurements and do not depend on subjective assessments. One consumer may personally prefer an item of clothing which is made of a certain material, while another consumer does not. The only thing which is potentially measurable is the specification—and even that may be difficult or even impossible to measure in practice.

However, for the time being we are stuck with (in my view) the inappropriate phrase "quality adjustment" and we continue with this nomenclature in the book.

The first implementing regulation (1749/96) of September 1996 contained one article on Quality Adjustment (QA):

Article 5 (Minimum standards for procedures of Quality Adjustment)

1. *HICPs for which appropriate quality adjustments are made shall be deemed to be comparable. Where quality changes occur, Member States shall construct price indices by making appropriate quality adjustments based on explicit estimates of the value of the quality change. In the absence of national estimates, Member States shall use estimates based on information provided by the Commission (Eurostat) where these are available and relevant.*
2. *Where no estimates are available, price changes shall be estimated as the difference between the price of the selected substitute and that of the item it has replaced. In no case should a quality change be estimated as the whole of the difference in price between the two items, unless this can be justified as an appropriate estimate. Where replacements have to be*

> *made after goods and services have been offered at reduced prices, those replacements should be selected according to their similarity of utility to the consumer and not according to similarity of price.*

This Article was drafted only after a great deal of argument and discussion in the Working Party. Para. 1 shows clearly that this was only a preliminary regulation as it says nothing about how quality adjustments should be made. It is perhaps an extreme example of the general "output-based" approach to the construction of HICPs, i.e. specifying the outcomes rather than the methods. In any case, Eurostat itself was not in the business of making quality adjustments, just as it was not in the business of collecting prices or even calculating price indices. The only assistance Eurostat was in a position to give was to ensure that the varying practices of individual member states were shared among the group so that lessons could be learned, pending any later, more detailed, regulation.

The second paragraph was slightly more precise, though it was argued over quite strongly. Its terms seem at first sight rather complex, but in fact the message is clear enough. An example should suffice. Suppose a certain product—let's say Product A (price €50)—disappears from the market and needs to be replaced. Product B (price €52) is chosen as the replacement, as it appears to be the closest in terms of specification to Product A. But it is not identical. The difference is a small but significant change to the product, e.g. the removal of a handle. It is decided that a quality adjustment should be made. The value of the handle can be easily estimated (say €3), and this is deducted from the price of product B (now adjusted to €55)—an increase of €5 rather than €2 on Product A. This is a fully acceptable method of QA.

Paragraph 2 of Article 5 prevents the use of a simple technique which avoids the need for valuing the handle. It would be easy to say that being of relatively low value the disappearance of the handle need not be regarded as a quality change, so the price change is taken at face value, i.e. €2 rather than €5. This is covered by the first sentence of Article 5(2): "where no estimates are available, price changes shall be estimated as the difference between the price of the selected substitute and that of the item it has replaced". The quality change should not be estimated as the full €2 price change, giving an effective no change in price.

This regulation remained as the only reference to QA for a decade, when Regulation 1334/2007 was adopted. This is examined at the end of this Section.

As the reader may well imagine, the act of QA introduces an element of estimation into a CPI, illustrating the fact that statistics is rarely an exact science. After all, the foundations of a CPI are a relatively small sample of products and their prices. The choices are not set in stone. Having said that, we need also to understand that of the various methods of QA, some may be better, or at least more appropriate, than others.

So let us look briefly at the methods of attacking the difficult QA issues.

It was recognised from the start that some rules must be laid down on this important topic in a regulation or guidelines. And they would inevitably be complex. A lengthy discussion took place at a WP meeting in September 2001 following some earlier exchanges of views at an HICP seminar in Baden (Austria) earlier that year. At that meeting, presentations were made, giving real examples in the fields of cars, computer software and televisions. At the WP meeting in July 2001 it was decided that the best way of handling these detailed studies was by means of a special QA Task Force, which would also be dealing with sampling, given the essential connection between the two topics. Over half the member states volunteered to join the new TF, which had its first meeting immediately after the September 2001 WP.

Guidance was given to the new TF in the following ways. First, it should select a limited number of product sectors and deal with them in detail, classifying the QA methods currently used in member states. The sectors selected for this study were: motor cars, books, compact discs, computer software, certain durables and clothing. It was felt that there could be a danger of developing ad hoc sets of pragmatic rules for each sector, perhaps resulting in a lack of overall consistency of approach. There needed to be a conceptual framework underpinning the various sectoral approaches. The conceptual framework would be for the full WP to decide rather than the TF, which would focus on the sectoral detail.

The meeting went on to decide on the way of managing the work of the new TF. It was decided that each of the four product sectors would be entrusted to TF members working in pairs, since it was felt that two individuals were better able to work efficiently together, keeping in close touch by means of a "CIRCA" limited-membership website.[2] CIRCA had been used for the first time in 2001 for the distribution of the WP documents.

[2] Communication and Information Resource Centre Administrator (an Internet-based groupware tool).

A related point is that the regular WP meetings by now had a standard agenda item called "Technical Forum". This was to allow a discussion of technical questions put forward by a member state. Not all WP meetings had such a topic to discuss, but a typical one concerning QA was discussed as follows:

Case Study: Cable TV Network

Old situation:

The operator of a cable TV system in a medium large town offered a package of 17 channels for €13 per month. The package comprised 6 national channels plus several from foreign countries.

New situation:

Customers may choose a standard package of 15 channels for €14 per month, or the standard package plus an extra 11 channels for a total price of €20.

The question is: What is the "true" price change? (assuming that the cable operator has a monopoly).

The paper suggests several possible options, such as (a) comparing the prices of the old and new packages directly or (b) comparing the two prices and quality adjusting, using the number of channels as a quality indicator.

QA methods depend to a large extent on the type of product. The simplest type of QA occurs where the only change is the weight of the product. This often applies to purchases of food items contained in packets or tins. The weight of the contents may be reduced from, say 150 to 125 gm (17%)—but the price drops by only 10%, say from €1.00 to €0.90. So the real price of the food has changed from €0.67 per gram to €0.72 per gram—an increase of 7.5%. So the actual price would be quality-adjusted upwards by 7.5%–€0.97. The fundamental point is that price as measured in a price index is the actual price for a stated quantity of the product.

But the above example is one of the easiest to deal with in QA. Let's move to the other end of the spectrum and consider a computer (PC). Allow me to give you a personal example. In 1997 I bought a laptop for £800. In 2019 I bought one for £400. If these were typical machines (and they were indeed nothing very special) it would imply a fall in price of 50% over 22 years. But this is to ignore the enormous changes in specification over those years; the original RAM memory was 32 MB; the hard disk size was 3.5 GB; it had a 200 MHz processor; it had Windows 95; The equivalent specifications on my 2019 machine are: RAM 4 GB; hard disk 9.3 GB; processor 1.8 GHz, and Windows 10. So the two products are not really comparable at all. Of course, this is over a long period of time, and pricing monthly for the HICP would see far fewer major changes.

Nevertheless, the essential problem remains: how to estimate the values of the various changes every month or so? One of the complications in the field of computers is that changes (which admittedly imply a cost to the manufacturer) are not necessarily useful to the average consumer. I guess that over 90% of the facilities offered by my current software are not used by me—yet I am paying for them. Should this be a further factor to take into account in QA methodology?

As I have said before, this is not a statistics textbook, so I am not going to devote pages to the QA techniques used by price statisticians in the HICP or other CPIs. I will however mention one particular technique which has sometimes proved useful. It is known as "hedonic regression".

When compiling a pure price index (such as the HICP), it is important to compare the prices of a product of unchanged quality (specifications) over time.

A hedonic price function uses regression analysis to predict the influence of product features on the sale price. In this way, price changes due to changes in the specification of certain features can be estimated and removed from the actual sale price. For example, a particular TV set may be one of the items for which prices are observed for the HICP. Among the specifications may be the screen size, the sound quality, LED or LCD, Wireless/USB/Ethernet connections, screen resolution, etc. If any one of these specifications changes, it may affect the price. But if the actual price is the one which is observed for the index, it is likely to overstate the rate of real inflation since the product specification is not unchanged as it needs to be.

Hedonic methods are in practice difficult to apply. They require a great deal of data; the results may be hard to explain to users; they are usually related to technical products as described above; and they are almost impossible to apply to services such as air fares.

Hedonic methods of quality adjustment have been used by some member states in their HICP calculations, but they are not governed by regulation and they have not achieved widespread acceptance.

It is not easy to monitor the effectiveness of QA methods as applied by different member states in different product groups at different times.

In the late 1990s there was still no detailed regulation on QA. As the first part of this Section said, the first Implementing Regulation had stated that QA should be done, without saying how; it also said what types of treatment should not be made. But there was still no official guidance on specific methods of QA. It was a serious worry and Eurostat and the member states were anxious to make some progress on this difficult topic.

One idea which gained traction was the concept of "Implicit Quality Indices" (IQIs). An IQI is an index formed as the ratio of an index of prices unadjusted for quality change to an index of prices adjusted for quality change. It provides an approximate measure of the aggregate quality change for which allowance has been made. The basic idea was straightforward. If the price of a product in Country A is €100 and the product is replaced by a product with different specifications, a quality adjustment should be made to the actual price. If the price is adjusted upwards to, say, €110, the QA is 10%. If such a ratio is calculated across an entire sub-index, it may give an average adjustment of, say, 8%. If we then compare this ratio with a similar ratio from Country B, and that country's ratio is 15%, there is an issue to be solved. The temptation may be to assume that Country B is making a different QA from Country A, and the reason should be investigated. Of course there may be good reasons for the discrepancy. The products in B's sub-index may be significantly different from those in A, and it would not be surprising if the IQIs were different.

The IQI is thus a measure of the effect of operational adjustments that have been made to the raw price data in order to obtain the price index. That is the aggregate effect of adjustments to remove non-price effects and arrive at the true price change. Where the only adjustments to the raw price observations are allowances for quality change, the IQIs provide an index of quality change in the universe.

An Action Plan, covering other QA aspects as well as IQIs, was agreed by the SPC in 1999, and work began in TF5—now devoted to both Quality Adjustment and Sampling. Member states and Candidate countries agreed to provide Eurostat with IQIs for some product groups on an experimental basis. Early results demonstrated the usefulness of the IQI approach for analysing whether the implied quality changes appeared reasonable for the products concerned, and for giving indications of potential non-comparability between countries.

Quality Adjustment continued to be argued over in the WP and TFs for several more years. This book mainly describes the development of the HICP until 2002, but in 2007 a new Regulation (1334/2007) on sampling, replacement and quality adjustment was adopted. QA is such a fundamental issue that I make an exception to my normal "2002-end" rule, and look ahead to the 2007 regulation. Here is the relevant text in full:-

Article 2: Definitions

"Quality change" means that a replacement has resulted in a significant difference in the degree to which the replacement product-offer serves the consumer purpose of the consumption segment to which it belongs, whenever the Member State judges so.

"Quality adjustment" means the procedure of making an allowance for an observed quality change by increasing or decreasing the observed current or reference price by a factor or an amount equivalent to the value of that quality change.

Article 5: Minimum standards for replacements and quality adjustment

1. *Quality adjustments shall be rated as follows:*
   (a) *A-methods: those which are considered to deliver the most reliable results, in terms of precision and bias;*
   (b) *B-methods: those which may deliver less precise or less representative results than A-methods, but are nevertheless considered also acceptable. B-methods shall be used in case A-methods are not applied; and*
   (c) *C-methods: all other methods, which shall hence not be used.*
2. *Standards concerning the rating of quality adjustment methods shall be developed and issued by the Commission (Eurostat) after consultation at the SPC, following a case-by-case approach with due regard to aspects of cost-effectiveness and the context in which they are applied. The rating of quality adjustment methods does not preclude the adoption of implementing measures on this subject in accordance with Article 5(3) of Regulation 2494/95* [the Framework Regulation].
3. *A- and B-methods shall be deemed to be appropriate quality adjustment methods. HICPs for which appropriate quality adjustments are made shall be deemed to be comparable. Other things being equal, A-methods shall be given the preference over B-methods.*
4. *In the absence of appropriate national estimates, Member States shall use estimates based on information provided by the Commission (Eurostat) where these are available and relevant.*

5. *In no case shall a quality change be estimated as the whole of the difference in price between the two product-offers, unless this can be justified as an appropriate estimate.*
6. *Where no appropriate estimates are available, price changes shall be estimated as the difference between the replacement price and that of the product-offer it has replaced.*
7. *Replacement product-offers:*
   (a) *shall be either 'essentially equivalent', if no quality change is observed between the replacement product-offer and the one it replaced in the sample, or 'equivalent by quality adjustment', if a quality adjustment is necessary for an observed quality change between the replacement product-offer and the one it replaced in the sample;*
   (b) *shall be selected from the same consumption segments as the replaced ones, so as to maintain the representation of consumption segments;*
   (c) *shall not be selected according to similarity of price. This shall in particular apply where replacements have to be made after goods or services have been offered at reduced prices.*

The reader will notice that some new expressions appear in this more recent regulation. In particular, the word "product-offer" which is used instead of the earlier word "product". It is defined in Reg 1334/2007 Article 2: *"Product-offer" means a specified good or service that is offered for purchase at a stated price, in a specific outlet or by a specific provider, under specific terms of supply, and thus defines a unique entity at any one time"*.

This is clearly a better description than simply using the word "product".

Another new expression is "consumption segment". It is also defined in the same Regulation article referred to above:

> *A "consumption segment by purpose" or "consumption segment" means a set of transactions relating to product-offers which, on the grounds of common properties, are deemed to serve a common purpose, in the sense that they:*
>
> - *are marketed for predominant use in similar situations,*
> - *can largely be described by a common specification, and*
> - *may be considered by consumers as equivalent.*

It is apparent from the above text (in particular paragraphs 5 and 6 which are almost identical to the earlier regulation) that fundamentally there is little change between the 1996 Regulation and its replacement, apart from the new system of classification of different methods of QA. This change was the result of many discussions over the whole period on the vexed subject of QA. And as long as words like "quality" and "utility"—both of which are implicitly subjective—are in use, the process of QA can at best be seen only as approximations of reality. Having said that, the HICP with QA is in general a more reliable indicator of inflation than it is without QA.

9.6 Tariff Prices

A tariff is a list of pre-established prices and conditions for the purchase and consumption of one and the same good or service or of similar goods and services that has been centrally fixed by the supplier, by the government, or by agreement, to exert influence on the consumption patterns by means of appropriately differentiated prices and conditions according to characteristics of consumers, the level, the structure or the timing of consumption. Tariffs are not negotiable for households.

A tariff price is a price within a tariff that applies to a component element or unit of consumption of the good or service in question.

These definitions are taken from Article 2 of Regulation 2646/98 which is examined in this chapter. As "tariff" is not a particularly common word, it is perhaps best to look at the formal definitions before continuing.

In practice we are all familiar with tariffs. A common one would be the price of domestic gas or electricity, where often there is a scale of charges depending on the level of usage. The first X units of consumption will be charged at A euros, the next set at B euros, and so on. Usually, it is the lower steps of the tariff which are most expensive, declining as usage increases. There will be several other types and example of tariffs discussed later in the chapter.

We start with the text of regulation 2646/98 and go on to illustrate how it is followed in practice.

The Preamble says:

Whereas HICP sub-indices involving tariff prices are, in practice, obtained directly from suppliers or computed by the Member States based on data on tariff prices and their underlying consumption patterns provided by suppliers;

> *Whereas there is considerable scope for procedural differences in the construction of sub-indices where changes in the structure of tariffs are made at the same time as changes are made to the tariff price of a particular element to the extent that consumers are obliged to make new choices in their consumption;*
> *Whereas it is therefore important to ensure that the relevant basic information can be obtained as to* ensure*that the resulting HICPs do not fail to meet the comparability requirement of Article 4 of Regulation (EC) No 2494/95* [the Framework Regulation];
> *Whereas, by virtue of Article 6 of Regulation (EC) No 2494/95, the basic information for the production of HICPs which should be obtained from the statistical units, consists of those prices and weights which it is necessary to take into account in order to achieve comparability;*
> *Whereas, by virtue of Article 7 of Regulation (EC) 2494/95, the statistical units called upon by the Member States to co-operate in the collection of or provision of* prices*data should be obliged to allow observation of the prices actually charged and to give honest and complete information at the time it is requested;*
> *Whereas by virtue of Article 4 of Commission Regulation (EC) No 1749/96, as last amended by Council Regulation (EC) No 1688/98 the HICP should be compiled to include the price change of a newly significant good or service;*
> *Whereas This Regulation Should not Require Member States to Carry Out New Statistical Surveys ..*

Now this preamble is considerably longer than most of the those in earlier regulations. Probably the reason is that this regulation imposes potentially difficult, and confidential, data requirements on the so-called "statistical units"; these are not the national statistics institutes but the providers of data where tariffs are involved, such as railway service providers, energy suppliers, sellers of telephone services (including smartphones), and so on. Many of these operate in highly competitive markets, and detailed information, not so much about tariff prices which are usually available to the public, but the underlying weights, which may be highly confidential. Sometimes it may be possible to obtain the required details from the appropriate industry regulating authority.

The definition of "tariff" quoted at the start of the chapter makes it evident that the collection of tariff prices may be complex and time-consuming compared with the collection of non-tariff prices.

We next examine other Articles of this Regulation.

Article 3 (Basic information) says:

The basic information shall be all tariff prices and ***weights*** *which reflect the structure of the consumption of the goods or services according to the characteristics of the consumers, the level, the structure or the timing of the consumption.*

The reason why "weights" is highlighted is that this is almost always the one aspect of tariffs that is not published and hence not always available to price statisticians. To take a popular example of smartphones: the price tariffs may be quite complex. There are often three particular tariffs in the whole set; time spent talking; numbers of text messages; and volume of data downloads or uploads. (There may be additional factors or subdivisions such as whether or not the phone being spoken to is on the same supplier network). The total cost of the service will depend on the size selected by the customer of each of the three factors. For a user who rarely downloads data it would not be worth having a large allowance for this factor. A user who downloads much data (perhaps including movies) will need a large allocation and would therefore be alert to the charges levied by different suppliers for this feature. Short of having the ability to examine the monthly bills of every phone customer—a prospect nobody would want!—the only way to estimate the overall "price" of a phone contract is to get the information, anonymised and doubtless averaged—either direct from the suppliers, or from an appropriate communications regulatory authority. This would provide for the average user a figure of x% of the overall bill for talk time; y% for the number of chargeable text messages and z% for the total volume of data downloads. This data should be provided on a monthly basis.

The expression *"characteristics of the consumers"* may refer to those tariffs which charge, for example, a lower price for children, students, or older people. This may relate to public transport or entry to museums, for example.

The "timing" aspect, mentioned in this Article, is very common, especially in the transport sector. Fares for trains, buses, etc. may be cheaper at night or at the weekend, for example. Or if the purchase is made in advance of the date of travel.

This Article essentially sets out the requirements following on from the definitions in Article 2.

Article 4 (Data sources):

1. *HICP sub-indices involving tariff prices shall be computed by the Member States from basic information as defined in Article 3 provided by the supplier.*
2. *The statistical units called upon by Member States to cooperate in the collection or provision of basic information are obliged to give honest and complete information at the time it is requested and allow the organisations and institutions responsible for compiling official statistics at their request to obtain information at the level of detail necessary to evaluate compliance with the comparability requirements and the quality of the HICP sub-indices.*

This wording harks back to that in Article 6 of the Framework Regulation (Chapter 3.3).

Article 5 (Procedure):

HICP sub-indices involving tariff prices shall be calculated using a formula which is consistent with the Laspeyres-type formula used for other sub-indices. They should reflect the price change on the basis of the changed expenditure of maintaining that consumption pattern chosen by households prior to the given change in the tariff. Where there is a change in the tariff and where, after that change:

1. *A component element or a unit of consumption remains unchanged with respect to its specification, then the price for that element or unit according to the old and the new tariff shall be directly compared, and the price difference taken into the HICP;*
2. *a component element or a unit of consumption remains unchanged with respect to its specification, or a new component is added which does not constitute a new good or service for the consumer, then the price change shall be computed with weights corresponding to the expenditure of preserving the pattern of consumption applying during a period, up to one year preceding the change. The adjustments of specification changes shall be consistent with quality adjustments made for other sub-indices;*
3. *a component element or a unit of consumption with a new and distinct specification constituting a new good or service for the consumer is added to the tariff, it shall be treated as 'newly significant goods and services' as defined in Regulation (EC) No 1749/96. If the expenditure on the new good or service is significant it shall be taken into the index by linking from the month when the new tariff comes into force using*

> *an estimate of expected immediate consumption or within a period of 12 months otherwise.*

Article 5 is the essential core of this regulation. To the uninitiated it probably makes little sense, and it is perhaps best understood by the use of some straightforward examples.

Take the case of domestic electricity prices. In this case, an electricity company's "tariff" could be the following:

A "component element" would be one of the above three elements of the tariff. The price of each component can be changed independently: the electricity company can change the standing charge, or the price of the first 200 units or the price of the units above 200. It can also change the 200-unit threshold (which is often the most difficult aspect for the price statistician to deal with).

A "unit of consumption" would be 1 kWh in the above example.

We can imagine three types of customer, distinguished by their different levels of electricity usage:

(a) a customer using 350 units in a month would pay a total of €58;
(b) a customer using 150 units would pay €33;
(c) a customer who used no electricity in the month would pay €3.

Using this example, if one of the tariff component elements were to change (say, the 200-unit threshold were changed to 250 units), the tariff would be re-priced on the assumption that consumers did not change their pattern of consumption as a result of the tariff change. Thus, the consumer who used 350 units per month would continue to use 350 units per month. The three types of customer above would therefore pay, under the new tariff, €63, €33, and €3 respectively. To put this another

Table 9.2 Price of electricity for domestic households

Standing charge per month	€3.00
First 200 units (kWh): cost per unit	€0.20
Subsequent units (kWh): cost per unit	€0.10

way, consumers are assumed to be insensitive to changes in the tariff; they do not change their consumption as a result of tariff changes.

A second possibility might be an increase in the standing charge, say from €3.00 to €4.00. In this case, all three customers would pay an extra €1.00 per month.

A further possibility could be the introduction of a second band of usage, for example a charge of €0.15 per unit for consumption between 200 and 500KwH. In this case, customer (a) would pay a total of €65.50 instead of €58.00, while there would be no change for customers (b) and (c).

So, provided the tariff information is kept up-to-date, there should, in this type of example at least, be few problems in calculating the price increases for different user-types.

A potentially more complex example may be the tariff applying to bus fares in a particular town. Very often, the tariff would include different "off-peak" and "peak" fares (the two periods being of course displayed publicly). But these periods may be changed at will by the bus company. Suppose the morning peak time was extended from 10.00 to 10.30. Under the rule that changes in tariff prices should reflect the price change on the basis of the changed expenditure required to maintain the same consumption pattern of households as before the change in the tariff, we must assume no change in the behaviour of passengers as a result of this change in the definition of "off-peak".

However, it might happen that some passengers, especially pensioners, whose timing is perhaps more flexible than for other passengers, would delay a journey normally undertaken at 10.10 to the slightly later time of 10.30 in order to continue to obtain the off-peak discount. This implies that the numbers of peak time passengers would decrease, and those in off-peak time would increase. The total numbers will remain unchanged. The practical problem is that not even the bus company would probably be able to estimate the changes needed. In such a case the NSI has two choices. One is to keep the tariff calculation unchanged until such time as the bus company has enough data on the numbers of passengers within each component after the change; or to make a rough estimate in the absence of such information.

Article 5 refers also to a component element *with "a new and distinct specification constituting a new good or service for the consumer"* being added to the tariff. This has certainly happened in the case of smart-phones. (Note however that the inclusion or improvement of a camera in mobile phones does not form part of a tariff as there is no specific charge for its use. It is however a quality change which must be dealt with according to the QA regulation.) But the typical smartphone tariff will have several elements which together form a tariff. As mentioned earlier, these may include talk time, number of text messages and volume of downloaded data (including movies).

Changes in any one of these elements are likely to affect the total cost of the package.

The only other articles in this Regulation are standard ones concerning quality control and comparability.

9.7 Treatment of Price Reductions

The phrase "price reductions" was coined as a catch-all phrase aimed at all the possible causes of reductions of prices, including sale prices, discounts of various kinds, special offers and so on. The background to this topic was one of mixed practices in member states. Some felt that a true measure of underlying inflation would be reached by excluding temporarily reduced prices such as those in seasonal sales and other temporary discounts. Others took the view that a comprehensive CPI should in principle include all prices, reflecting what consumers actually pay.

For example, in the UK the regular bi-annual "sale" prices (i.e. widespread discounts in the New Year and summer periods) were ignored in the Retail Prices Index, despite their growing importance compared with total annual sales. And during the 1990s there was a growing trend for stores to introduce more and more different kinds of inducement, not restricted simply to straightforward price reductions, These inducements would take forms such as "buy xx for the price of yy", "free delivery", "discounts for pensioners", "goods close to the expiry date", etc. And sometime these types of inducement would last for relatively short periods of time in individual outlets.

Partly because of the rapidly changing types of discount, it was decided to frame the rules with a set of Guidelines rather than a Regulation. The details could be changed much more easily. Guidelines have to be agreed by the SPC but they have no legal status. The guidelines were adopted in December 1998 and were generally agreed to be useful.

However, it was decided less than two years later that the complex basic rules underlying these Guidelines could be transformed into a simpler

Regulation, and this duly appeared in November 2000 (Regulation 2602/2000).

An example of the complexity of the original Guidelines is:

Inducements in the form of 'extras' (extra quantities of the product concerned, inclusion of a different product for 'free' or other extra favours) should be disregarded if they are not significant. The market value of the inducement may be deducted if known but it should then be added back if the offer is withdrawn.

The preamble of the 2000 Regulation includes the following:

(2) There is considerable scope for procedural differences in the treatment of price reductions and the relationship between price reductions and purchase price. A harmonized methodology for the treatment of price reductions in the HICP is necessary to ensure that the resulting HICPs meet the comparability requirements of Article 4 of Regulation 2494/95 [the Framework Regulation]. *It will also improve their reliability and relevance.*

(3) *Prices used in the HICP should be purchaser prices actually paid by households to purchase individual goods and services in monetary transactions, including any taxes less subsidies on the products, after deductions for discounts for bulk or off-peak purchases from standard prices or charges, and excluding interest or services charges added under credit arrangements and any extra charges incurred as a result of failing to pay within the period stated at the time the purchases were made.*

(4) In the event of changes in specifications, prices should be treated in accordance with the rules regarding quality adjustment set out in Commission Regulation (EC) No 1749/96.

In marked contrast to the earlier Guideline, the 2000 Regulation contains only three specific Articles concerning price reductions:

Article 2 Purchaser prices

Unless otherwise stated purchaser prices used in the HICP shall in general take account of reductions in prices of individual goods and services if such reductions:

(a) *can be attributed to the purchase of an individual good or service;*
(b) *are available to all potential consumers with no special conditions attached (non-discriminatory);*
(c) *are known to the purchaser at the time when they enter into the agreement with the seller to purchase the product concerned; and*
(d) *can be claimed at the time of purchase or within such a time period following the actual purchase that they might be expected to have a significant influence on the quantities purchasers are willing to purchase.*

In particular, reductions in the prices of individual goods and services which are likely or expected to be available again at standard prices or are available elsewhere at standard prices shall be taken into account in the HICP. Standard price means the price without any conditions or qualifications and not described as a special price.

Article 3 Inducements

The market value of something temporarily offered to consumers to persuade them to purchase a particular product, hereinafter referred to as an 'inducement', may be deducted if known. That market value shall be added back at the time the offer is withdrawn. Inducements in the form of extras, such as extra quantity of the product concerned, inclusion of a different product 'free of charge' or other benefits, shall be disregarded if they are not significant.

Article 4 Specification change

Where specification changes, prices shall be treated in accordance with the rules on specification changes, and in particular those regarding quality adjustment in Article 5 of Regulation (EC) No 1749/96.

Since the language used in these Articles is non-technical, there seems no need to have any explanatory notes as with most other articles.

9.8 Timing of Price Entry into the HICP

Since the early days of the HICP, pricing technology has changed considerably. Much more use is made of two new sources: the internet (using "web scraping"), and barcode scanner data. These are fascinating tools and fast progress is being made to maximise their usage. In addition, a fast-growing proportion of consumption is made via internet purchases. But in the early days there were really only two ways of gathering price data. The main method was for price collectors to visit retail outlets such as supermarkets and ordinary shops and other retail outlets such as hairdressers. In some cases, prices were obtained via the telephone, especially for services such as plumbers, electricians, painters, etc. and also for travel companies such as airlines.

For the HICP, there was no requirement in those days to enforce specific time windows on member states. As long as prices were collected at some point(s) in each month, the Framework Regulation was followed: *Art 8: "The required frequency of price collection shall be compiled once a month"*. So some countries might collect prices in the middle of the month, some near the beginning and some nearer the end. At times of low inflation (which were mainly in the region of 2% when the HICP was launched) this discrepancy perhaps did not matter much. But if a certain product was rising much faster in prices than the average, such as petrol prices for instance, the difference between the price at the beginning and end of a particular month might be significant, and could affect the resulting overall HICP. In addition, the sample size was not prescribed in any regulation. The only criterion was "monthly collection". Some countries collected prices on a single day in the month, others on two or more days, sometimes adjacent, sometimes not. In particular, some countries collected the prices of fresh food items at least twice in the month at different times.

The specification of price collection timings was not made until 2006 (Regulation 701–2006)—beyond the usual scope of this book. Before then, member states were left to their own decisions, based on national conditions such as weather, temperatures and regional differences—as well as budget constraints.

When it came to certain services, there are some problems which were discussed at length in the WP.

Consider package holidays. Typically, a customer of a travel agency may book a holiday for next summer in the middle of winter. The customer may have to pay the full amount in advance, or, more likely, a deposit when booking and the rest at a time closer to the date of the holiday. Which month or months should these prices enter the HICP?

Another, and rather different, example is the booking of a ticket for a theatre performance, a sports event or a railway season ticket. These payments would usually be for the full price, but sometimes the services may not happen, or begin, until a future date. It could also be the payment of an electricity bill, covering future estimated consumption spread over several months or even a whole year.

Such questions posed many difficulties for the WP delegates. And member states found that they were using different methods from their neighbours. Here was something important to be harmonised.

There are three main approaches to the issue. Firstly, what may be called the "legal" approach. At what date do consumers have a legal right to the service they have paid for? That could be an appropriate date for entering the HICP.

A second approach is to consider the usage of the service. If it can't be "used" for six months (like a package holiday) perhaps it shouldn't be in the index until it is "used".

A third approach is the "payments" approach. If customers have paid for a service—whether or not it is to be "consumed" today or in the future—they are out of pocket at the moment of payment, and given that inflation is all about money, it should be recorded as of the date of payment.

The solution finally adopted was to allocate the payment to the month in which the service may first commence. In other words, for a single event like a package holiday, it would be registered for the month of the holiday, not the month of payment. For a railway season ticket the full price paid would be registered for the first day of the ticket validity. This solution, while not suiting everybody, had at least the advantage of logic and simplicity, and it is still in force. A strong body of opinion would have preferred the payments approach, since consumers usually have to pay whatever the charge is at the time when it is demanded, regardless of the time when the service is consumed. Of course, CPIs are designed for different purposes, some for what are termed "macroeconomic" purposes and others for "microeconomic" purposes. The HICP was clearly and explicitly designed for macroeconomic purposes, although it has also been used in other ways. My own view is that inflation is all about money, so whenever money changes hands, such as a deposit, it should enter the price index—if it is to be used as a measure of consumer price inflation. However, as always with practical statistics, the deciding factor may well be practicability. We cannot always measure with any precision the transactions that we would wish to.

9.9 Treatment of Outliers

Outright lies—or outliers? To be serious, the question of outliers is a common problem with CPIs. An outlier is a value (usually we are talking about prices) which is so far from the normal range of prices for a particular item that it is probably wrong. In modern times, we may expect the frequency of outliers to be reducing, since more and more prices are obtained electronically, such as from the internet or from scanner data. As everybody knows, electronic data cannot be wrong! In the earlier HICP days, however, the vast majority of prices were collected physically by collectors and written down on a price collection form. So it was only to be expected that many prices were written quickly—and distortions occurred. Or the price was misread by the person transferring it to the computer programme.

But sometimes outliers are the reality. Wealthy consumers may sometimes buy goods or services way beyond the reach of the average consumer. But even when a particular price is checked and verified to be correct, if it is well outside the normal range, should it still be permitted to stay in the sample? The purist may say that it should, but perhaps the statistician should say not. Because the HICP (or any CPI) is a sample statistic aiming to measure average prices paid. If one outlier price affects the average significantly, the argument is that it should not be included in the sample.

Usually, if a particular item at a particular outlet has a recorded value which is significantly lower or higher than the average for that item, and it is confirmed to be accurate, then in subsequent months if similar prices are recorded they should be accepted as genuine and kept in the sample.

It also needs to be borne in mind that there is an inbuilt skew in such data. Prices cannot fall below zero, but there is no limit to the maximum for a price. So if outliers are included, it may introduce an upward bias to the HICP. If the average price of a certain item is small, say €2, the lowest possible price is €0.01, which is 99.5% below the average. The same percentage amount above €2 is €3.99, which may well be possible. This implies that the thresholds for permissibility for outliers may need to be greater for the upper threshold than for the lower threshold, in percentage terms at least.

It appeared that the treatment of outliers needed to be agreed. To be treated as an outlier, the price concerned must be beyond a certain limit with respect to the average price. What should such a limit be: 50% different, 100% different ..?

There is no regulation covering this matter. However, under the "compliance monitoring" heading (see Chapter 12) it was agreed informally that there is a strong need to check all prices before they are finally admitted into the calculations.

CHAPTER 10

Weights

10.1 Background

So far, the technical chapters of this book have focussed on prices: the products for which prices are collected, along with their classification, the regional and temporal aspects of price collection, and so on. But to construct a price index, we also require weights for the products grouped at various levels of aggregation. For the uninitiated, "weights" refers to the importance to be attached to the various groupings of products. We would not calculate a price index for food by taking a simple average price of tomatoes, butter and fish. Some products are much more "important" than others to the extent that consumers spend more on them—either because they are more expensive or because they are more popular—or a combination of the two. It may sometimes be that expenditure (or sales) data are not available, in which case it may be necessary to use physical quantities as weights. The techniques used to weight the prices of the products in the HICP are complex, and in this chapter I illustrate how the HICP weights are obtained and how they are calculated and aggregated.

One of the early discussions in the WP concerned the question of whether the "basket" of products in the HICP should also be harmonised among the member states. It would have had to be some sort of European "average" basket, not corresponding to the exact basket of any individual country. One view was that if the basket was not harmonized, the resulting indices would not be harmonized either. This is a superficial

J. Astin, *Measuring EU Inflation*,
https://doi.org/10.1007/978-3-030-68806-6_10

idea, though in some ways a natural one. Harmonizing the index might surely imply a harmonized basket of goods. The response made by Eurostat was that if one country consumes a lot of meat and another country consumes a lot of fish, and if meat prices rise faster than fish prices, then inflation (other things being equal) would be higher in the first country than in the second. And the design of the index should show this effect.

It should be noted that if all prices changed more or less equally, regardless of the product, the use of weights would make no difference to the index. Weights are needed only in order to give more importance to those prices which rise (or fall) significantly faster than the average. We often read in the news that (for example) "inflation has risen by 1.5% in the latest month. This rise was driven mainly by higher air fares and the price of petrol". In more technical terms, such a statement implies that the relatively high weight for air fares and petrol had the effect of emphasising (rightly) the price increases of those two products in the overall index. In practice, it has often been noted that relatively small changes in weights throughout the index tend to have only a small effect on the overall index. That doesn't mean that we don't need to pay much attention to the accuracy of weights. But it does imply that the accurate measurement of prices has more influence on the overall index than the accurate measurement of weights—in most normal circumstances. Imposing the cost of high precision for all weights by frequent and comprehensive updating would not have been acceptable.

10.2 Weights Regulation

Chapter 3.3.3, in describing the Framework Regulation article on sources of data, paid some attention to the provision of weights. This section goes into detail of the statistical treatment of weights rather than their sources.

It was clearly going to be necessary to have a regulation on weights. The preliminary discussions took place in TF2 in early 1995. It took nearly two years to reach the stage of a third draft regulation ready for consideration by the WP, in late 1996. The draft represented a pragmatic compromise involving a minimum of resources between national CPIs whose weights were updated annually and those updated only every five to seven years.

This was the Eurostat introduction to the draft regulation on weights for the WP discussion in February 1997:

The Working Party is invited to vote on this draft regulation on weighting in order to meet the deadline of May 1997 for the SPC. It has been amended to take account of comments received on the draft circulated in January. The aim is to give a "minimum" guarantee of the quality of weights used to construct the HICP and to minimise any disparity between HICPs arising from different up-date frequencies. The Framework Regulation requires that HICPs are sufficiently accurate in terms of their comparability, relevance and reliability, and, as these depend on the quality of weights as well as prices, users can reasonably expect a guarantee of this. It is for NSIs to provide such a guarantee but Eurostat has indicated that it can support guarantees which are based on the scrutiny of a limited number of weights where there is a significant risk of errors affecting the overall HICP.

Resources were to be focussed especially on those weights which were critical to the reliability of the HICP. There were clearly some concerns about the reliability of this approach. Nonetheless, the WP voted in favour of the draft regulation with near unanimity. It was submitted to the SPC at its meeting in May 1997 and was adopted as a Commission Regulation (2454/97) on 10 December 1997.

The regulation itself was quite short with only one technical article, reproduced below. But the Preamble is interesting:

Whereas Article 8 (3) of Regulation (EC) No 2494/95 [the Framework Regulation] *requires the weighting of HICPs to be updated with a frequency sufficient to meet the comparability requirement* ***but does not require family budget surveys to be carried out more frequently than once every five years****, except in Member States which are acknowledged as experiencing changes in consumption patterns such as to make more frequent surveys necessary;*

Whereas consumer price indices from which HICP weightings are derived are updated at different frequencies with the result that the HICPs based thereon may fail to meet the comparability requirement of Article 4 of that Regulation;

Whereas an operational measure of non-comparability is required in order to establish which weightings should be updated in order to ensure comparability;

Whereas Article 9 of Regulation (EC) No 2494/95 requires HICPs to be price indices of the Laspeyres type;

> *Whereas, when relative prices of different goods and services change, consumers' expenditure patterns can change to an extent that makes it necessary for weightings of the corresponding expenditure groups, and in particular their underlying quantities. to be updated in order to ensure their relevance.*

The first highlighted phrase (author's highlighting) was a clear statement designed to allay fears in some member states that they might be forced to conduct family budget surveys (FBS) more frequently. Indeed, while many countries held these surveys quinquennially, some had much longer intervals, even as long as ten years.

The second highlighted phrase illustrated that not all item weights were equally important. Precedence for updating had to be given to those product groups which had the larger weights and thus more likelihood of affecting the overall HICP by more than the permitted 0.1% comparability threshold.

Article 3 was the principal technical article:

> ***Minimum standards for weightings***
>
> 1. *Each month Member States shall produce HICPs using weightings which reflect consumers' expenditure patterns in a weighting reference period ending no more than seven years before the preceding December.*
> 2. *Each year, Member States shall carry out a review of weightings in order to ensure that they are sufficiently reliable and relevant to meet the comparability requirement established in Article 4 of Regulation (EC) No 2494/95. The review may be confined to weightings at the level of sub-indices and their major components.*
> 3. *In the review, Member States shall check whether or not there have been any important changes since the weighting reference period in current use regarding price developments of each major component index relative to the HICP, or sustained market developments in each major component group.*
> 4. *Where reliable evidence shows that changes referred to in paragraph 3 indicate a weighting change that would affect the change in the HICP by more than 0.1 percentage point on average over one year against the previous year, Member States shall adjust the weightings of the HICP appropriately. Member States shall not be obliged to take account of any changes occurring within a two-year period ending in December before the review.*

5. *Any adjustments made pursuant to paragraph 4 shall be implemented by Member States, at the latest, in the index for January following the year of the review.*

Paragraph 1 is the practical expression of the point in the Preamble about the frequency of having FBSs no more than every 5 years. So why 7 years in this Article? This is because it can take up to 2 years to analyse the immense amount of data arising from an FBS, and to make any necessary adjustments. So while the frequency remains at 5 years, the "oldest" FBS data to be used in the HICP could be a further 2 years.

Paragraphs 2–4 put the onus on member states to check the weights every year and to make corrections in those cases where there is clear evidence that they have reduced or increased compared with the previous year's figures. This applies particularly to the larger weights, which have most influence on the overall HICP. Typically, these changes can involve such products as changes in fuel prices, rail fares—or simply changes in indirect taxes such as VAT.

There is no objection to any Member State adjusting the HICP weights every year. Paragraph 5 simply puts a time limit on the making of any changes to weights resulting from the annual reviews.

See also Sect. 10.9 on the special rules for insurance.

[Note also the comment in Chapter 3.3.3 concerning the use of the word "weightings" as opposed to "weights".]

It may be noted that the regulation in fact contained very little in the way of instruction on how to obtain weights. It represents very clearly the policy of "output-based" regulations rather than "input-based", as discussed in Chapter 5.4.

Another oddity in the Regulation (2454/97) is the absence of references to sources of weights data other than Family Budget Surveys. A considerable amount of the data required cannot in fact be obtained—or at least obtained reliably—from the FBS. Data from the national accounts is a particularly rich source for some products.

Again, the HICP approach is to specify the requirements from member states, but to leave it to each country to select its own most reliable sources of weights. Naturally, these tend to be rather similar between countries, for the basic data. The main source is indeed the FBS.[1] This is also the source of much of the data which are used in the national

[1] In the UK now known as the Living Costs and Food Survey (LCF).

accounts, and the latter is also supplemented by data from other sources, such as industry figures of expenditure on alcoholic drinks and tobacco products—which are almost always understated in the FBS surveys.

See also Sect. 10.6 for detail on sources of weights data.

10.3 Price Updating of Weights

So as to achieve a common weight reference period, the item weights for all member states needed to be expressed at the same prices as the annual chain index countries. This is done by "price-updating" the HICPs and their sub-indices; that is, to express the movements in the HICP and its sub-indices by reference to the average level of prices in 1996 (that was the index reference period laid down in the Framework Regulation) and subsequently to each December for subsequent periods. Price-updating is simply a scaling exercise which in itself has no effect on the measured rate of inflation. However, it allows and provides for the construction of indices for groups of countries such as the Monetary Union or indeed the EU as a whole.

10.4 Regional and Outlet-Type Weights

A further complication in the construction of HICP weights is that the basic national data sources for the weights need to be subdivided into regional aspects and also into outlet types.

This requirement is a reflection of normal sampling rules. A national statistic such as the HICP should reflect price changes on average over the whole country. Usually, it is to be expected that different parts of the country, such as cities, rural districts and regions generally, may be expected to show regular differences in many fields of economic data, including the rates of inflation. These differences may be partly a reflection of the types of product which are purchased in different places—such as theatres and concert halls in large cities but not so much in the countryside. Or it may reflect the varying income and expenditure levels in different regions of a country. One might, for instance, expect inflation to be somewhat lower in low-income regions—though this is not necessarily so. Regarding outlet types, it is generally the rule that price levels—and possibly price changes too—are different in supermarkets and corner shops. And supermarkets tend to proliferate in the larger urban districts. Increasingly, purchases are made on the internet, where prices are often lower than in shops, and perhaps also with lower inflation rates.

Because of all these types of variation, sampling schemes for the price surveys must be carefully designed and monitored. For each "section" of the sample, a weight must be assigned, reflecting the value or volume of purchases made in that section. Thus, if surveys indicate that 10% of retail sales are made over the internet, then roughly 10% (by weight) of prices should be collected from internet sources. The same applies to geographic samples.

Thus, a weight at the lowest level would reflect the price of a certain group of products purchased in a certain region of the country and in different types of outlet. All of these figures, when grossed up, should reflect the total national aggregate of consumer expenditure.

10.5 Elementary Aggregate Indices

So-called "elementary aggregates" are the lowest level of groups of products for which data on expenditure are generally available. The weights regulation did not prescribe any specific requirements for these various levels. Clearly, a small country like Luxembourg would be unlikely to have reliable estimates of expenditure relating to particular groups of products separately classified by both regions and outlet types. The larger the country, the larger is likely to be the range of elementary aggregates.

How are the elementary aggregates defined? The preliminary stage is to work down from the main heading, which in the case of the HICP corresponds to a particular level in the COICOP/HICP classification of consumer expenditure (see Chapter 6). This could be, for example, non-durable household goods (COICOP/HICP 05.6.1). It would be necessary to have a weight for this heading, derived usually from a Household Budget Survey (HBS). It is then entirely within the hands of the NSI to determine which sub-elementary aggregates products to price within each COICOP/HICP heading. COICOP/HICP has many to suggest, and the list is not comprehensive. Examples from 05.6.1 are: polishes, waxes, softeners, tablecloths, clothes hangers, etc. It is the task of the NSI to select which of these products to price in the HICP, and normally this would be the same as, or very similar to, the products in the same group in the national CPI—assuming such a group exists.

The obvious criteria for selection of sub-aggregates are the popularity and/or price of the product. The HICP regulations laid down no specific targets for the number of products to be priced in each elementary aggregate; this is left to the informed decisions of the NSI statisticians who are best placed to arrive at a suitable choice. And, as mentioned above, they would normally start with the list used in the national CPI equivalent heading.

After the product level has been established, the next stage is to disaggregate the national data into the categories described in the previous section.

So finally an elementary aggregate description would be along the lines of "Product group 05.6.1 in supermarkets in UK cities".

10.6 Data Sources for Weights

(a) **Household Budget Surveys**

For any consumer price index, the weights must refer to the expenditure on different products by households. The most obvious (and also the most expensive) way of acquiring such information is by asking a sample of households to report their expenditure in some detail over a given period. It would be normal good practice to select a representative sample of households. What do we mean by "representative" in this context? Given that the HICP should reflect expenditures and prices over all regions of the country and all main product groups, the sample of households should be selected in such a way as to maximise the chances that their expenditures fulfil the above requirements. And, unless the survey form requires the respondents to specify the "point of purchase" for each product category (i.e. supermarket, corner shop, internet, etc.), we must assume that overall the survey results will approximately match any known proportions of such sales. To put this another way, it is clear that it would be a mistake to confine the household survey to high-quality districts in an expensive part of the country—or the opposite. The households must be selected in a statistically random way. But, as usual, this is not as simple as it may seem. The households themselves may indeed be selected randomly, but not necessarily the response rates. It has been found over the years that the higher the household income the lower the response rate. To some extent this problem can be overcome by selecting relatively more households with probably above-average income than would be the case if selected randomly. But this introduces an element of subjectivity into the process. As mentioned earlier, statistics is rarely an exact science!

(b) **National Accounts and other data sources**

Some member states used their National Accounts as the main source of weighting information, others used household budget surveys, but both sources are invariably used to some extent. Indeed, the source of probably most of the weights used in the National Accounts are based on HBS results, sometimes adjusted for taxation, or for estimated under- or over-reporting. For example, as mentioned earlier, the HBS results consistently under-report expenditure on alcohol and tobacco. Alternative sources for these products can usually be obtained from national taxation databases. HBS results may also be supplemented by market research and other data where these are available. In the end, it is the quality of the estimates rather than their origins that is important.

10.7 Household or Expenditure Weighting?

These practical issues are not the end of the story. Turning now to the matter of what are often referred to as "democratic" and "plutocratic" weights (see below), this is a topic which has to be given serious attention in designing any price index; it certainly was in the case of the HICP.

Analysis of the HBS reports will enable the statistician to calculate—for each respondent household—the proportions of total expenditure on the various product groups, such as food 15%, air tickets 3%, and so on (with doubtless more detail than suggested here). But we are interested in these proportions over the whole country. There are two ways of calculating this. Firstly, we could take the simple arithmetic average of all HBS respondents for all the proportions as calculated above.

The second way would be to add all the expenditures (not the proportions) separately, to get a grand total of the expenditures on each product group. We could then calculate the overall proportions for each group. This will normally give a significantly different result from the first method. Why is this? It is because the first method gives effectively an equal weight to each household, whereas the second method gives more weight to the expenditures of the wealthier households.

The first method is often referred to as "democratic" weighting, and the second as "plutocratic" weighting. (My personal preference is to use more precise expressions such as "household-weighted" and "expenditure-weighted".)[2]

The international "Practical Guide to Producing Consumer Price Indices"[3] (paragraphs 4.14–4.16) explains the main usages of the two approaches: *"The use of plutocratic weights is generally considered more appropriate for consumer price indices which have been constructed to be a general macroeconomic indicator... Democratic weights.. are not considered appropriate for an index used as a general measure of inflation"*. The HICP, being of the macroeconomic type, uses the "plutocratic" (expenditure-weighted) method. The differences can be quite substantial.[4]

In any case, not all weights can be obtained with sufficient accuracy from the HBS. For example, it is well known that expenditures on items such as alcoholic drinks and tobacco products are greatly underestimated. Much better estimates can be obtained from National Accounts sources—which fits well with the macroeconomic uses of the HICP. In general, the National Accounts data on consumer expenditure can be used to supplement HBS data for consumption categories that tend to be wrongly reported in the HBS, and where the HBS data suffer from a significant partial non-response rate.

10.8 Aggregate Weights—Laspeyres or Lowe?

Chapter 8 (index formulae) refers to the technical aspects of the aggregation of the elementary aggregate indices to the higher aggregates, including the all-items HICP, using a "Laspeyres-type" index as laid down in the Framework Regulation. CPIs rarely use a "pure" Laspeyres index for the simple reason that the reference weights do not in general refer to the time period for which the index is calculated. It is simply not practicable to carry out a Household Budget Survey covering a certain year and introduce the resulting weights in that same year, as a true Laspeyres index

[2] See Astin, J., and Leyland, J. " Towards a Household Inflation Index", 2015.

[3] "Practical Guide to Producing Consumer Price Indices", United Nations, 2009.

[4] Flower, T., and Wales, P. "Variation in the Inflation Experience of UK Households: 2003–2014" (Economic Trends, UK Office for National Statistics, December 2014).

would require. The base year weights are price-updated (see Chapter 8.4) and re-based only at intervals. The name of the resulting index type is a Lowe Index.

10.9 Special Case: Insurance Weights

Section 10.2 of this chapter describes how the regulation specified that the weights for the HICP should be reviewed every year, and that changes should be made where there is evidence that the 0.1% comparability threshold may be compromised. If that happens, the weights should be adjusted.

In the case of insurance, this was argued to be an inadequate provision. It happens not infrequently that a major disaster, such as flooding, occurs in a particular year, resulting in a significant change in the insurance company service charges, which form the basis for the insurance index. The standard method of calculating weights could quite easily result in a negative weight in some years. This is a situation which had to be avoided. A later Regulation (1617/99) dealt with insurance generally, and included a new rule on insurance weights. The 1999 Regulation requires that the annual service charges (for all insurers in each category) are averaged over a three-year period, which helps to smooth out annual variations, and hence minimise the chance of a negative insurance weight.

This topic is dealt with more fully in the next chapter.

CHAPTER 11

Treatment of Special Products

In this chapter we examine a number of important products which do not follow the same sort of patterns of sale and/or consumption as most "ordinary" products. The products concerned are:

- Health, education and social protection services
- Owner-occupied housing
- Proportional service charges
- Insurance
- Data processing equipment
- Miscellaneous products.

11.1 Health, Education and Social Protection Services

Readers will recall that this large area of consumer expenditure was not covered in the Interim Indices of Consumer Prices in 1996, nor in the HICPs as first published in 1997. This is mainly because of the widespread variation amongst member states in the treatment of these products (and often because of their differing legal and administrative managements). But clearly it was necessary to cover them without too long a delay,

J. Astin, *Measuring EU Inflation*,
https://doi.org/10.1007/978-3-030-68806-6_11

and work at the Task Force and Working Party levels began at quite an early stage. The culmination of these discussions was Council Regulation 2166/1999.

A key issue which perhaps should be mentioned first is the definition of which payments should be covered. In the case of prescription medicines, one extreme is that the consumer pays nothing, while at the other extreme the consumer may have to pay the full price. Between these limits, various possibilities exist, such as variable discounts depending on the medication or on the status of the patient, such as their age. Some countries covered in their national CPI the full, undiscounted cost of such medicines, even if the consumer did not pay the full amount. Given that the HICP had already been decided to be covered on the basis of Household Final Monetary Consumption Expenditure (HFMCE—see Chapter 7.5) it was agreed that only actual payments would be covered.

A similar situation existed for consultations with a general practitioner (GP) or "family doctor". In some countries such consultations were free of charge, in others not. Again, it was agreed that if they were free, no monetary transaction took place and thus no payment would be imputed. Similar arguments applied to hospital stays and medical operations. The end result was at least simple in theory: the HICP would cover only actual payments made (even if this involved a larger payment followed by a whole or partial refund, in which case only the net amount paid would be covered).

Naturally, payments made outside any national health service, i.e. payments to private practitioners, would be covered in full. Where a patient was partially covered by a medical insurance policy, the premiums for such a policy, if paid by the final consumer, would be covered in the "insurance" heading of COICOP (see Sect. 11.4 of this chapter), while any partial payments by the consumer to a medical practitioner would be covered in the HICP under the COICOP medical heading.

It was agreed that these principles would also apply, mutatis mutandis, to the education and social protection expenditure headings. A considerable amount of preparatory discussion, both in TF2 and in the WP, took place before the draft regulation was submitted to the SPC. Some details from the discussions follow.

Work began effectively in 1997 on a proposed Regulation which would cover education, health and social protection services. From the point of view of consumer prices, these activities share some similarities. For example, they are often provided either free of charge or at prices lower than the full price. Examples of these are school and university education, medical services; and nurseries and play schools in the field of social protection.

Other shared aspects of these services are the instances where previously "free" services become payable—and vice versa. This could apply to dental services or school textbooks for example.

Another type of event within these sectors is the question of fees whose level depends partially or fully on the income of the person acquiring the good or service. For example, the practice of fixing nursery school fees according to the income(s) of the parent(s) (see Chapter 6.4).

Given the fact that many of these attributes were shared in the three sectors of public service concerned, it was decided to aim for a single regulation covering all three sectors. Initial discussions taking place in the TFs focused on each one of the sectors. After sufficient progress had been achieved, the resulting work was brought together by Eurostat and moulded into a composite Regulation for the WP to consider. These WP discussions began in the middle of 1998 and culminated in a draft ready for proposal to the SPC in 1999.

The TF discussions focussed mainly on the following topics:

(a) The choice of COICOP sub-indices to be calculated and published;
(b) The frequency of checking and updating of weights;
(c) How to deal with situations where a price is imposed when formerly a service was provided free of charge;
(d) How to deal with cases where partial (or even full) reimbursements were made, for example in the provision of medicines;
(e) The proposed date(s) of introduction of the rules in the forthcoming regulation;
(f) Whether or not the rules should apply only to services or also to goods, such as school textbooks;
(g) How to deal with income-related prices;
(h) The treatment of institutions and their residents, such as retirement homes;
(i) Details of classification, for example whether or not kindergartens should be included under the heading of education or social protection.

A number of draft regulations were discussed in successive WP meetings in 1998 and 1999, culminating in a draft which was supported by a majority of the WP in March 1999. This was presented to the SPC at its meeting in May 1999. Unfortunately, the draft did not reach a qualified majority vote. There were in fact no votes cast against the draft, but only 57 votes were cast in favour; the remainder abstained. The qualified majority (62) not having been reached, the draft was submitted to the Council, where it received approval. The original planned date was left unchanged: the regulation came into effect on 31 December 1999.

The main parts of the Regulation (2166/99) are given below.

The preamble included the following:

(2) *Commission Regulation (EC) No 1749/96 defines the coverage of the HICP as those goods and services which are included in household final monetary consumption expenditure; goods and services in the health, education and social protection sectors are part of the coverage of the HICP; household final monetary consumption covers the expenditure incurred by individuals living in institutional households and should be grouped in accordance with the COICOP/HICP categories as laid down in Commission Regulation (EC) No 2214/96;*

(3) *by virtue of Commission Regulation (EC) No 1749/96, in particular Article 3 and Annex la thereof, extended coverage in the health, education and social protection sectors should be implemented in December 1999 and take effect with the index for January 2000, whereby the methodological details of inclusion should be specified in accordance with the procedure laid down in Article 15 of the framework Council Regulation (EC) No 2494/95; the timetable of inclusion for hospital services and social protection services provided within the home, retirement homes and residences for the disabled should be specified in accordance with the same procedure;*

(4) *there is considerable scope for procedural differences in the treatment of goods and services in the health, education and social protection sectors in the HICP; a harmonized methodology for such goods and services is necessary to ensure that the resulting HICPs meet the comparability requirement as laid down in Article 4 of Regulation (EC) No 2494/95;*

(5) *the treatment of goods and services in the health, education and social protection sectors is consistent with the definitions laid down in the European System of Accounts (ESA) 1995 set out in Council Regulation (EC) No 2223/96.*

This preamble, in short, is saying that the new measures for these sectors must not depart from the methods set out in the HICP Framework Regulation and also must adhere to the definitions in the ESA. The details of how these principles were to be followed are set out in the following technical Articles.

Article 2 (Definitions):

1. ***Reimbursements*** *refer to payments to households by government units, social security administrations or non-profit institutions serving households (NPISHs), that are made as direct consequences of purchases of individually specified goods and services, initially paid for by households.*
2. *Payments of* ***claims to households by insurance companies*** *do not constitute reimbursements.*
3. ***Other payments or rebates to households*** *by government units, social security administrations or NPISHs in the form of assistance to reduce household expenditure, such as housing allowances to tenants or payments due to sickness, disability, the care of elderly relatives or scholarships to students, are considered as social benefits in cash. They are treated as income transfers to households and do not constitute reimbursements.*

A common type of reimbursement would be partial or full reimbursements for medicines paid to pharmacies on prescription.

Article 3 (Coverage):

1. *Goods and services in the health, education and social protection sectors on which household final monetary consumption expenditure is incurred shall be covered in the HICP and grouped in accordance with the COICOP/HICP categories as laid down in Commission Regulation (EC) No 2214/96.*
2. *All providers of goods and services in the health, education and social protection sectors, such as government and private institutions, NPISHs or private self-employed persons, shall be covered in the HICP independently of their status. This excludes individuals or groups of individuals as producers of goods and non-financial services exclusively for own final use.*

   This paragraph makes it clear that "own production" is not covered in the HICP. This would include food production used exclusively for supplying the producer's own household (see Chapter 3.1).

3. *In accordance with COICOP/HICP, Education (Division 10) includes* ***education services only****. If an all-inclusive price for education services in combination with educational materials or education support services, its components shall be separated and allocated to the COICOP/HICP classes concerned. Where such an all-inclusive price cannot be separated into the prices of the components concerned, the all-inclusive price shall be allocated to COICOP/HICP Division 10.*
4. ***Borderline cases*** *between education services at the pre-primary level and child-minding social protection facilities, such as wet-nurses, crèches and play-schools, shall be allocated to COICOP/HICP Division 10 if the child's age of entry is not less than three years and the activities consist of organised instruction in a school-type environment designed to bridge the gap between the home and school atmosphere. If, on the other hand, the main objective is not a pedagogical one, but to provide child-minding assistance and support, the service concerned should be allocated to COICOP/HICP class 12.4.0.* [Social protection]
5. *Where* ***hospitals****, in addition to basic services as defined in COICOP/HICP 06.3, make other goods and services available to in-patients on a separate charge basis, the latter shall not be allocated to class 06.3.0 but to the COICOP/HICP classes concerned.*

Article 4 (Prices):

1. *The HICP sub-indices concerned shall be calculated using a formula which is consistent with the Laspeyres-type formula used for other sub-indices. They should reflect the price change on the basis of the changed expenditure of* ***maintaining the consumption pattern of households*** *and the composition of the consumer population in the base or reference period.*
2. (a) *The purchaser prices of goods and services in the health, education and social protection sectors to be used in the HICP shall be the amounts to be paid by consumers* ***net of reimbursements****.*
   (b) *Changes in purchaser prices which reflect* ***changes in the rules determining them*** *shall be shown as price changes in the HICP.*
   (c) *Where purchaser prices are* ***index-linked****, changes resulting from changes in the index shall be shown as price changes in the HICP.*
   (d) *Changes in the purchaser prices resulting from* ***changes in purchasers' incomes*** *shall be shown as price changes in the HICP.*

   (This last section (d) covers the type of situation discussed in Sect. 11.6 of this Chapter.)

3. *Where **quality changes**, prices should be treated according to the rules applied in the context of specification changes, and in particular those regarding quality adjustment pursuant to Article 5 of Commission Regulation (EC) No 1749/96.*
4. *Where goods or services, in the health, education and social protection sectors, have been made available to consumers free of charge and subsequently an actual price is charged, **the change from zero to an actual price, and vice versa**, shall be reflected in the HICP.*

An example of the latter change could be the introduction of a fee for out-patient clinic services for the first time. The detailed method of how such a change should be incorporated into the HICP was not part of a regulation but, like a number of other detailed technical issues, dealt with purely as an advisory matter. Most of these are now covered in the HICP Methodological Manual (2018).[1] The basic answer to this particular problem is to:

- Estimate the expenditure incurred by consumers due to the introduction of the new charge during the current year;
- Calculate what would be the 'price of the new total basket' including the new charge and compare the result with the 'price of the old total basket';
- Compare the 'new' and 'old' baskets to get a price index.

Of course, a similar method can be used in other parts of the basket, such as parking charges.

5. *Where goods or services in the health, education and social protection sectors, jointly provided with other goods and services, have been made available to consumers **free of charge** and subsequently have been charged for on a separate basis, the change shall be reflected in the HICP.*
6. *Where relevant, the procedure provided for in Article 5 of Commission Regulation (EC) No 2646/98 concerning tariffs shall apply mutatis mutandis.*

[1] Eurostat "HICP Methodological Manual," 2018, Luxembourg. ISBN 978-92-79-76861-3.

Article 5 (Basic information):

The basic information shall be all purchaser prices of goods and services in the health, education and social protection sectors and their components, together with weightings which reflect the level, the timing and the structure of the consumption of such goods and services, according to the price-determining socio-economic characteristics.

Note: the latter category may include, for example, wealth, income, number of dependent children.

Article 6 (Data sources):

1. *The HICP sub-indices concerned shall be computed by the Member States from basic information as defined in Article 5.*
2. *The statistical units, such as government agencies, social administrations or NPISHs, called upon by Member States to co-operate in the collection or provision of basic information, are obliged to give honest and complete information at the time it is requested and allow the organisations and institutions responsible for compiling official statistics, on request, to obtain information at the level of detail necessary to evaluate compliance with the comparability requirements and the quality of the HICP sub-indices.*

Article 9 (Implementation):

The provisions of this Regulation shall be implemented by the Member States in December 1999 and shall ***take effect with the index for January 2000****, apart from the following, which shall be implemented in December 2000 and shall take* ***effect with the index for January 2001****:*

(a) *hospital services (COICOP/HICP 06.3);*
(b) *social protection services provided within the home, such as home cleaning, meals, transport for the disabled (part of COICOP/HICP 12.4.0);*
(c) *retirement homes, residences for the disabled (part of COICOP/HICP 12.4.0).*

In fact these three sets of temporary exclusions were of necessity postponed by one year because of delays in the administrative process—in particular reflecting the fact that the draft regulation was not approved by the SPC in May 1999, and it had to be referred to the Council, as noted above.

Table 11.1 shows the changes in HICP product coverage made with the publication of the January 2000 index. Member states reported on the changes they made with the January 2000 index (X indicates changes, C indicates compliance already before January 2000) in implementing extended coverage according to HFMCE as follows:

(a) Including domestic expenditure by non-residents, excluding expenditure by residents abroad.
(b) Individuals living in institutional households, poor and rich, urban and rural.

11.2 Owner-Occupied Housing (OOH)

This has for many years been a huge problem area for price statisticians. When it first began to be discussed in a Eurostat Task Force in 1994 it was clear that opinions were very divided. Naturally, most delegates took as a model the way in which OOH was treated in their national CPI.

The basic problem in reality is simple. Are owner-occupied houses capital items or consumption items or some sort of combination of the two? The European System of Accounts (ESA) classifies OOH as a capital item. For some CPI statisticians, that was sufficient reason to maintain this approach for the HICP. The result would be to keep OOH outside the scope of the HICP.

But approaching the problem from the point of view of households, it is not so straightforward. When somebody buys a house, they usually have in mind the prospect of its future (hopefully increased) value. We all accept that if we buy a car, even an expensive car, eventually it will become almost worthless. But we still buy it. If it were the same with houses, maybe we would prefer to rent rather than buy. On the other hand, if we don't maintain the house properly, eventually it would become almost worthless (apart from the land it occupies).

The arrangements for paying for a house also cause problems. Typically, a house buyer pays a deposit to the current owner, or to the builder if it is a new house. The buyer will usually need to borrow all or most of the remaining cost with the help of a mortgage from a bank or other lender. Or there may be a sum available from the sale of a previously

Table 11.1 Changes in coverage made with January 2000 HICP

	Increase of total expenditure covered by HICP (%)	*Geographic coverage (a)*	*Population coverage (b)*
Belgium		X	X
Denmark		C	C
Germany		C	X (*)
Greece		X	X
Spain	7	X	X
France	4.5 (product coverage)	C	C
Ireland	5.2 (product coverage) 6.9 (domestic concept)	X	X (*)
Italy		C	C
Luxembourg		X	C
Netherlands	5.8 (population and geographic coverage)	C	X
Austria		X (**)	C
Portugal	7.3 (population and geographic coverage)	X	C
Finland	3.8 (population and geographic coverage)	X	X
Sweden		C	C
United Kingdom	3.5 (tourists) 5.0 (product coverage) 1.0 (Household coverage)	X	X
Iceland	6.7 (population and geographic coverage)	X	X
Norway		X	

Source HICP Compendium 2001, Table 6

(*) Individuals living in institutional households are not covered because of their small relative importance

(**) From 1996 to 1999 the Austrian HICP related to the domestic concept but included not only household consumption expenditure but also all foreign consumption expenditure. In order to adjust this concept the weight of division 07 (traffic) was reduced by 0.7 percentage points and the weight of division 11 (hotels and restaurants) was reduced by 1.0 percentage points, both figures relating to 1998 expenditure

owned house. The mortgagor will have a contract to repay the mortgage, with interest, over a period of years—often as long as 25 years or even more. The rate of interest may be variable, or it may be fixed. The repayments, usually monthly, are normally a mix of capital and interest. But sometimes they are interest only, the capital element being paid off by means of an insurance policy after perhaps many years.

All of this can provide measurement difficulties for the statistician.

Such arguments raged in the WP for many months. The first step was the provision of a paper to TF2 in 1994. It was in fact a UK document of 1992 summarising the treatment of OOH in countries worldwide. It showed that of 11 EU member states, 6 used the imputed rents method, 1 used mortgage interest and 4 omitted OOH entirely from their national CPIs. The imputed rent method was based on the idea that the value of the house to its owner could be measured by the rent which they would have to pay if in fact it was rented. The trouble with this approach—popular though it is—is that (a) the rent is purely imaginary: the owner does not transfer any money from one pocket to the other to cover the cost of their house. And (b) how is such a rent to be estimated if it doesn't exist? The use of mortgage interest was disapproved by several delegates on the grounds that interest is neither a good nor a service, and for this reason is not classed as consumer expenditure in the National Accounts.

It was clearly going to be a long haul for the WP! Shortly afterwards, TF2 commissioned a lengthy report from the Oxford University economist John Muellbauer. It gave a good deal of academic insight into the issue. Later, in 1996, a further academic assessment was provided by the late Professor Peter Hill, a national accounts expert, working as a consultant to Eurostat. It was during the discussions on this topic that Hill proposed a general rule for the HICP—the idea of HFMCE (Household Final Monetary Consumption Expenditure), discussed in Chapter 7.5. Adherence to this rule would automatically exclude the use of imputed rents, since these were not actual monetary expenditures.

If expenditure on cars is measured by the net method—i.e. the purchase price effectively offset by the sale proceeds of a previous car (which it is in the HICP)—then why not adopt the same method for houses? But there was a snag here. Most houses owned by consumers are sold to other consumers. If the cost were included, it would have to be shown also as a negative; in fact the net transaction cost would be zero for the household sector. On the other hand, some houses may be sold to buyers outside the household sector—to companies for example.

And some houses are purchased by consumers from sellers outside the household sector—such as local authorities.

Why not then include only transactions such as these? Properties new to the household sector. It would also of course include newly built houses.

The Hill report came out strongly in favour of including the net capital costs of OOH in the HICP. And this formed the core of Eurostat's first recommendation to the SPC in March 1997. No decisions were made then.

In 1998 a new Task Force (TF12) was established to examine further the OOH issue. This was its remit:

"Task Force 12 shall assess each of the following three alternative options for treatment of owner-occupied housing in the HICP:

(a) *the scope of the HICP should be extended to include the net acquisition of dwellings;*
(b) *the net acquisition of dwellings is classified in ESA 95 as capital formation and should therefore be excluded from the HICP;*
(c) *the net acquisition of dwellings should be excluded from the HICP on the above grounds, but a separate index on the net acquisition of dwellings should be developed as a matter of priority."*

After several meetings, TF12 presented a report to the main Task Force, TF2, at its meeting in April 2000. The report included a draft recommendation for the SPC, which was duly presented to its meeting in September 2000. The recommendation comprised a choice of one of three options:

Option 1: A new HICP sub-index for OOH should be developed on the basis of the acquisition price of dwellings new to the household sector.

Option 2: A similar type of index should be developed, initially on an experimental basis in each Member State, but with a view to its subsequent inclusion within the HICP. Following an assessment of the index after a certain time, the SPC would be asked to approve its inclusion in the HICP, or to maintain it as a separate index, or to discontinue it.

Option 3: No specific action; maintaining the status quo.

Note that none of the options included the use of imputed rents to measure the value of OOH. As well as several member states, the EMI had made it clear that it would not accept this as a solution.

The SPC recognised that owner occupier costs should be measured, and it agreed on a modified version of option 2: a net acquisition index should be developed on an experimental basis in each Member State. The HICP Working Party should have a clear mandate and timetable to develop the methodology, together with a financial commitment by the Commission. A pilot time series should be developed, addressing methodological and measurement issues. After a certain time, following the analysis of the series and the problem of weighting, a decision should be made if this index is to be incorporated into the HICP.

Following this ruling, a Task Force continued in Eurostat to plan and prepare for the experimental OOH index recommended by the SPC.

The HICP still (2020) does not cover owner occupiers' expenditure. Council Regulation (EC) No 1687/98 stipulates in Annex I(a) that "imputed rentals of owner-occupiers" (COICOP 04.2.1.) and "other imputed rentals" (COICOP 04.2.2.) should be excluded from the HICP. That is still the case.

When I left Eurostat in 2002, this Task Force was still engaged in its discussions. It was not until 2013 that a Regulation was published[2](see details in Chapter 15.10).

11.3 Proportional Service Charges

This sounds complex—and it certainly can be!—but the idea is straightforward. An example of a proportional service charge is the charge made by a foreign exchange dealer which is often related to the value of the transaction: the higher the value the lower may be the unit charge. The larger the job, the bigger the fee.

As may be deduced from the late date of the Regulation covering this topic (1920/2001), the matter was for a long time the subject of debate and alternative views. The earlier regulations from 2214/96 right up to 1749/99 of July 1999, contained a COICOP product coverage list which explicitly excluded payments expressed as a proportion of charges.[3]

[2] Commission Regulation 93-13, 2013.

[3] (COICOP/HICP 12.5.A—Banking Services).

Discussions began in TF2 and the WP from 1999. It was agreed in these discussions that it would not be right to exclude such payments; draft regulations were prepared and discussed at several meetings over the following two years. Finally, in September 2001 came Commission Regulation 1920-01, which amended Regulation 2214/96.

The rules cover for the most part—but by no means entirely—the financial sector, such as commissions for the sale and purchase of stocks and shares. (The prices of stocks and shares themselves, not being consumption products, are excluded from the HICP.)

The relevant clauses of the Preamble set out the rationale for including this type of charge in the HICP:

Whereas …

(2) *Commission Regulation 1749/96 defines the coverage of the HICP as those goods and services which are included in household monetary consumption expenditure and requires coverage of COICOP/HICP class 1.5.1 'Financial services n.e.c.' in full by December 1999 without specific exclusion of charges expressed as a proportion of the transaction value.*

(3) *Commission Regulation 2214/96 requires a harmonized sub-index for COICOP/HICP expenditure class 12.6.2. 'Other financial services n.e.c.'*[4] *excluding interest payments and charges expressed as a proportion of the transaction value.*

(4) *There is considerable scope for non-comparability by excluding service charges that are expressed as a proportion of the transaction value; a harmonized methodology for the treatment of such charges is necessary to ensure that the resulting HICPs meet the comparability requirement as laid down in Article 4 of Regulation (EC) No 2494/95.*

(5) *The treatment of service charges that are expressed as a proportion of transaction values should be consistent with the treatment of goods and services in the health, education and social protection sectors as laid down in Council Regulation (EC) No 2166/1999.*

This preamble tells a story in itself! Paragraph 2 is an admission of the failure to achieve complete coverage. Paragraph 4 clearly implies that this is an important omission, while Paragraph 5 seems to be saying that if it can be done in the health, education and social protection sectors it can be done in the financial sector. Note that the latter Regulation did not appear until 1999, only two years before this Regulation. At least the priorities were right!

We now look at the main articles of Regulation 1920/2002.

[4] n.e.c.—not elsewhere classified.

Article 2 (Definitions):

1. *Interest payments and interest-like charges cover nominal interest payments and all elements included in the calculation of effective interest.*
2. *Where service charges are defined as a proportion of the transaction value, the purchaser prices are defined as the proportion itself, multiplied by the value of a representative unit transaction in the base or reference period.*

This Article raises some important issues. Though definitions of somewhat abstruse words and phrases are given, they needed to be explained to make any sense to the index compiler. Perhaps they didn't go far enough! What comprises an "interest-like" charge? What is a "representative unit transaction"? Eurostat gave some explanations to the WP and the SPC.

"Interest-like charges" would include, for example, charges to consumers from delaying or advancing the booking of transactions in accounts, premiums or discounts on credits, commitment fees, overdraft provisions and credit provisions.

The "representative unit transaction" (RUT) is best understood by an example. Suppose the product in question is the purchase via a broker of a block of shares. A typical RUT may thus be the purchase of a portfolio of 1000 shares with a value of €7500. The service charge is a flat fee of €10, plus a single rate of 5% of the value of the transaction. The total cost to the purchaser in such a transaction would therefore be €7885. The HICP is not concerned with any change in the stock market valuation of these shares. That is a capital issue and does not contribute to consumer price inflation. What forms part of the HICP are changes in the purchase costs, i.e. the service charge and the flat rate fee. If the service charge were raised from €10 to €12, and the flat rate from 5 to 6%, the cost of the RUT would rise from €385 to €462—an increase of 20%. This is a price rise that would be included in the HICP.

Article 3 (Treatment of service charges):

1. *The HICP sub-indices concerned shall be calculated using a formula which is consistent with the Laspeyres-type formula used for other sub-indices. They shall reflect the price change on the basis of the changed expenditure of maintaining the consumption pattern of households and*

the composition of the consumer population in the base or reference period.

(a) *The purchaser prices of services to be used in the HICP shall be the actual charges levied directly on consumers in exchange for the service provided. The HICP shall include charges expressed as a flat fee or flat rate.*

(b) *Changes in purchaser prices which reflect changes in the rules determining them shall be shown as price changes in the HICP.*

(c) *Changes in the purchaser prices resulting from changes in the values of the representative unit transactions shall be shown as price changes in the HICP.*

(d) *The representative unit transactions shall be expressed in physical terms, except where this is not appropriate or possible, in which case they shall be expressed in the currency of the Member State.*

(e) *The change in the values of the representative unit transactions may be estimated by the change in a price index which represents appropriately the unit transactions concerned. Where they exist, HICP sub-indices or aggregate indices shall be deemed appropriate for this purpose.*

2. *Where the specification changes, prices shall be treated in accordance with the rules on specification changes, and in particular those regarding quality adjustment as laid down in Regulation (EC) No 1749/96.*
3. *Where services have been made available to consumers free of charge and subsequently an actual price is charged, the change from zero to an actual price, and vice versa, shall be reflected in the HICP.*
4. *Where services jointly provided with other goods or services have been made available to consumers free of an explicit charge and subsequently are charged for on a separate basis, this change shall be reflected in the HICP.*
5. *Where relevant, the procedure provided for in Article 5 of Commission Regulation (EC) No 2646/98 concerning tariffs shall apply mutatis mutandis.*

While not expressly stated in the Regulation, the interpretation of the phrase "*representative unit transactions shall be expressed in physical terms*" would mean something like an apartment or a piece of land. Where this is not possible, simply an amount in euros could be used.

Two Articles (4 and 5) follow, but are not reproduced here. They refer simply to changes in the detailed contents of COICOP headings in Regulation 2214/96, which relate to the types of product dealt with in this Regulation.

Stock market transactions are by no means the only type of transaction subject to the rules of this Regulation. Other examples include:

- Payment services
- Safe deposit services
- Dealing in precious metals
- Property management
- Consultancy
- Foreign exchange brokers
- Book-keeping services.

11.4 Insurance

This is another difficult subject for CPI practitioners, on the grounds of both principle and practice.

With this topic we begin by noting that, in the world of economic statistics, life **assurance** is not regarded as an item of consumption and hence not appropriate for inclusion in a consumer price index. This is because the premiums paid in respect of life assurance are regarded as a form of saving. They are moreover not recommended for coverage by international authorities such as the international CPI Manual[5] and the UN guide.[6] However, there are several other types of insurance, notably travel insurance, motor vehicle insurance, medical insurance and several others, including civil liability insurance. All of these are in principle covered by the HICP.

We need to define exactly what is meant by "insurance". It's clearly very different from a tangible product like food, but different also from intangible products such as medical services. There is no certain benefit gained from purchasing insurance: the situation which is the subject of an insurance policy may never materialise. A car driver may never have

[5] ILO/IMF/OECD/UNECE/Eurostat/The World Bank "Consumer price index manual: Theory and practice" Geneva, International Labour Office, 2004.

[6] United Nations, "Practical Guide to Producing Consumer Price Indices", 2009.

an accident. But nevertheless, insurance is not necessarily a waste of consumers' money. It may be thought of as a payment for "peace of mind"—a phrase used by at least one UK insurance company. The insurance policyholder is paying a premium in the expectation that if a certain event occurs, the insurance company will compensate the policyholder for losses suffered as a result of the event in question.

For example, in the case of a motor accident causing damage to the policyholder's car, the insurance company would normally pay for the repairs to the car. It is worth pointing out that after such an accident, the policyholder would normally be financially neither better off nor worse off than before the accident. They have not gained financially as a result of the accident. But also they have not suffered financial loss (other than the possible payment of an "excess" charge to the insurance company).

It should also be mentioned that a substantial part of motor vehicle insurance is generally prescribed by law, whether the consumer wants it or not. That is also included in the HICP.

The treatment of insurance is covered in Commission Regulation 1617/99. The definitions used in this Regulation are especially important, given the complexity of the subject matter.

Article 2 (Definitions):

For the purpose of this Regulation the terms given below are defined as follows:

1. *'gross insurance premiums': the amount paid by the policyholder for a specific insurance policy to obtain insurance cover;*
2. *'claims': the amount which the insurance company pays to the policyholder and other parties in settlement of injuries or damages suffered by persons or goods;*
3. *'premium supplements': the income earned by insurance enterprises by investing their insurance technical provisions, which comprise prepayments for insurance premiums, provisions for outstanding claims, and provisions against outstanding risks;*
4. *'actuarial premiums': allocations by the insurance company to technical provisions against outstanding risks;*
5. *'services charge': gross insurance premiums plus premium supplements minus claims minus changes in the actuarial provisions.*

What the Regulation doesn't do is to define what is meant mean by terms such as "product" and "specification". There is surely a clear "**product**" in the case of non-life insurance, even if it may be difficult to define. And this lack of definition brings problems in describing insurance policies so that their prices may be compared in ways which are somehow similar to price comparisons in the case of tangible products. In the context of quality adjustment, such descriptions have been called **"specifications"**, and indeed this is the way in which the WP decided how to address this issue. The method used was not in fact new, as those member states which included insurance in their national CPIs (by no means all) were already coping with these problems.

Prices must be monitored in a similar way as other prices in the HICP, namely by monthly surveys. An example of a possible item specification might be:

> The monthly or annual premium for the insurance of a particular brand and model of a car, diesel or petrol, with an engine capacity of 1600cc, for a car which does not exceed 10,000 km a year, owned by a 35-year-old male driver, having had a licence for 10 years with no accident claims in the past 5 years; living in the capital city.

This is similar in principle to the case of private medical insurance, where the pricing of premiums is done on a case-by-case example basis. An example could be:

> the cost of providing medical cover for listed types of operation or treatment up to an annual total of €2500 for a male aged between 40 and 50. The policy covers half of the total cost of treatment; the first €200 is payable by the insured person.

Travel insurance can be particularly difficult to price because "items" are often bundled together in varying ways. Loss of luggage, accidental injury, transport delays, inclusion of travel fares or hotel prices (which may themselves differ in coverage of meals included, sea view, etc). Moreover, individual policies tend to change in their composition over quite short time periods. All of these circumstances can make it very difficult to select "items" for pricing.

Prices will usually be obtained from a selection of different insurers; this is comparable to pricing products in a range of different retail outlets. It may be possible to collect such prices by telephone to the insurance company, or from the internet.

11.4.1 Data Sources—Insurance Companies

Current premium income from policyholders is not the sole source of insurance companies' income. A secondary source is known as "premium supplements". This comprises income received from investments made by insurance companies which act partly as a cushion against future exceptional claims. An adjustment also has to be made for changes in "actuarial provisions". These are the allocations by the insurance company to technical provisions against outstanding risks.

The "service charge"—which can be reasonably accepted as the value of the services supplied by insurance companies to policyholders—is thus taken as the gross premium income plus premium supplements, minus the value of claims and any changes in actuarial provisions. This is an approach frequently used in consumer price indices, and is probably the most appropriate approach for an index such as the HICP, designed as it was for macroeconomic purposes. It is also the method used for classifying insurance premiums in the ESA (European System of Accounts), which underlies the methods used for compiling each country's national accounts.

There is an additional—and serious—practical difficulty with measuring premiums on the "net" basis in that there is no practical way of obtaining the necessary information from insurance companies, at least not on a monthly basis. Some CPIs simply track the price of the gross premiums paid by policyholders, without taking account of the fact that the greater part of these premiums, in total, are returned to households after claims have been paid. But we couldn't look solely at the experience of individual policyholders; the HICP is an inflation index which reflects the overall experience of the household sector. So the real cost to the household sector is the total value of the premiums paid, less the total value of the claims paid out.

The solution adopted—after a good deal of WP discussion concerning such matters as the scale and frequency of very large claims, such as major floods or fires—was a practical one: prices would be measured according to gross premiums, whereas weights would reflect the value of net premiums. This was felt to be justified on the grounds that over the longer term the trends in the prices of gross and net premiums would be likely to be fairly similar. The underlying implicit assumption that service charges change in parallel with premium income, may be defensible in the longer term. However, sudden changes which may affect this supposed relationship may need to be taken into account. An example is a change in the taxation of insurance companies which affects only the service charge. In such a case it is advisable to make an adjustment to the premium which takes account of the change. In principle, it must be admitted that using actual service charges as the basis for the weights, and gross premiums as the basis for prices, makes no logical sense. It is unsatisfactory, but it is widely accepted as a second-best measure.

The rationale for this "net" approach is set out briefly in the preamble to Regulation 1617/99. The defence of the approach is made purely on a practical rather than a theoretical basis:

> *Whereas there is considerable scope for procedural differences in the treatment of insurance in the HICP; whereas a harmonized methodology for insurance is necessary to ensure that the resulting HICPs meet the comparability requirement of Article 4 of the Framework Regulation 2494/95;* ***whereas, in practice, it is not possible to observe the service charge for a particular insurance policy on a monthly basis ...***

Article 3 of the regulation clarifies this: "*The weights for insurance shall be an* ***estimate*** *of the aggregate expenditure by households on* ***service charges*** ..."

It goes on to acknowledge that such estimates are likely to vary widely from one year to the next, by laying down that "the weights shall reflect the average aggregate expenditure during three years". Indeed, it could happen that if only annual figures were to be used, there would sometimes be negative weights as a result of an exceptional event or events, such as major flooding. The weight is thus taken as an estimate of the annual average over a three-year period. This information comes direct from insurance companies, not from household expenditure surveys, as is generally the case with weights estimation.

The full text of Article 3 is as follows:

Article 3 (Treatment of insurance weights)

1. *The weights for insurance shall be an* ***estimate*** *of the aggregate expenditure by households on* ***service charges*** *for insurance covered by the HICP expressed as a proportion of the total expenditure on all goods and services covered.* ***The weights shall reflect the average aggregate expenditure during three years.***

2. *Expenditure financed out of claims shall be treated as being incurred by the policy holder or other parties to the claim and not by the insurance company. The weights of the HICP sub-indices shall include such expenditure where it is incurred by or on behalf of the household sector.*

There is just one further technical Article:

Article 4 (Treatment of insurance prices)

1. *The prices used in the HICP for the compilation of insurance price indices shall be the gross insurance premiums.*
2. *The gross insurance premium shall be taken as the full premium that is payable for the policy and shall not be adjusted, even if the premium or the cover value of the policy is index linked.*
3. *Subject to paragraph 2, for each insurance policy in the target sample the price-determining specifications shall be kept constant. Where those specifications change, prices shall be treated according to the rules applying to quality adjustment laid down in Article 5 of Regulation 1749/96.*

Note that Article 4.2 says explicitly that the gross premium should not be adjusted even if the premiums and cover values of a policy are index-linked. That is not to say that the gross premium is taken to be unchanged: the new index-linked value should be used, but no other adjustments made.

11.5 Data Processing Equipment

Personal computers (PCs) and other data processing equipment were in an early but fast-developing phase in the early 1990 s when the HICP regulations were first developed. The treatment of these products in the HICP posed serious problems since they were not only complex but subject to frequent specification changes. In addition, they were generally expensive—as well as popular.

It was therefore decided that it would be more useful to agree on a set of "guidelines" rather than a full Regulation, since the latter were intended to have a reasonably lengthy life and thus unsuitable for a fast-changing set of products. Guidelines were relatively quick and easy to produce and implement.

Thus, in December 1998 the SPC approved a document entitled *"Guidelines for the Treatment of Data Processing Equipment and notably Personal Computers in HICPs"*.

After a short preamble, the Articles themselves are also short:

Article 1 (Aim)
The aim of these guidelines is to specify how data processing equipment should be included in order to ensure that the HICPs are reliable and relevant to meet the comparability requirements as laid down in Article 4 of Regulation 2494/95 [the Framework Regulation].

Article 2 (Reliability and relevance)
As there are sustained market, price and quality developments in data processing equipment and since the prices for personal computers in particular tend to move differently from the all-items HICP,

(a) *Member States should cover personal computers and associated items in their HICPs. Where direct sellers are a significant source of supply, they should be covered in addition to other outlets. Prices may be obtained from magazines instead of or as well as direct observation in outlets.*
(b) *The annual review of HICP weights foreseen by Regulation 2454/97 should not be confined to the weight at the level of the sub-index for data processing equipment but should be applied to weights at the level of its major components among which there should be a component-index for personal computers.*

Article 3 (Implementation)
These guidelines shall be implemented by Member States in December 1998 and take effect with the index for January 1999.

11.6 Miscellaneous Products

This chapter is concerned with products which have special features requiring them to be dealt with in unique ways. So far, we have covered only major items. But there are other, less important, products which nevertheless pose challenging problems. They include:

- Books
- Package holidays

- Delivery charges
- Products with income-related prices.

Each of these products, widely purchased, brings with it some interesting and not obvious price measurement problems. Let's look at them in turn.

11.6.1 Books

Bearing in mind the criterion that like must always be compared with like, how do we deal with books, which are in a continual state of flux? Of course, there are some which are reprinted annually, or at least very often. Dictionaries are an example. But even then, the contents change to account for newly popular words. Nevertheless they are basically similar.

But what about works of fiction? Again, some popular works last for years, and apart from relatively minor differences such as the number of pages due to changes in page or font size, again they are basically the same. But it becomes much more of a problem with works of fiction which may sell well on first publication but then more or less disappear from the shops. Or can we simply specify a "paperback fiction work of around 250 pages", and treat them as if they were identical products? But some are of much higher "quality" than others. Do we choose to ignore that and just think of them as a collection of numbered pages?

A TF report was discussed by the WP in July 2002. It was based on a considerable amount of statistical enquiry and study, covering the procedure currently used in member states.

At the time I left Eurostat (a month later) no final decision had been made on the TF report. But there was a clear recommendation for the so-called "replacement strategy". This is a sampling method which reproduces consumer behaviour in a plausible and realistic way, because it requires that products that are selected are those currently most sold.

For books (also for music CDs and software games) the method can be applied easily, because ranking lists, hit lists and bestseller lists are widely available; they give current and credible figures of volume and consumer preferences. The replacement method gives the possibility of getting a grip on the heterogeneous book market in a simple and practicable way. Using and applying ranking lists makes it possible to keep the sample representative in an objective way.

11.6.2 Package Holidays

By this term I mean a holiday—usually abroad—whose package usually comprise travel from the home country and back, and a period, of say, two weeks, in a hotel, with (some) meals provided. Summer holidays are often purchased in the winter months, sometimes in full, sometimes with a deposit. With winter holidays, such as skiing, it is the other way round.

Two main questions arise. First, in which month does the price appear in the HICP? The time(s) of the payment(s) or the time of the holiday? And what if the holiday is split over two calendar months?

Second, how to specify the holiday? Bear in mind that we are interested in comparing the prices of two identical holidays occurring in different months. A summer holiday in a certain resort in Spain for a given length of time in a given hotel may cost more the closer the time of booking comes to the time of the holiday. Or the hotel may have sold out and a different one substituted. There are many variable factors at play.

The answer to the first question was answered fairly easily as there was an agreement on payments for services generally; the decision was taken that the price of any service, whether a football match, a rail season ticket—or a package holiday—would be entered into the index in the month in which the service can first occur.

Up until the time I left Eurostat in 2002 there had been no definitive rules or regulations on this matter, though there had been a certain amount of work done in TFs. Nevertheless, the first HICPs were required to have coverage of package holidays, and data were indeed supplied. Judging from the range of weights applied by different countries (ranging from 1.4 to 50.0 per thousand) there were almost certainly wide variations in methods in member states.

11.6.3 Delivery Charges

Although by definition a charge for the home delivery of a good is quite different from the nature of the good itself, it is always closely associated with the good: you can't have a delivery of nothing! So it became fairly obvious that when the price of a delivered good includes the cost of delivery, or if the cost of delivery is added on later, the two charges must be combined into a single price for the good itself. Delivery charges alone do not figure in ECOICOP.

In the earlier days of HICP, internet shopping was far from commonplace as it is today. White goods like refrigerators and cookers were chosen from shop displays, and ordered from the shop—with delivery added or included. So price observation was not particularly difficult. The collector merely had to make sure that the price was including delivery or not including delivery, and ensure that like was always compared with like; this would be specified in the pricing list.

Nowadays of course the picture is very different—especially with the experience of COVID-19, when home deliveries of food and many other items have rocketed.

The basic issue is that home delivery for a good or a variety of goods is often different from the price of the same good(s) in the shop. The product whose price is being monitored must be clearly specified as being with or without delivery—just as with the refrigerator above.

The same rules apply to purchases by mail order and phone, even though they are not classified as "e-commerce".

11.6.4 Products with Income-Related Prices

Products with income-related prices are nearly always services. There are perhaps not so many of these, but they can in total be quite important.

Let's take an example that was often discussed in the Working Party or Task Forces: **fees for private nursery schools**.

A typical situation is that the school will provide clients with a price list which shows that as the client's income changes the fee also changes: the higher the income, the higher the fee.

The question for price statisticians is this. If a certain client's income rises, and they have to pay a higher fee, does that count as "inflation" and raise the HICP level, or does it not? It is not a straightforward matter. The quality of the service has not changed, and the list of income-related fees has not changed. All that has changed is the income of the client. Can that be a cause of inflation?

There were strong views on either side, but eventually it was felt that it is in fact inflationary. It is not as if the clients choose to spend their higher income on, say, better-quality wine. That is nothing to do with inflation. It is that in order to maintain an unchanged experience (or even "utility"—though I don't like the word!) the client has to pay more. That sounds like inflation—and that is what the WP thought too. Of course, if the fees themselves rise, regardless of incomes, that is also inflation.

PART III

Wider Issues of Organisation and Management

CHAPTER 12

Quality Control

A major part of the role of the European Commission is to propose and draft legislative documents, such as the HICP regulations. Following the official adoption of regulations, it is another major task of the Commission to ensure as far as possible that all the member states are implementing the regulations correctly. While temporary impediments may require the use of "derogations" (see Chapter 3.3.1), member states are otherwise required to implement the regulations adopted and published in the Official Journal of the EU. The derogation process was laid down in some detail:

(1) The Member State should explain to Eurostat, in writing, and in good time, why it is seeking a derogation, for which (part of the) Regulation, and for how long. The maximum time of derogation that can be granted is one year.
(2) Eurostat will consult the EMI, in writing, on each proposed derogation.
(3) Eurostat will advise the member state in writing confirming whether or not the derogation has been granted and for how long.

The HICP could be viewed as a new "brand" on the CPI market. It needed an appropriate quality image appealing to its users. Quality assurance was an essential factor in forming such a quality image, and the way

J. Astin, *Measuring EU Inflation*,
https://doi.org/10.1007/978-3-030-68806-6_12

to achieve this would be by means of "compliance monitoring". It was essential that compliance monitoring was carried out in a way that would help to form such a quality image and provide the HICPs with an official and accepted stamp of approval.

We were given some encouragement in this aspect of quality management by the launch in the late 1990s in Eurostat of a system called Qualistat, which was set up to encourage all units in Eurostat to make efforts to achieve various "quality" improvements in their outputs. These targets included the following aspects:

- Relevance
- Accuracy
- Timeliness
- Accessibility
- Interpretability (metadata, etc.)
- Coherence.

These were all intended primarily for Eurostat staff themselves, but also of course to the staff involved in the HICP work in member states. Several of these aspects (such as timeliness) were covered in any case in the regulations.

The big question was: how could the Commission (and for this read Eurostat as far as the HICP and other statistical regulations are concerned) be sure that every member state was actually following the rules laid down in the regulations? And were the rules sufficiently clear as to permit judgements of this nature?

It was made clear in the Maastricht Treaty itself that member states would have the responsibility of ensuring that they would follow the rules laid down by the Commission or Council. Art 109(j) of the Treaty says: "*The Commission and the EMI shall report to the Council on the progress made in the fulfilment by the Member States of their obligations regarding the achievement of economic and monetary union*". Clearly the Commission (Eurostat) would need to be able to satisfy itself that member states were indeed fulfilling their obligations if they were to be able to report positively to the Council as required.

The 2000 Report from the Commission to the Council[1] set out some details of the ways in which member states were implementing the regulations.

It was argued that ultimately HICPs are non-comparable only to the extent that actual practices used in their construction differ in the results they give. If identical practices are followed, the indices will be comparable regardless of differences in the assumptions and arguments that are advanced in support of particular practices in specific contexts. Two or more practices may give results that do not differ systematically. In this case the practices should be allowed regardless of their underlying rationale. Where different practices lead to systematic differences in results, above the 0.1% comparability threshold, then agreement must be reached on which practice should be used. Such agreements should be made by reference to the assumptions and arguments supporting the alternatives, but in the absence of a clear conceptual framework they may have to be based on a simple consensus that a particular practice should be used in the interests of comparability.

In 1999 Eurostat made an internal report on the whole issue of quality control and compliance monitoring. Some of the essential points included the following.

> *The purpose of 'compliance monitoring' is to* ***ensure*** *that HICPs meet the legal requirements and to* ***assure*** *the users of the indices that this is being achieved. The first question is: how should quality be ensured? The second one is: how should quality be assured to the users of the indices?*
> *The main ingredients of the organisation of Eurostat's compliance monitoring may be seen as a cyclical process of continuing improvement:*
>
> - *Identify key quality targets on the basis of existing legal rules, agreements, user requirements and CPI quality standards in the Member State concerned (initial plan);*
> - *Review of requirements and monitoring of compliance (action to test the initial plan);*
> - *Evaluation of compliance and performance (reflection on what more needs to be done);*
> - *Co-operative development of improved methodology and practice (conclusion on what should be done);*

[1] "Report from the Commission to the Council on harmonization of consumer price indices in the European Union" (COM 2000) 742 final Brussels, 21.11.2000.

- *Identify new or improved quality targets on the basis of new developments of the situation concerning legal rules, agreements and user requirements (new plan based on user and producer feed-back).*

Cost effectiveness of the monitoring process is of paramount importance and every effort will be made to minimise the burden on NSIs. A sequential procedure is envisaged, where detailed checks are made only when initial checks indicate that there is a cause for concern.
The HICPs and the harmonised inflation rates are expressed to one decimal place. The threshold for accepting non-comparable practices was set at 0.1 percentage point on the annual rate, unless for a particular aspect of HICP construction a different threshold is warranted. The threshold also ensures a focus on 'effective' corrective action rather than costly action with the aim to cover all eventualities.

Serious thought as to the methods of implementing compliance monitoring began some time after the launch of the HICPs in 1997.

The earliest type of compliance monitoring was done on paper in the form of quite detailed questionnaires sent to member states (and later to candidate countries).

In 1999 Eurostat distributed a "Compliance Monitoring Questionnaire" to all member states. The questionnaire covered all regulations so far adopted and asked member states to give detailed information on their compliance. Below is an example of a small part of this questionnaire. The example omits several tables showing lists of questions for the whole COICOP range. It is 21 pages long! But it demonstrates the wide range of detailed questions for member states.

"D. NEWLY SIGNIFICANT GOODS AND SERVICES

5. Please describe briefly the procedures you have put in place to systematically seek to identify newly significant goods and services.
6. In Table 3 [not shown here] please fill in those newly significant goods and services you have included since the last review to the Council. Please indicate which of the three options you have chosen in each case.

E. QUALITY ADJUSTMENT AND SAMPLING

Please fill in Tables 5 and 6. (Not shown).

9. How do you control the precision of your HICP/CPI? Do you estimate a sampling variance? if yes, please fill in the following table. [Not shown].

Please give:

(a) The period to which latest estimate refers
(b) A brief description of the estimation procedure which was used
(c) The result of your estimation procedure
(d) Comments (if possible, please indicate the software you have used)

10. Please calculate Implicit Quality Indices (IQIs) for the following sub-indices and products thereof. If this is not possible, please compute other approximate measures of the impact of repeated quality adjustment procedures.

H. TREATMENT OF TARIFF PRICES

22. Please list the component elements or consumption units according to Article 5 of the Tariffs' Regulation used for:

    - telephone services (COICOP 08.1.2/3) and
    - railway services (COICOP 07.3.1A).

23. Please describe briefly changes made on the grounds of the Tariffs Regulation.
24. To which extent was the Tariffs Regulation helpful to improve the calculation of sub-indices containing tariff prices?

I. TREATMENT OF INSURANCE

The draft Regulation on insurance lays down that the net/gross-concept should be used for the calculation of the sub-index on insurance in the HICP.

25. Please describe your procedure and sources of information to calculate the single components of the service charge as defined in Article 2 No 5 of the insurance Regulation (gross insurance

> premiums plus premium supplements minus claims minus changes in the actuarial provisions)".

Later, it was agreed with the WP that a more intensive style of compliance monitoring was necessary. Plans were drawn up to begin a series of visits to NSIs by Eurostat HICP staff. Clearly, such visits would be expensive in terms of staff time and costs and would need to be strictly limited. One way of prioritising was to limit the inspections to the larger member states whose contributions to the MUICP were the highest. It was decided that two such assessments would be made each year. The so-called "assessors" would comprise at least one from the Eurostat HICP team. Reports would be made (confidentially) to the Commission.

Questions were still sent to the NSIs ahead of such visits, and they would have to be returned, as drafts, to Eurostat before the start of each visit.

Typically, the visits would last one or two days, and were generally felt to be worthwhile. Care had to be taken by Eurostat to be, on the one hand, not too intrusive, but, on the other hand, searching. After the visit, Eurostat would write a note of the discussion and a description of any changes made or planned as a result of the visit. This would be sent to and agreed by the member state concerned.

CHAPTER 13

Country Aggregation

Although each EU member state is required to compile its own national HICP, following the HICP regulations, it should be recalled that the most important focus of the HICP project was (and is) to have an overall macroeconomic inflation index not only for the whole of the EU, but, in particular, for the member states of the Monetary Union (MU). The latter is indeed the principal motivation, since it is the MUICP (Monetary Union Index of Consumer Prices) that the Maastricht Treaty set as the prime inflation measure for the forthcoming European Central Bank (ECB) in its role in monitoring euro area inflation and as the ECB's main inflation indicator for use in its task of interest rate setting. This is why the ECB (or its predecessor the EMI) was always present at the meetings of the Working Party and of some of its Task Forces.

The national HICPs of the euro area countries are of course the essential building blocks for the MUICP: if the national indices are not produced accurately and to the published timetable, the MUICP would be compromised. The method of aggregating the HICPs of the MU member states is thus another key aspect of the entire process.

Before the HICP project was begun, Eurostat operated a system under which EU member states would supply it with their monthly national CPI which would be published in a single document by Eurostat, published monthly (except August) together with the weighted

J. Astin, *Measuring EU Inflation*,
https://doi.org/10.1007/978-3-030-68806-6_13

average of all the current member states. Annual averages were also calculated and published. Clearly, the use of averages of figures compiled in differing ways gave rise to largely meaningless results, and one of the critical decisions which needed to be made in calculating the EU or MU average HICP was the choice of country weights. A number of possibilities was discussed in the WP. These included national population; national GDP, etc. Up until this time, Eurostat used the country weights which were provided by the National Accounts unit in Eurostat. The data received from the National Accounts was "private final domestic consumption expenditure". This included owner occupiers' expenditure, including imputed rents, which was (is) of course excluded from the HICP.

Eurostat planned to calculate country weights from 1999 using the final expenditure of households on national territory excluding owner occupiers. But the National Accounts unit at Eurostat wasn't able to provide the data needed. However, a nearby source came to the rescue: the unit responsible for Purchasing Power Parities (PPP) was able to provide the data needed.

But this solution was not generally acceptable by others; the solution reached was embodied in a WP document presented by Eurostat in 1996, following a number of internal Commission discussions and also agreed with the EMI. In brief, the decision was as follows:

> *As defined in the two draft regulations on product and geographic coverage, the HICP refers to household final monetary consumption expenditure (HFMCE) which takes place on the economic territory of a Member State. The country weight should reflect a Member State's proportion of this aggregate in the EMU total. Since National Accounts do not give the value of HFMCE on the economic territory, the closest approximation needs to be chosen, which is currently the aggregate 'a51: Private consumption expenditure on the economic territory'. This aggregate covers final consumption of households as well as collective consumption of private organisations and non-profit institutions serving households (NPISH). The proportion of the latter is about the same in all Member States, hence the aggregate a51 is considered to be the best current estimate for HFMCE. Once all Member States report their National Accounts data according to ESA 1995, it will be possible to distinguish between private and collective consumption, and hence to use 'final consumption expenditure of households on the economic territory' as a better estimate of HFMCE.*

This procedure of course also involved the conversion of national currencies with an agreed method:

> *The decision on the participating countries of EMU will be taken at the beginning of May 1998. At the same time, the conversion rates of the national currencies in relation to the euro will be announced. These rates should be used to convert the values of final consumption expenditure of households into euros to calculate the country weights for the MUICP. Once the National Accounts of the participating countries of EMU are expressed in euros this conversion will no longer be necessary.*

The monthly and annual aggregation of the national HICPs are carried out by Eurostat and the results are published in its monthly press release.

Quite apart from the statutory requirement to publish these aggregated indices, they provide a useful tool for those interested in comparing European inflation with other countries, especially larger countries such as China, USA, India and Japan. Indeed, the USA has since 2006 been producing its own version of the HICP, allowing closer comparisons with the EU. This series is available on the Eurostat website.

It may be noted that at the end of January 2020 the UK formally withdrew from membership of the European Union. For several years the UK had published its HICP under the name Consumer Price Index (CPI), and indeed this index is still (2020) used by the Bank of England as the main inflation indicator for its interest rate-setting system and monetary policy in general. Given that the UK no longer has any formal input into Eurostat's Prices Working Group (which deals with all HICP matters) it remains to be seen whether the Bank of England will remain committed to the HICP/CPI for the future. This was of course the first time that an EU member state had left the union, so there were no precedents to follow.

CHAPTER 14

Expansion of the EU; Establishment of EMU and Euro

14.1 Preparations for the Accession of Candidate Countries

In the early days of the HICP, the EU member states were the largest and most important group of countries involved in the project. At the time of the HICP launch in early 1997 there were 15 member states. In addition, the 2 non-EU members of the EEA (European Economic Area) were also legally obliged to participate. They were Iceland and Norway. But also in 1997 the process of harmonizing CPIs in the then "candidate countries" (hereafter CCs) was started. From early 1998 the CCs' statisticians were attending the WP meetings as observers. And "back-to-back" meetings were held for 1-day sessions after the main WP meetings. These meetings were not interpreted and were entirely informal. They were however attended by the vast majority of the CCs. At that time, they were: Cyprus, Czech Republic, Estonia, Hungary, Latvia, Lithuania, Malta, Poland, Slovakia and Slovenia—a total of 10 countries. From 2001, the CC delegates were participating as full members of the WP meetings, though without any voting rights on draft regulations.

The implementation of the HICP in the CCs was in four stages. In 1999 they began producing indices which were effectively similar to the HCPs, i.e. mainly by removing a number of product groups. From January 2000, HICP standards began to be incorporated. This extension was increased as from December 2000.

J. Astin, *Measuring EU Inflation*,
https://doi.org/10.1007/978-3-030-68806-6_14

In early 2001 Eurostat made an analysis of the main differences between the national CPIs in the CCs and the HICP. At that stage, 3 countries were using imputed rents to measure owner occupier housing costs; 2 countries had significant differences in weights; 2 countries included gambling costs; 1 country covered the expenditure of foreign visitors; 1 country used a different method of rounding in the calculations and 1 country had a significant number of differences in product coverage.

By January 2002 most of the CCs were producing HICPs with virtually all the requirements. By 2003 most of them managed to meet the same release schedule as the EU/EEA member states.

Much of the cost of this work was financed by PHARE—an EU organisation focussed on assistance to the CCs (PH stands for Poland and Hungary). This project was devoted to a range of different means for delivering technical know-how:

- Technical assistance missions of EU price experts
- Attendance at HICP WPs and back-to-back meetings
- Organization of workshops and seminars on specific HICP topics
- Secondments of CC staff to Eurostat for 5½ months each.

Between 1999 and 2002, my unit at Eurostat hosted eight such secondments—to the mutual advantage of the CC staff and Eurostat.

WP meetings were held with the objective of the gradual adoption of the HICP by the CCs. Initially CCs were simply provided with the documents from these meetings, but after 1997 they were invited as observers. From 1998, special sessions during the meetings were held for the CCs to exchange their views and problems on this issue. Although they were not represented in TFs and Study Groups, they were invited to Eurostat seminars where technical problems were discussed.

The 10 CCs joined the EU on 1st May 2004. Later, in 2007, Romania and Bulgaria joined the "club". Today (2020) there are more candidate countries: Montenegro, North Macedonia, Serbia and Turkey. All but the first of this group provide monthly HICPs which can be found on the Eurostat website. The UK left the EU in January 2020, but it continues to produce the HICP (known by the name CPI in the UK) though it is not legally required to do so. UK HICPs are (at the time of writing, 2020) still published on the Eurostat website.

14.2 Establishment of European Monetary Union 1.1.99

This massive European financial development took place in two stages. The Maastricht Treaty of 1992 required the establishment of a Monetary Union which would—among many other requirements—use a harmonized CPI to measure inflation—see Chapter 1. A deadline for the establishment of the Monetary Union was set for January 1999. Before this could happen, every participating country would have to meet all four of the "convergence criteria". These were: price stability, government budgetary provision, exchange rate stability and interest rate convergence. This implied that some form of harmonized CPIs needed to be ready by early 1996.

The timing precluded the use of the HICPs, which were insufficiently developed, and this is why the IICPs were used for the assessments up to early 1997. The final stage of Monetary Union (Stage 3) was established on 1 January 1999, and from that date the euro replaced the previous EU currency, the ECU (European Currency Unit). Since 1979 the ECU had been used to price some international financial transactions and capital transfers. It was now replaced, at parity, by the euro.

The period before the decision on Stage 3 of Monetary Union posed a question on the revisability rules for the HICP. Normally, each revision should be agreed by the Member State concerned and Eurostat in accordance with the provisions of the guidelines for such revisions—see Chapter 15.9. During the crucial period for the decision on Stage 3 of Monetary Union, special rules were applied. Eurostat would, during this period, agree only such revisions that were due to a mistake or a correction of **last month's** provisional results. The restriction was applied immediately after the publication of the HICPs for December 1997 and was removed at the publication of the HICPs for January 1999.

Consequently, the release of HICPs for December 1997 was, for each Member State, the only possibility until the release of HICPs for January 1999 to seek agreement with Eurostat for the implementation of revisions due to any other reason than "mistake" and "correction of provisional figure".

14.3 Introduction of Euro Currency 1.1.02

In the early days of Maastricht, there was relatively little talk of the use of the euro as a general currency for the population. The emphasis was on its use as preparation for the Monetary Union. As time went on, however, and the euro was being successfully used as a currency for banking and other government purposes, people began to realise that it would eventually become a currency in everyday use and would replace all the national currencies. Some thought it would not be accepted by large groups of the population, especially older people who would not be happy to have to convert from the currency they had used all their lives.

The day chosen for the introduction of the euro was of course planned well ahead. The preparations for this event were huge, but are not relevant to the theme of this book. The date of introduction was 1 January 2002; from then until 1 March 2002 shopkeepers and other retailers were allowed to accept either the old national currency or the new euros and cents.

But there was an inflation aspect to the changeover. Those countries whose currency had a relatively low value per unit, such as the Belgian franc, feared that retailers would round up their euro prices to accommodate the exchange rate. For instance, an item like a chocolate bar which cost 50FB (Belgian francs) would have translated into a price of about €1.24. It was felt that at least some retailers would charge the more convenient amount of €1.30. Thus inflation could rise. It was being referred to as "changeover inflation".

Studies took place in several countries during the following months to check if this was actually happening. The consensus was that for low-price articles it did indeed happen quite often. But it is the more expensive items that dominate the HICP or any other CPI. Computers or cars would not be affected by such petty roundings.

The flash estimate for January 2002 published by Eurostat has some interesting information:

"Consumers and policy-makers are concerned that the changeover to the euro may have been widely used as an occasion to increase prices. This note gives some information on the impact of the changeover on the HICP.

Capturing price changes in the HICP

The first priority for Eurostat is to ensure that changeover inflation is correctly captured by the HICP. Nearly all National Statistical Institutes have accepted Eurostat recommendations on how to treat the euro changeover in the index. Changeover inflation will be correctly captured within the HICP.

The flash estimate for January 2002

The estimation procedure for the MUICP flash estimate issued today combines historical information with partial information on price developments in the most recent months to give a total index for the euro-zone. Ex-ante simulations have shown the procedure to be reliable (15 times correctly anticipating the full estimate, 8 times differing by 0.1 and once differing by 0.2 over the last two years). Nevertheless a major structural change such as the introduction of the euro is likely to affect the performance of the estimation procedure. Thus the January 2002 flash estimate carries a greater uncertainty than past performance would indicate.

The flash estimate for January 2002 is within the range (± 0.1) which would have been expected making a simple extrapolation of the seasonal pattern, developments in recent months up to December 2001 and January's fuel price changes.

The fact that the flash estimate for January 2002 is higher than the actual figure for December 2001 cannot necessarily be taken as evidence of a significant euro changeover effect when all the other possible influences, described below, are taken into account.

There is thus as yet no detectable evidence pointing to a euro changeover effect."

A briefing note issued by Eurostat made some interesting remarks:

"1. **Separating out conversion inflation**

There could potentially have been price increases due to several factors relating to the changeover to the Euro. In particular:

(a) *changes to price levels to achieve targeted price levels after conversion to the euro as suppliers re-positioned their products in the market,*
(b) *changes to price levels to target so-called psychological or convenient prices in euros (e.g. prices ending in 49, 99 or 00 cents),*
(c) *price increases aimed at windfall profits in the knowledge that consumers are not yet fully familiar with prices expressed in euro,*
(d) *price increases resulting from applying incorrect conversion rates.*

Ideally Eurostat would be able to quantify changeover inflation where it exists, and break it down by source. In practice the most that can be done is to assess the situation on the basis of informed assumptions. Such assessments carry the risk of attributing price changes to the euro-changeover when they may be due to other factors, such as those outlined below.

Potential effects coming from sources (a), and (c) are impossible to separate out. This would require the distinction of their likely effects from price changes which would have taken place anyway. There is no operational tool to establish such a distinction. Potential effects coming from (b) and (d) could be assessed by means of simulation models involving various working assumptions and on the basis of additional price observation.

Many National Statistical Offices have made or are making studies of changeover effects. For the time being most of the studies which have been released rely on data collected before the changeover.

2. ***Other factors influencing the HICP in January 2002***

Comparing January 2002 price levels with those of December 2001 or January 2001 is complex, due to a number of factors in addition to the changeover to the euro.

Tariffs and taxes

Many tariffs change on 1 January. Examples can be found in the health sector, in postal services, passenger transport by road (buses, taxis, etc.), water supply, sewerage and refuse collection and other services related to housing, and some catering services. The volatility of alcohol and tobacco price indices between December and January seems to be linked to changes in the taxes on those products.

Sales

The winter sales also play an important role when comparing December and January prices. In January 2002 the sales period in some Member States has been postponed because of the euro changeover. This may lead to an over assessment of the effects of the changeover, for example for clothing, if not taken into account.

In addition, implementation of the Regulation on the treatment of sales prices in the HICP will be completed when Spain and Italy introduce actual sales prices within their HICPs for the first time. As a result of the way in which this is being implemented, this will not affect index levels or rates of change during 2002 or beyond.

Weather
The unusually bad weather in much of Europe in recent months could also be expected to affect prices, especially those of fresh fruit and vegetables. The December indices for vegetables already showed signs of price increase in some Member States. It will be possible to know whether this has persisted when the detailed data for January is available.
Financial services
The HICP extended its coverage of financial services from January 2002.
Some country-specific issues
The annual rate of change for the Netherlands to January 2002 will be affected by the increase in VAT and 'green' taxes on energy in January 2001, though this will not be visible in the month-to-month change between December 2001 and January 2002. In Germany some 'green' taxes and taxes on insurance and tobacco increased in January 2002. Taxes on tobacco in France also increased in January 2002. Licence fees for televisions and radio have been abolished in the Flemish part of Belgium but this may not have a full impact in January 2002. In many countries, indices for package holidays and air transport usually fall in January after increasing in December.
In total
Taken together the product groups mentioned above account for some 20–25 percent by weight of euro-zone HICP.
Volatile price indices
Beyond changes between December and January, it should also be recalled that some prices have a tendency to be volatile whatever the time of year. Examples are prices for energy, coffee, oils and fats, fruit and vegetables.
New weights
In January 2002, as happens each January, the HICP will take the latest expenditure data provided by National Statistical Institutes into its internal weights.

3. *The HICP during 2001*

The development of the HICP during 2001 was influenced strongly by changes in energy and food prices and, to a lesser degree, also by changes in prices for services and non-energy industrial goods.

In the first months of 2001, when inflation rates climbed significantly and reached a peak at 3.4% in May, the energy sector together with unprocessed food, in particular meat, were the components with the biggest upward effect on inflation.

After that peak, rates steadily decreased up to the end of the year. This was mainly due to the rapid decline of fuel prices, while unprocessed food continued to have an upward impact.

Services had lower than average inflation rates during the first half of the year, while they were higher than average towards the end of the year."

CHAPTER 15

Administrative and Other Issues

I now come to the final chapter of this book. There are always some loose ends to be included in any book of this nature, and this is the place to do it. Most of the subjects covered are more of an administrative nature than statistical, but, as I said at the start, this is not a statistics textbook but a historical perspective of the early days of the HICP.

15.1 The European Commission and Eurostat

It may be helpful for readers to have some background information about the organisations responsible for organising and making decisions about the HICP project. What follows is far from being a comprehensive description of the European Commission and of Eurostat, but it should be sufficient to understand the administrative system which lay behind the development of the HICP.

The European Commission (hereafter "Commission") is the principal body of what is now known as the European Union. Its main functions are:

Proposing new laws

The Commission is the sole EU institution tabling laws for adoption by the Parliament and the Council:

Managing EU policies & allocating EU funding;

Enforcing EU law

J. Astin, *Measuring EU Inflation*,
https://doi.org/10.1007/978-3-030-68806-6_15

Together with the Court of Justice, ensuring that EU law is properly applied in all the member countries.

Representing the EU internationally

Speaking on behalf of all EU countries in international bodies, in particular in areas of trade policy and humanitarian aid;

Negotiating international agreements for the EU.

The Commission resembles to some extent the Civil Service (i.e. permanent non-political officials) in individual countries. The staff are appointed by means of regular competitions and appointed normally for unlimited periods. The individual members of staff are treated in a similar way to many national civil servants: with annual reports on their outputs and behaviour; chances for promotion to jobs with greater expertise and/or responsibilities, and so on. The staff are divided into several broad groups, ranging from those at the very summit—Directors-General—to those with junior support duties.

The Commission is divided into a range of departments ("Directorates-General" or DGs) each with specialised functions. Examples are: ECFIN (Economic and Financial Affairs); AGRI (agriculture). Most are dealing with functional areas of the EU, while others have administrative functions such as informatics, translation services and so on.

One of these generalist DGs is Eurostat, whose formal name used to be the Statistical Office of the European Communities (SOEC). Most of the staff of Eurostat are professional statisticians, assisted by clerical and secretarial staff and other layers of management and expertise, such as informatics. Eurostat has to work within similar procedures as the other DGs. It is organised into broad subject divisions, such as Agriculture, Transport, etc. During the 1990s, the early years of HICP development, there were six Directorates in Eurostat, of which the HICP work was carried out in Directorate B—Economic Statistics.

All too often, it seems, members of the public appear to believe that all of the legislation emanating from "Brussels" is the work of the Commission and its staff. As I can testify, this is nowhere near the truth. One of the first tasks facing us in Unit B3 was to start up a new international group of price statisticians (the Working Party) to lay the groundwork and eventually agree on the detailed rules for the new HICP. All of this work is described and discussed in the earlier chapters of this book. No decisions of any importance were made unilaterally by anybody in Eurostat or the Commission. The Working Party of national statisticians—often presented with drafts emanating from the more informal Task Forces—discussed succeeding drafts of the various HICP regulations, and informal votes were finally obtained. Only when a "qualified majority" (i.e. a majority based on the weighted votes of all member states) was obtained, would the drafts be submitted to higher levels of authority. Any disputed regulations would be sent to the Council of Ministers where a qualified majority would be obtained, or the draft was returned to Eurostat. So the whole process was a democratic one. Not all countries were satisfied with all regulations, of course—but that's what you get with democracy.

15.2 The Process of Drafting the Implementing Regulations

This section contains information about the procedures used for the adoption of the implementing regulations.

There are two types of EC Regulation, both of which are a fundamental part of Community law, and are directly applicable in all Member States. Indeed, they take precedence over any related national laws wherever there is a potential or actual conflict. The two types of law are Commission regulations and Council regulations. The HICP regulations were usually Commission regulations, for which the procedure was both less complex and faster than with a Council regulation. The process is known as "comitology". The procedure is outlined in Article 14 of the Framework Regulation, which is given at the end of this section.

As far as the specifics of the HICP are concerned, the process of developing regulations can be summarised as follows:

1. Initial draft text drafted by Eurostat, usually after some preliminary discussions in a Task Force.
2. Further drafts discussed in Task Force meetings, resulting in a version ready for presentation to the Working Party (WP).
3. Further drafts are prepared following WP discussions, culminating in a draft which is put to an informal WP vote. Informal in the sense that it carries no legal weight. Normally, the voting is on a simple "per capita" basis. But it was decided that in the case of this exceptionally important subject—the whole HICP project—that the votes be counted with the standard weights appropriate to the size of each country—"qualified majority" voting. A "qualified majority" is a way of ensuring that the votes of the larger member states count

for more than those of the smaller ones. For example, Germany had 10 votes while Luxembourg had only 2. On this basis it was laid down that a "qualified majority" was 62 votes out of a maximum of 87 (approximately 70%).

4. Drafts which have been approved by the WP are then submitted, together with an explanatory memorandum, to the Statistical Programme Committee (SPC) of Directors-General of statistics in the member states.
5. Before the SPC meets, each NSI Director-General is asked to inform Eurostat whether or not they are likely to vote for the draft regulation at the forthcoming SPC meeting. If, unusually, the result of this enquiry indicates that there is unlikely to be a qualified majority, the draft is returned to the WP for further discussion.
6. At the SPC meeting, it can happen that unexpectedly there is a failure to reach a qualified majority. In one case, a D-G, who had earlier signified that they would vote for the regulation, did not do so at the actual meeting; this resulted in a failure to reach a qualified majority. In this case the rule was that the draft regulation was not returned to Eurostat, but had to be submitted directly to the Council. If it is approved by the Council (which was always the case with such HICP regulations) it will then become a regulation of the Council rather than of the Commission.
7. If the Council itself fails to reach a qualified majority within three months, then the draft regulation is returned to the Commission which may then adopt the proposal itself.
8. Finally, before formal adoption, a Council Regulation proposal is also submitted to (a) the EMI (later the ECB), (b) to the European Parliament and (c) to the Economic and Social Committee for their official approval. These approvals are recorded in the Preamble to the published Regulations. Commission regulations do not require such approvals, as they are based on the existing Council Regulation 2494/95 which does include them. They are known as "Implementing Regulations".

Chapter 3.3.1 presented the administrative articles of the Framework Regulation. Article 14 is an administrative article of great procedural importance. The current section is concerned with the specific procedures surrounding the adoption of the HICP regulations; such procedures are generally referred to as "comitology", a phrase we have met a few times in earlier chapters. The specific procedural steps regarding the adoption of the HICP regulations were described above. Below is the underlying legal text of the Framework Regulation (2494/95).

Article 14
Procedure

1. The Commission shall be assisted by the Statistical Programme Committee, (hereinafter referred to as 'the Committee').

2. The representative of the Commission shall submit to the Committee a draft of the measures to be taken. The Committee shall deliver its opinion on the draft within a time limit which the Chairman may lay down according to the urgency of the matter. The opinion shall be delivered by the majority laid down in Article 148 (2) of the Treaty in the case of decisions which the Council is required to adopt on a proposal from the Commission. The votes of the representatives of the Member States within the Committee shall be weighted in the manner set out in that Article. The Chairman shall not vote.

The Commission shall adopt the measures envisaged if they are in accordance with the opinion of the Committee.

If the measures envisaged are not in accordance with the opinion of the Committee or if no opinion is delivered, the Commission shall without delay, submit to the Council a proposal relating to the measures to be taken. The Council shall act by a qualified majority.

If, on the expiry of a period of three months from the date of referral to the Council, the Council has not acted, the proposed measures shall be adopted by the Commission.

Article 14 is thus an administrative article of great procedural importance. It should be remembered that EC regulations can take precedence over national laws in member states, and therefore great care must be taken in the process of consultation, agreement, voting and adoption. It is not a simple procedure and it can take a long time.

15.3 Legal Terminology

Below is a sentence taken from a draft regulation:

An elementary aggregate shall refer to the expenditure (or consumption) covered by the most detailed level of stratification classified according to such criteria as commodity group, geographic location and outlet type.

We statisticians soon learned that the legal experts which we had to consult in Eurostat did not like to see examples in the text. They are fine in the explanatory notes, but they are not usually allowed in an actual regulation. So the second part of the above definition had to go! Lawyers also love the word "shall": this is their word for "must". It sounds rather old-fashioned (Ten Commandments?) and perhaps slightly kinder than "must". The statistician who drafted the above text knew about this, of course, and decided to anticipate the "shall". However, on this occasion, for some unknown reason, the lawyers did not like it, so the final definition starts with "*An elementary aggregate refers to …*". It finishes with "*… stratification of the HICP*". So essentially, the proposed wording of the draft eventually found its way into EC law. This happened quite regularly, though usually there were some minor legal alterations (though very rarely altercations!).

Let's now look at the general issues involved in translating technical statistical material into the language of legal texts without losing their meaning or making them impossible to apply in practice. This topic was addressed in a paper which I presented at an IAOS (International Association for Official Statistics) conference in 2014.[1]

When it came to the nitty-gritty business of drafting the regulations, we had to start thinking like lawyers as well as statisticians. The regulations had to follow certain procedural formats. This was sometimes a chore, but in fact there were some advantages.

Many countries have Statistics Acts. These are usually concerned with aspects of the governance of official statistics, the organisation of national statistical work, the standards expected of official statistics and of statisticians themselves. They are rarely concerned with operational aspects of statistics: methods of collecting data, organising data, statistical methodology and presentation. These matters are nowadays normal in the EU approach.

This section is devoted to the latter aspect, focussing on the challenges and the pitfalls presented by the transformation of statistical concepts, procedures and practices into legal language.

The HICP project was the earliest legally based statistical harmonization projects launched by Eurostat, and consequently there were few, if any, precedents to fall back on.

[1] Astin, J. "The Transformation of Statistical Principles and Procedures into the Language of Legal Acts", IAOS Conference, Da Nang, Vietnam, 2014.

The importance of legal scrutiny was mentioned above. One of the early lessons learned was that the regulation articles would have to comply with standard headings and placed in a specific order. Generally this was not a problem, but sometimes it took a little imagination to squeeze a particular topic into a standard heading. For example, two standard headings were "Basic Information" and "Data Sources". To the statisticians, this sounded rather like two identical things.

Thus, in the Framework Regulation, the "Basic Information" article began: "*The basic information shall be those prices and weightings of goods and services which it is necessary to take into account in order to achieve comparability of indices*". The next article "Sources", said: "*The statistical units called upon by the Member States to cooperate in the collection or provision of price data shall be obliged to allow observation of the prices actually charged and to give honest and complete information at the time it is requested*". In fact, this article provides the legal backing required to compel, if necessary, shop managers to allow price collectors to operate on their premises. As far as I am aware, it has never been used in the courts.

In fact, the Article headings' requirements gradually began to perform a useful task, in that it forced the drafters of the texts (we statisticians) into more logical ways of thinking than might otherwise have been the case. It gradually became clear that although one may classify statistics as a science, statisticians—especially in the field of economics—do not always think or behave like scientists.

Most legal acts, and the HICP regulations were no exception, start with a so-called "preamble". In the EC regulations, these were of two types. Firstly, short clauses beginning with "Having regard to ..."; followed by a series of rather more complex "Whereas ..." clauses. The "Having regard to" clauses were left to the lawyers to deal with: they referred to the legal foundation of the regulation, including the Treaty establishing the European Community, and with references to the opinions given by the European Parliament and other bodies.

The "Whereas" clauses, on the other hand, were a useful and rigorous check on the entire contents of a regulation. They explain, down to the required level of detail, why the regulation is needed and how its content can be justified. This needs some illustration.

The "Whereas" clauses normally had to be drafted after the main articles themselves had been drafted. This meant that not only did the answer to the question "Why have this regulation?" have to be provided, but each article must be justified.

The drafting of the "Whereas" clauses sometimes exposed the need for an additional Article, or even the lack of need for an Article already drafted. The aim was always to be able to match the Whereas clauses with the Articles—a most useful discipline. The Eurostat legal scrutineers' beady eyes usually managed to spot any mismatches!

The standard articles on Definitions provided another useful discipline to the statisticians drafting the regulations. It was first necessary to decide which words or phrases actually needed to be defined. This wasn't always easy. There were two criteria. Firstly, the word had to be one which was considered too technical for a non-expert to understand. Secondly, a word with a commonly understood meaning may need to be defined if it had a special meaning in the context of the regulation.

One of the great difficulties in drafting a comprehensive set of legal acts on a complex technical subject like the HICP is that at the beginning of the journey one has little idea of what lies ahead. For sure, it would have been (and indeed was) possible to write down a list of most of the topic headings which would need to be covered by the regulations: sampling, price collection, treatment of seasonal products, quality adjustment, index formulae and so on. Less easy was putting these many topics in priority order, given that a series of regulations was planned. Even though the Framework Regulation was produced in record time, and the first implementing regulation soon after, it turned out that much of the latter regulation needed to be amended in later regulations in the light of experience gained mainly through discussions in the WP and its subsidiary TFs. Time was always in short supply, given the constant pressure of producing fresh regulations. Until the time when I left Eurostat, a total of fourteen regulations (of which four were Council and ten were Commission) and three sets of guidelines had been produced in nine years. This left little time for cross-checking for consistency. For example, in the definition of "comparability" (Chapter 3.3) there is no difference between "one part in a thousand" and "one tenth of one percentage point"—but to the non-expert reader it may appear that the different wordings have been used for some arcane reason. Other examples of minor differences in wording can be found scattered throughout the regulations. Sometimes such inconsistencies might be picked up by the legal scrutineers, but this could not always be relied upon.

15.4 HICP Advisory Committee; CEIES

It was mentioned in Chapter 2 that at the very first WP meeting in 1993, there were discussions on the desirability or otherwise of establishing some form of permanent Advisory Committee to oversee the direction of travel of the HICP. Indeed, the SPC were informed by the Eurostat Director-General at an early stage that this was indeed planned. In fact many, if not most, member states had their own advisory boards overseeing the production of their national CPI. Such bodies would typically comprise people representing users, such as trade unions, employers' associations, pensioner groups, etc., as well as independent economists and statisticians. The main purpose of an HICP Advisory Committee would be to help to guarantee the impartiality and general standards of methodology of the index.

Opinions in the WP over the coming years seemed divided. For example, at a WP meeting in 1998 it was noted that not all delegates were convinced that an Advisory Committee was needed. There were clearly unspoken concerns that such a body may challenge or frustrate the actions of the WP and may turn out to be an administrative impediment. The functions and terms of reference for such a Committee had to be further elaborated and the institutional framework better defined. It would also have to be made clear whether such a group would be comprised of users or experts—or both. Its independence was also critical.

Meanwhile, the influential European Advisory Committee on Statistical Information in the Economic and Social Spheres (CEIES) had been established in February 1991. In 1992 the CEIES formed a subcommittee to examine the question of CPI harmonization. The subcommittee presented a report to the CEIES at its meeting in March 1993. This read as follows:

> *The harmonization of the CPIs in the Member States is an important task. The theoretical and empirical deficiencies of various types of the CPI of many of the Member States have been known for a long time, hence the need for harmonization. The importance of the deficiencies of current concepts and practice and the urgency to overcome them has been augmented by the role of the CPI as a central measure of convergence in the Maastricht Treaty, though this is by no means the only reason to attack this problem soon. Despite policy requirements at the national and Community level, the well-grounded interest of the private sector in having a valid and reliable measure of inflation must be mentioned here.*

> *A central and indispensable element of any harmonized CPI should be that it is free from political influence. This holds not only for the methodology of calculating the index, but also for its coverage. In addition, the production of the index should be guided by the principle of cost effectiveness (in particular to small and medium sized firms).*
> *As to the details of a 'Community CPI' it is not yet possible to fix any criteria. In principle the Community CPI should include all forms of consumer expenditure. Exceptions to the general rule should be permitted only (a) on the condition that special circumstances can be shown to exist and (b) their consequences for the CPI and its development under a wide range of different circumstances have been shown* not *to have a deleterious effect.*
> *… A harmonized CPI may obtain more support from Member States if it were to be developed and published alongside the national CPI. It may be better to give the harmonized index a special name to distinguish it from the national CPI.*
> *The [subcommittee] urges that the work on the harmonization of the CPI be started without delay.*

The CEIES was from the start regularly invited to attend the WP meetings.

Eurostat was in turn invited to the first meeting of the CEIES HICP subcommittee in December 1992. Following that meeting, the subcommittee reached the following conclusions:

> *The harmonisation of CPI in EC countries is an important task. The theoretical and empirical deficiencies of various types in the CPIs of many of the member states have been known for a long time; hence the need for harmonization. The importance of the deficiencies of current concepts and practices and the urgency of their overcoming has been augmented by the role of the CPI as a central measure of convergence in the Maastricht Treaty, though this is by no means the only reason to attack this problem soon. Despite policy requirements at the national and Community levels, the well-grounded interest of the private sector in having a valid and reliable measure of inflation must be mentioned here.*

The subcommittee's subsequent 1993 report also included the following:

> *In principle the Community CPI should include all forms of consumer expenditure. Exceptions to the general rule should be permitted only (a) on the condition that special circumstances can be shown to exist and (b) their consequences for the CPI and its development under a wide range of different circumstances have been shown* not *to have a deleterious effect.*

The CEIES continued to attend the WP for some time and contributed many useful ideas in the discussions. To the CEIES it seemed obvious that an international version should be established for the HICP.

A seminar was organised by the CEIES in Berlin in October 2001 on "Inflation in Europe – Different Measures and their Users". About 80 participants from various European (including Eastern European) countries attended, including representatives from Eurostat.

The existence of the CEIES HICP subcommittee and its close interest in the activities of Eurostat doubtless modified the interest in Eurostat establishing its own Advisory Committee, and in fact no further steps were taken in this direction.

15.5 Funding and Contracting

It was clear from the start of the HICP project that there would be costs involved, and probably very high costs. Nothing comes free! Of course, the costs of the staff involved in the project in Eurostat and other Directorates of the Commission would be "free" in the sense that the work became part of the normal work of the staff involved. But for the member states there would inevitably be extra costs, for example in making changes to their monthly price surveys, changes to the Household Budget Surveys, changes to their computer systems and so on.

There was nothing new in the concept of Eurostat making payments to member states for work necessary for the accomplishment of specific tasks. For instance, in my Price Comparisons Division, which was handling the HICP project, there were two other ongoing projects which required provision of data from each member state. One was the Purchasing Power Parities (PPP) work, later to be named the European Comparison Programme (ECP), which fed into the wider International Comparison Programme (ICP) which compiled PPPs for countries around the globe. The same Eurostat unit was also responsible for the analysis of data on civil service salaries in member states, as this formed the basis of the annual salary adjustment for EC staff.

So the fact of having financial contracts with member states was nothing new. For the HICP work, it would be the task of individual member states to estimate the probable costs of carrying out new work, especially at the setting-up stage of the project.

Eurostat's job was to evaluate the sizes of the various estimates and negotiate as necessary with individual member states, after having its own estimates of the level of funds likely to be available for this work.

Despite the complexity of the project, the negotiations turned out to be largely straightforward, though of course the size of the payments made to each member state varied considerably. This was due partly to the size of the country and partly to the degree to which a country would need to adjust its various systems. Article 13 of the Framework Regulation was clear that funding would be limited to a maximum of two-thirds of the additional costs, at least during the first two years.

The actual amounts varied from year to year. In the first two years, 1994 and 1995, the payments were of the order of 350,000 ecu in total (the ecu ("European Currency Unit") being the precursor of the euro). Most countries would benefit from part of this pot. After the first regulations had shown much of the detailed work that would be required, the financial assistance increased. The bulk of the funding was made during the period 1996–1999, which took the total funding to over 6m ecu.

A pause in funding followed, since most of the changes which required financial assistance had by this time been accomplished. There were however a number of difficult technical issues which needed some researching into both theory and methods. It was decided to launch a public call for tender in 2000 which was split into a number of different Lots. These concerned the following subjects:

- Quality Adjustment methods
- Quality Adjustment database
- Sampling
- Regional aggregation
- Missing price observations
- Compliance Monitoring plans
- Development of a House Price Index.

The winners of these tenders included some NSIs and some private sector consultancies. The total amounted to some 300,000 ecu. The work began in 2001 and was completed within a year.

In addition to these financial contracts, Eurostat accelerated its process for the funding of staff to be seconded to the Prices unit for short-term assignments mainly in the HICP field. Many of these secondments were from the candidate countries, starting in 1999. All of these seconded staff had been working in the price statistics field in the NSIs of their home country. The candidate countries' secondments were funded by the PHARE process—see Chapter 14.1.

15.6 Seminars, Workshops and Study Groups

Earlier chapters have described in some detail the work of the HICP Working Party and its many Task Forces. These were indeed the workshops which produced the HICPs. But sometimes we felt it necessary to stand back from the battleground and spend some time in calm discussions of some of the more difficult concepts underlying the HICP. So we decided to hold occasional WP seminars where we would decamp to a pleasant town in the EU, book a conference room in a decent hotel and have a one or two days discussion, plus, if possible, the chance of a local guided tour. It was also a good way of finding time for offhand chats among the attendees. In fact, for me, one of the most remarkable results from our HICP project was the way in which statisticians from all the member states (and later the candidate countries) were able to talk to each other in person and discuss matters of mutual interest, professional and other—when in the past there had been little or no contact between them. It was a great and lasting benefit to everybody.

Reports were written after the seminars summarising the main issues discussed, and they often led to improvements in methods in the HICPs.

Due mainly to time and cost constraints, the WP seminars were infrequent. The first—lasting for nearly three days—was held in the Austrian spa town of Baden in May 2001. We felt that if Beethoven could complete his 9th symphony here, the least that we 58 statisticians could do would be to make some serious progress in quality adjustment! As chairman, I explained that the main aim was to get away from the usual crowded 15-item agenda of the typical Working Party meeting, and instead to discuss in depth a few selected topics, without the pressure of making decisions on an impending regulation. The usual type of minutes would not be written, but instead short summaries of conclusions and agreements. No interpretation was provided. Given the size of the group, the first couple of hours were taken up with short private discussions between each delegate and Eurostat in turn. During that period, the seminar would begin its general discussion.

In the case of that first seminar in Baden, the topics selected for discussion were quality adjustment and sampling.

The last of these seminars before I left Eurostat was held in the small seaside town of Egmond aan Zee in the Netherlands in July 2002.

The subject of this two-day seminar was Chapters 2–5 of the US National Academy of Sciences (NAS) recently published book "At What Price?".[2] These chapters covered conceptual bases of price indices; the domain of CPIs; quality change and new products and new outlets. All very important issues for the HICP. The seminar aimed to draw ideas from the book which should influence the future direction of the HICPs, and to have an impact on the HICP concepts document which was currently being developed. Each chapter was presented by a member of the panel, followed by a panel discussion, a general discussion and a summary by the presenter. Most of the regular WP delegates attended the seminar, and a panel of nine was nominated to help focus the discussions.

Workshops were another type of meeting format. They were focussed mainly on the candidate countries. Some of these workshops were held in the capitals of those countries, and be chaired by a member of the Eurostat prices team.

After the adoption of the first Implementing Regulation (1749/96) there was general agreement that intensive studies needed to be made, not into specific types of methodology, such as quality adjustment, but into the particular problems faced by specific product groups. After much discussion it was decided to form a number of special Study Groups, each of which would be dedicated to studying the particular problems of certain product groups. The groups selected were:

- Cars
- Clothing
- Data processing equipment
- Data capture (esp. scanner data)
- Sampling
- Durables
- Rents.

[2] "At What Price? Conceptualizing and Measuring Cost-of-Living and Price Indexes", National Research Council, USA, 2002.

Each group would be a small one of around five statisticians from the member states, and would be led by a selected member state.

The main aim was not so much to define the ideal method but to establish which currently used methods lead to non-comparability, and hence to narrow down non-comparability by pinpointing extreme methods—and of course eliminating them as far as possible.

They were given rather tight timetables to make their studies and disseminate their reports. Most of the groups held their first meetings in early 1997, and made preliminary reports to the WP and TF2 soon afterwards. Full reports were discussed at a WP meeting in July 2001.

An example of a preliminary report is given below.

Study Group 4: Scanner data

Aim: Explore the use of scanner data for improving the comparability and reliability of HICPs.

Work divided into 7 parts, allocated to Member State groups:

(a) Sampling Purposive versus probability; non-comparability; SA errors; first result: do not use random SA if distribution is very skewed.

(b) Missing prices Define appropriate limits for missing prices; non-comparability as a result of different imputation methods.

(c) Price collection Effect of the number of days of price collection per months; unit values as continuing price measurement.

(d) El aggs Number of elementary aggregates.

(e) Weights Effect of the updating of weights at different aggregation levels.

(f) Quality adjust Hedonic regressions for TVs was carried out by UK; similar studies for other durables.

(g) New approach Superior indices.

One member will provide a bibliography of research on scanner data.

15.7 Reports to the Council of Ministers

Mention has been made in earlier chapters of the requirement for the Commission (of which Eurostat is a part) to make progress reports on the HICP development to the Council of Ministers (known normally by the shorthand "Council"). This section describes these reports and the topics they contained.

First, though, some description of the roles and methods of the Council and its relationship with the Commission (see also the short note on the Commission itself at the start of this chapter).

The European Commission is part political body and part administration. Unlike some other EU bodies, it is permanent and is therefore the institution that is most often identified with the EU. The Commission has three responsibilities that are central to the EU's operation: it proposes legislation designed to implement the objectives outlined in EU treaties; it manages EU policy and the EU budget and it acts as the guardian of the treaties, monitoring compliance with EU law.

The Council of the European Union, known usually as the "Council of Ministers", or merely "Council", is the main law-making body of the EU. While the Commission represents the general interests of the European Union, the Council represents the governments of the member states. National delegations meet at three levels of the Council: working groups, which is where Commission proposals land first and where technical experts from the member states discuss the merits of each policy initiative; the Committee of Permanent Representatives (COREPER), composed of the ambassadors of each of the member states to the European Union, which tackles political issues that the working groups are unable to resolve; and ministers from member states, who have ultimate decision-making authority. In practice, most issues are agreed before they reach ministerial level.

Many of the laws made in the EU are the responsibility of the Council.

The Framework Regulation (2494/95) was a regulation of the Council. This is because it established the HICP project in the certain knowledge that later "implementing" regulations would need to be made. Implementing regulations, made under the umbrella of the Framework Regulation, can be proposed by the Commission and enacted without further involvement with the Council. This procedure depends on the agreement of the Regulatory Committee specifically authorised to do so. This Committee, known in the 1990s as the Statistical Programme Committee (SPC) and now known as the European Statistical Service Committee (ESSC), is comprised of the heads of national statistics in each member state. This procedure is known as "comitology". This topic is described in detail in Section 2 of this chapter.

The Commission had a legal responsibility to make reports to the Council on the state of progress of the articles laid down in the Framework Regulation. The legal basis for these reports was contained in Article 15 of the Framework Regulation:

> ***Article 15***
> ***Review***
> *After consulting the Committee, the Commission (Eurostat) shall, within two years of the date of entry into force of this Regulation and again within two years thereafter, submit a report to the Council on the HICPs established pursuant to this Regulation and in particular on their reliability and compliance with the comparability requirements.*
> *In those reports, the Commission shall state its views on the operation of the procedure described in Article 14 and shall propose any amendments it considers appropriate.*

The Commission also had a legal responsibility (alongside the EMI/ECB) to make regular reports to the Council on progress on the Maastricht "convergence criteria". The first of these two reports were formally drafted by DG2, the Economic and Financial Directorate of the Commission, though in reality most of the text was drafted by Eurostat, who were legally the body delegated to carry out the functions set out in the regulation. The second was drafted also by DG2 but with significant contributions from Eurostat.

The first HICP report from the Commission to the Council was made on 27 February 1998 (actually slightly later than the 2-year deadline in the Regulation). It is available as a public document.[3]

The Executive Summary began as follows:

> *As required by Council Regulation (EC) No 2494/95 and with the co-operation of Member States 'Harmonized Indices of Consumer Prices' (HICPs) for each Member State are now produced and published monthly together with an aggregated index, the 'European Index of Consumer Prices' (EICP). These indices have been accepted by both the Commission and the European Monetary Institute as providing satisfactory measures for the assessment of convergence. Although certain differences in their constructions remain to be fully harmonized considerable progress has been made in removing differences in the concepts, methods and practices followed by*

[3] COM (1998) 104 final.

Member States in constructing their national Consumer Price Indices (CPIs). Those indices continue to be published in most cases and used in national contexts. Their construction will reflect improved practices developed in the harmonization process but their use for international comparisons is peripheral. The Commission and the European Monetary Institute are looking for further improvements in the quality and comparability of the HICPs for their use in monetary policy and the monitoring of inflation in the Economic and Monetary Union.

The second of these reports was made on 21 November 2000.[4]

Both of the reports served a useful purpose in summarising the state of progress towards full harmonization. The executive summary included the following paragraphs:

The initial HICPs, although fairly comprehensive in coverage, were for the most part the common denominator of the national Consumer Price Indices (CPIs). Since then, with considerable effort and co-operation by Member States, coverage has been extended to almost all of consumers' expenditure. In particular the difficult areas of health, education and social protection services are now largely covered, as are insurance and financial services. These and the geographic and population coverage are included according to agreed definitions thus ensuring comparability despite major institutional differences. Other improvements in comparability have come from agreements on the treatment of 'tariff' prices, such as electricity and telephones, and the willingness of Member States to update weights and to ensure that prices of new goods, such as mobile phones and PCs, are included. Although the Regulations imposed no requirements on Member States for an annual comprehensive updating of weights three Member States have moved to annual updating and others are either considering this or are planning an early updating. As a result HICPs have rather more up-to-date and relevant weights than was the case with CPIs before harmonization.…

The Commission (Eurostat) believes that the HICPs represent a considerable co-operative achievement resulting in markedly improved measures of inflation not only for informing monetary policy for the Monetary Union but also for the Governments of Member States. Nevertheless, there still remains much to be done to ensure the overall reliability, relevance and comparability of the indices. The forward programme of work with Member States therefore seeks to consolidate and explicate (with practical guidelines) existing standards and, where there remains potential for systematic differences such as

[4] COM (2000) 742, Brussels, 21.11.2000.

in quality adjustment, to develop the necessary new standards. It also seeks to develop operational monitoring systems sufficient to assure users that all HICPs and the MUICP meet the established standards and those yet to be agreed.

In addition to the regular monthly News Releases, Eurostat has, over the years, published or contributed to various reports describing aspects of the HICP and its construction. Several of these have proved useful to the author in providing details of the development of the HICP. Readers will doubtless also find them useful reference books. See Section 8 of this chapter for more detail. Most are also listed in the "Suggestions for Further Reading" near the end of this book.

1996—the year in which the first Interim Indices of Consumer Prices were published—saw the first of several "Convergence Reports", as mentioned above. These reports were prepared in accordance with Article 109j(l) of the Maastricht Treaty, which required the Commission to report to the Council on the progress made in the fulfilment by the member states of their wider obligations regarding the achievement of Economic and Monetary Union (EMU).

These reports were the first steps of the procedure set out in Article 109j which required the Council, deciding (not later than 31 December 1996) whether a majority of the Member States fulfilled the necessary conditions for the adoption of a single currency, and whether it was appropriate for the Community to enter the third stage of EMU.

The 1996 convergence report describes the price stability requirement of the Treaty and to comment on the results following the first publication of the IICPs in March 1996. The report said: "*Though not strictly comparable, IICPs are for the time being considered to constitute a more comparable basis for the assessment of inflation convergence among Member States than the national CPIs*".

The 1998 convergence report described very briefly the considerable advance of the previous two years:

Considerable progress has been made in harmonizing methodologies. The HICPs currently provide the best statistical basis for international comparisons of consumer price inflation. Under the Council Regulation, the Commission has so far adopted three detailed regulations (No 1749/96, No 2214/96, and No 2454/97) establishing specific implementing measures governing the production of the HICP.

15.8 HICP Compendiums and Manuals

During the early years of HICP development, my Eurostat team had been fully occupied in dealing with the programme of regulations, together with compliance monitoring, administration and related topics. We saw the need for a publication which would draw together all of this work in a single volume. It would not only be very useful for our own team but also for price statisticians in the member states. It also fulfilled a basic need to have a reference document containing all the regulations and guidelines adopted so far.

The outcome was a thick volume of around 350 pages entitled "Compendium of HICP Reference Documents".[5] It was published in December 2001. The Foreword, by the Eurostat Director-General, Yves Franchet, began as follows:

> *To achieve the objectives set by the Treaty of the European Union, and more specifically Economic and Monetary Union, we need high-quality statistical instruments which provide the Community institutions, governments and economic and social operators with a set of harmonized and reliable statistics on which to base their decisions. The Harmonized Indices of Consumer Prices (HICPs) are the result of several years' work. They draw on the experience and expertise of EU National Statistical Offices' price experts and user representatives from the European Central Bank, national central banks and the Commission's Directorate-General for Economic and Financial Affairs. The European Commission is deeply grateful to all partners, and especially National Statistical Institutes, for the perseverance and expertise with which they helped Eurostat to accomplish the harmonization task which is still continuing. The result of this collaborative effort is the achievement of a harmonized methodology, built on a solid legal basis, that provides a high degree of comparability, reliability and timeliness. Given the growing interest for and importance of the HICP, it seems opportune to share with users a comprehensive reference for the harmonized methodology. This Compendium is, therefore, intended to support not only those concerned with managing, understanding and analysing the European economy, but also those generally interested in inflation measurement issues. The set of compiled texts includes technical and non-technical documents, as well as the whole legal framework to date...*
>
> *I recommend this Compendium to all those with an interest in price indices.*

[5] Eurostat, "Compendium of HICP Reference Documents", 2/2001/B/5, 2001.

Most of the Compendium reproduces the Reports from the Commission to the Council on the harmonization of CPIs in the EU of 1998 and 2000 (see Section 7 above) together with all the Regulations and Guidelines made up to the date of publication. These sections take up all but 25 pages of the volume. The remaining section is a paper by Eurostat describing in some detail the main technical elements of the HICP, such as the macro and micro formulae, the weight reference period, indices for elementary aggregates, newly significant products and so on. In fact, the 2001 Compendium could be considered as a useful practical companion to this book! It is available on the Eurostat website.

Eurostat also published in 2004 a "Short Guide for Users".[6]

The 2001 Compendium was replaced by a revised edition in 2013.[7] It includes all of the Regulations and Recommendations published up to that date, and revisions to earlier regulations. It is also available on the Eurostat website.

The 2013 volume was the last "Compendium" on HICPs to be published. But five years later, a new volume described as the "HICP Methodological Manual"[8] was published. Unlike the earlier Compendiums, it was more focussed on detailed HICP methodologies than on Regulations as such. This is explained in the introduction:

> *The HICP Methodological Manual represents a comprehensive overview of methods that are used in the compilation process for the harmonised index of consumer prices (HICP). The manual intends to be a practical guide to all steps necessary to produce an HICP and is thus useful for statisticians who are new to the field of price statistics and statistical offices aiming to set up a similar inflation measure. Users of the HICP, such as businesses, policy-makers and researchers may also find this manual useful to help them understand and interpret HICP data. The drafting of the HICP Methodological Manual has been co-ordinated by Eurostat and supervised by a dedicated task force that was composed of experts from the statistical institutes of France, Germany, Italy, Luxembourg, the Netherlands, Norway, Portugal, the United Kingdom and the European Central Bank. The task force met*

[6] "Harmonized Indices of Consumer Prices (HICPs); a Short Guide for Users", Eurostat, Luxembourg 2004. ISBN 92-894-7081-X.

[7] "Compendium of HICP Reference Documents", Eurostat, Luxembourg, 2013, ISBN 978-92-79-29368-9.

[8] "HICP Methodological Manual", Eurostat, 2018, Luxembourg; ISBN 978-92-79-76861-3.

several times during the two years of the drafting process and discussed the content of every single chapter in depth. Two dedicated workshops, in which all EU Member States participated, were held to discuss the draft manual. The drafting work was carried out by a team of international experts and Eurostat.

The present author had no involvement with the Methodological Manual, but I would strongly recommend it as an excellent technical companion for readers of this book.

15.9 Revisions of the HICP

The national CPIs of many countries are often non-revisable, even after mistakes have been discovered. The usual reason for this approach is that one of the important uses of CPIs is in contracts for wages or other services, where the effects of a revision could be complex and even liable to legal action. The HICP, on the other hand, was not designed for uses such as the above: its raison d'être was to be an indicator of macroeconomic inflation, principally for use by central banks and the ECB. Of course, it cannot be doubted that it has been and perhaps will continue to be used as a reference for contracts and wage settlements, but that was never its purpose. Accordingly, the HICP is defined as a revisable index. This is laid down in a Commission Regulation.[9]

It was also, as it happened, the last HICP regulation to be made before my own departure from Eurostat!

The regulation is perhaps surprisingly lengthy. This is due to the need for a high degree of precision in its wording. For example, much depends on whether a proposed revision is because of a mistake or for some other reason. And the very word "mistake" has to be carefully defined. Some may prefer the slightly less emotive word "error"—but this word does not appear in the regulation.

So let's begin by looking at the definitions.

A "mistake" is defined *as "an unintentional breach of an established rule affecting at least one HICP series*". The expression "HICP series" is not itself defined, but the context clearly implies that it could range from a set of low-level sub-indices to the all-items HICP series. These definitions are aimed at mistakes made within a member state, rather than

[9] Commission Regulation (EC) No. 1921/2001, 2001.

in Eurostat, though in principle the latter could also be included. Article 2 of the Regulation requires that member states shall notify Eurostat of the action taken to prevent similar future occurrences.

A "revision" is defined as "*an ex-post change in a HICP series, index level, rate of change or weight, that has been made publicly available through printed or electronic media by the Commission (Eurostat) affecting the results to one decimal place*". This could be due either to the discovery of a mistake or to the existence of new or improved information, such as a more up-to-date weighting structure. This is an important definition, since it sets a limit on what should and should not be corrected. Readers will be aware that the entire HICP structure is based on the concept of "comparability", which is interpreted as being valid to within one decimal place. So this use of the same criterion seems reasonable.

A "provisional" result is defined as "*a result which is, subject to revision, expected to be finalised in a later month*". This implicitly acknowledges that if a mistake has been detected it may not be possible to correct it in time for the next publication. A "provisional" figure is thus a warning that a revision is likely to be made some time soon. In fact, Article 9 of the Regulation states that "*when an index is published as provisional, it shall be finalised in the following month's publication*".

The greater part of the Regulation is concerned with the process of making revisions to published data. The essence is in Article 3.1: "*The officially published HICP series may be revised*". Article 4.1 goes on to say: "*Mistakes shall be corrected and resulting revisions shall be implemented without unnecessary delay*". Rather obvious, but it has to be stated clearly.

Rather less obviously, Article 5 is concerned not with mistakes as such, but with the appearance of new or improved information: "*Revisions resulting from new or improved basic information which are considered by Member States necessary in order to improve the accuracy of an HICP shall be implemented provided the Commission (Eurostat) does not oppose the timing of the revisions to be made*".

New or improved information is essentially concerned with data, be they prices or weights. It could be that data relating to a particular sub-index has become available or more accurate, and its incorporation into the country's HICP calculation could make a "significant" (0.1 percentage point) difference to one or more indices. Eurostat would clearly not wish such changes—whose frequency is unknowable in advance—to be made often, as this would tend to reduce user confidence in the HICP. So some coordination at the centre is necessary to prevent this from happening.

Article 6 finally describes another type of event which may call for changes in the published HICP series. Recalling that the development of the HICP took several years—and will never be complete!—it happens that changes in methodology or coverage are implemented from time to time, usually at the start of a new calendar year. The previously published data are in such cases not revised. In other words, the new system is applied from the set date and the previously published data are not revised to reflect the new methods.

Thus, Article 6 says: "*Unless otherwise stated*:

> *1. changes in the system of harmonised rules shall not require revisions;*
> *2. changes in definitions, methods, or practices resulting from the HICP regulatory framework shall take effect with the index for January each year in all Member States concerned*".

However, given the fact that earlier data are not changed, the effect on the calculated rates of inflation at any or all levels cannot be ignored. Put simply, the comparison of annual figures which are compiled using different methods may give misleading results. Hence, the rest of Article 6 goes on to say:

> *3. the impact of any such changes shall be assessed for the 12 months starting with the index for January in which the changes take effect;*
> *4. if the changes are likely to affect the average annual rate of change of the all-items index over the 12-month period following the change by at least one tenth of a percentage point then the impact on the all-items index shall be estimated for each of the 12 months;*
> *5. where in addition any COICOP/HICP division, group or class index is likely to be affected respectively by at least three, four or five tenths of a percentage point calculated as in Article 6(4), the impact on the index series concerned shall be estimated for each of the 12 months.*

Put simply, this means that although the actual index numbers for the earlier year are not altered, an analysis providing estimates of the changes from one year to the next (and for each individual month) must be made (normally by Eurostat).

Article 7 describes in some detail how these estimates should be made. It includes the following instruction:

The estimates referred to in Article 6(4) and (5) shall be publicly available, with appropriate notes on their quality. These estimates shall not replace the official HICP.

On a more practical note, Article 8 requires that a revision mark of some sort must be shown in a publication against any figure which has been revised. The type of mark (e.g. a letter "p" for "provisional") is not specified, but it must remain for just one month only.

15.10 Main HICP Developments after 2002

As explained in the Preface, this book covers the early years of development of the HICP up to the middle of 2002 when I left Eurostat. I am not attempting to detail the large amount of work which continued after that date and indeed to the present day: that will be for another person to record. Here I refer only to changes in the HICP regulations which occurred after 2002.

15.10.1 New Implementing Regulations

The long list of (mainly) Commission Regulations implementing the rules laid down in the original Framework Regulation (2495/95) was extended as follows:

Reg 1708/2005: This Commission Regulation established a common index reference year of 2005 = 100, following the original 1996 = 100 which could not legally be changed without fresh legislation.

Reg 701/2006: This Council Regulation laid down more detail for the timing of monthly price collection. It was now restricted to at least one working week period at or near the middle of the calendar month.

Reg 1334/2007: This Council Regulation made significant and fundamental amendments to the first Implementing Regulation (1749/96) in respect of sampling and quality adjustment. It introduced the new concepts of "product-offer" and "consumption segment".

Reg 330/2009: This Commission Regulation provided detailed rules for the treatment of seasonal products.

Reg 1114/2010: This Commission Regulation laid down fresh rules regarding the quality of weights, including their date relevance.

Reg 93/2013: This Commission Regulation established a new index: the Owner-Occupied Housing Price Index (OOH-HPI). The index refers to dwellings new to the household sector plus other goods and services that households acquire as owner occupiers. It is a quarterly index but may also be provided monthly. The Regulation also established an OOH-HPI Methodological Manual.[10] It also established a simpler House Price Index (HPI) which is not restricted to housing new to the household sector, but measures the changes in the transaction prices of dwellings purchased by households.

Reg 119/2013: This Commission Regulation established a new variant of the HICP: the HICP-CT, where CT stands for "constant tax". The idea is that when prices rise, for example, as a result of an increase in Value Added Tax (VAT), the new price would enter the HICP in full and contribute to the measure of inflation. From the point of view of the consumer this is absolutely correct. But from the point of view of inflation analysis and also for the assessment of convergence in the member states it may be considered in a different light. As the Preamble (Paragraph 3) said:

> *For inflation analysis and for convergence assessment in Member States, it is necessary to collect information on the impact of tax changes on inflation. To this end, HICPs should additionally be calculated on the basis of constant tax rate prices instead of observed prices in the form of harmonised indices of consumer prices at constant tax rates (HICP-CT).*

The regulation also required Eurostat to compile all the same sub-indices for the HICP-CT as was done for the main HICP.

The taxes to be taken into account in HICP-CT were as follows:

- Value added type taxes (VAT)
- Taxes on specific services
- Excise duties and consumption taxes (other than those included in taxes and duties on imports)
- Car registration taxes

[10] Eurostat, "Technical Manual on Owner-Occupied Housing and House Price Indices", 2017.

- Taxes on entertainment
- Taxes on insurance premiums
- Other taxes on specific services
- Other taxes on products not elsewhere classified.

15.10.2 New Framework Regulation

Regulation 2016/792 (May 2016) (EU Parliament and Council) took a major step by repealing the original Framework Regulation (2494/95) and replacing it with a fresh and updated version.

15.10.3 Consolidated Implementing Regulation (2020/1148)

This was a huge step. Over 19 years, there had been a total of 19 implementing regulations, based on the 1995 Framework Regulation. Much thought had been given to consolidating all the regulations into a single entity, even during my period in Eurostat. But there was no time available for this major task. But in 2020 all of the implementing regulations were repealed, and replaced with a new consolidated **Regulation 2020/1148**, dated 31 July 2020. The ink is hardly dry! It thus simplifies the task of all those who need to look at the whole range of current legislation in its entirety.

Concluding Remarks

I was fortunate in having at my disposal a large number of documents of many types relating to the subject of this book, both on paper and in electronic format. Without this library my task would have been virtually impossible.

A great deal has happened to the HICP in the eighteen years since I retired from Eurostat, and I am sure there is another book ready to be written! The preceding sections alone demonstrate this. Doubtless more countries will join the EU (and maybe a few will leave!) so the process will continue. The USA has set an example by compiling its own HICP. The HICP has been described by many as a "state of the art" index, and there seems no reason why it should not be compiled by many other countries beyond Europe. Indeed one of my major consultancy tasks after I had left Eurostat was to assist the African organisation COMESA (Common Market for Eastern and Southern Africa) to design its own 19-nation harmonized CPI, based to a large extent on the HICP. Who will be next?

J. Astin, *Measuring EU Inflation*,
https://doi.org/10.1007/978-3-030-68806-6

Suggestions for Further Reading

(Note: Where these references occur in the main text as footnotes the relevant page number is given in each case. There is no special ordering.)

1. Stadlbauer, Josef. "Consumer Price Indexes in the European Community—Comparison of existing indexes and Approaches to Their Harmonisation", Eurostat Luxembourg, 1975 (Fn p. 12).
2. Teekens, Rudolf. "Consumer Price Indices in the European Community", Luxembourg, 1989 (Fn p. 13).
3. Turvey, Ralph. "Consumer Price Indices: An ILO Manual", International Labour Organization, 1989 (Fn p. 13).
4. Treaty on European Union (Maastricht) 1992. ISBN 92-824-0959-7 (Fn p. 14).
5. Astin, J. and Sellwood, D. "Harmonization in the European Union: A Review of Some Technical Issues", Ottawa Group, Voorburg, 1997 [All Ottawa group meetings and papers on ottawagroup.org].
6. Astin, J. "Quality Adjustment in CPIs—A Personal View", Ottawa Group, Washington DC, 1998.
7. Astin, J. "The European Union Harmonized Indices of Consumer Prices", Ottawa Group, Reykjavik 1999.
8. Council Regulation 2494/95; OJ No. L 257, 27.10.1995 [HICP Framework Regulation].

J. Astin, *Measuring EU Inflation*,
https://doi.org/10.1007/978-3-030-68806-6

9. "Final Report of the Advisory Commission to Study the Consumer Price Index", US Senate Committee on Finance, 1996 [Boskin Report] (https://www.finance.senate.gov/imo/media/doc/Prt104-72.pdf) (Fn p. 147).
10. "Report on Convergence in the European Union in 1996", COM(96) 560 final, Brussels, 1996.
11. Commission Convergence Report to Council 1998. https://ec.europa.eu/economy_finance/publications/european_economy/convergence_reports_en.htm.
12. Commission Convergence Report to Council 2000 (link as above).
13. Commission Report to Council on harmonization of CPIs, 1998, Brussels (COM(1998) 104 final).
14. Report from the Commission to the Council on Harmonization of Consumer Price Indices in the European Union (COM 2000) 742 final, Brussels, 21.11.2000.
15. "At What Price?—Conceptualizing and Measuring Cost-of-Living and Price Indexes", National Research Council, USA, 2002 (Fn p. 244).
16. "Household Budget Surveys in the EU. Methodology and Recommendations for Harmonisation", Eurostat, Luxembourg, 2003. ISBN 92-894-5435-0.
17. "Compendium of HICP Reference Documents", 2/2001/8/5, Eurostat, Luxembourg, 2001 (Fn p. 250).
18. "Compendium of HICP Reference Documents", Eurostat, Luxembourg, 2013. ISBN 978-92-79-29368-9 (Fn p. 251).
19. "Harmonized Indices of Consumer Prices (HICPs); a Short Guide for Users", Eurostat, Luxembourg 2004. ISBN 92-894-7081-X (Fn p. 202).
20. Flower, T. and Wales, P. "Variation in the Inflation Experience of UK Households: 2003–2014" (Economic Trends, UK Office for National Statistics, December 2014) (Fn p. 182).
21. Astin, J. and Leyland, J. "Towards a Household Inflation Index", 2015, https://rss.org.uk/policy-campaigns/policy/price-indices (Fn p. 182).
22. HICP Methodological Manual. ISBN 978-92-79-76861-3 Eurostat, Luxembourg, 2018 (Fn p. 2).
23. Astin, J. "The Transformation of Statistical Principles and Procedures into the Language of Legal Acts", IAOS Conference, Da Nang, Vietnam, 2014 (Fn p. 236).

24. "Technical Manual on Owner-Occupied Housing and House Price Indices" (ec.europa.eu Technical-Manual-OOH-HPI-2017) (Fn p. 256).
25. "Consumer Price Index Manual: Theory and practice", ILO/IMF/OECD/UNECE/Eurostat/ World Bank, International Labour Office, Geneva, 2004.
26. "Practical Guide to Producing Consumer Price Indices", United Nations, 2009, Table 10.2 (Fn p. 127).
27. Johnson, P. "UK Consumer Price Statistics: A Review", https://uksa.statisticsauthority.gov.uk/wp-content/uploads/2015/12/images-ukconsumerpricestatisticsarevie_tcm97-44345.pdf.
28. "Methods of Compiling Cost-of-Living Index Numbers", Studies and Reports, Series N (Statistics) No. 6, ILO, Geneva, 1925 (Fn p. 11).
29. "The Computation of Consumer Price Indexes (Special Problems)", ILO, Geneva, 1962 (Fn p. 11).
30. "Household Budget Surveys in the EC: Methodology and Recommendations for Harmonisation", Eurostat, Luxembourg 1993 (Fn p. 68).
31. "Consumer Price Index Manual: Concepts and Methods", ILO, Draft Jan 2020 (Fn p. 81).
32. "Classifications of Expenditure According to Purpose" (UN Statistical Papers, Series M No. 84, 2000) (Fn p. 100).
33. "Classifications of Expenditure According to purpose: COFOG, COICOP, COPNI, COPP", Series M: Miscellaneous Statistical Papers, No. 84, New York: United Nations. ST/ESA/STAT/SER.M/84. ISBN: 92-1-161420-1 (Fn p. 102).
34. "Classification of Products by Activity", Council Regulation 451/2008 (Fn p. 130).

Glossary

Acquisition, Payment or Use Methods of timing the price entry into the HICP: month of acquisition or of payment, or over the usage life of the product.

Aggregation The process by which CPIs for lower-level aggregates are combined to obtain CPIs for higher-level aggregates.

Barcode scanner An optical scanner that can read printed barcodes, decode the data contained in the barcode and send the data to a computer.

Benefits-in-kind Benefits which employees receive but which are not included in their salary such as company cars and medical insurance.

Candidate countries Countries applying for entry to the European Union; known also as pre-accession countries.

Carli Index An elementary price index covering two periods to be compared, being the arithmetic mean of the price relatives (or ratios) between the two periods.

Chain index An index number series for a long sequence of periods obtained by linking together index numbers spanning shorter sequences of periods.

COICOP A United Nations product classification: Classification of Individual Consumption According to Purpose.

COICOP/HICP A variant of COICOP designed specifically for the HICP.

J. Astin, *Measuring EU Inflation*,
https://doi.org/10.1007/978-3-030-68806-6

Comitology A process by which EU law is modified or adjusted and takes place within "comitology committees" chaired by the European Commission.

Compensation index A price index specifically designed as a tool for indexing or guiding changes in wages and salaries. Sometimes referred to as an "uprating index".

Comparability HICPs which include weights for each product category accounting for more than one part in a thousand of the total expenditure covered by all categories shall be deemed comparable (from Reg. 1749/96).

Compliance monitoring The process of checking that member states are following the rules laid down in the HICP regulations.

Consumer Expenditure Deflator A price index designed to remove the effects of inflation from data on consumer expenditure.

Cost of Living Index (COLI) A price index that measures the change between two periods in the minimum expenditures that would be required to achieve a constant standard of living (i.e. level of utility or welfare).

Democratic index Also known as a "household-based" index. A form of CPI in which each household is given equal weight in the calculation of the index irrespective of the size of its expenditure (see also "Plutocratic index").

Derogation In terms of EU legislation a derogation implies that a member state, with permission, delays the implementation of an element of an EU Regulation into their legal system over a given timescale.

Domestic coverage The use of weights covering all consumption expenditure on the national territory regardless of the nationality or normal residence of the consumer (see also "National coverage").

Dutot index An elementary price index covering two periods to be compared being the ratio of the arithmetic mean prices in each of the two periods.

EEA European Economic Area: a group of European countries including the European Union plus some other countries. The non-EU countries must comply with the HICP regulations.

European Central Bank (ECB) Established in 1998 as successor to the European Monetary Institute (EMI).

European Index of Consumer Prices (EICP) The aggregate index of all EU members' HICPs weighted together.

Elementary aggregate The smallest aggregate of items for which expenditure data are normally available and used for an HICP calculation to compute an elementary price index (see below).

Elementary price index A price index for elementary aggregates.

Economic and Monetary Union (EMU) The group of EU member states which share the common currency of the euro.

European Monetary Institute (EMI) The central bank for the EU was established in 1994 by the Maastricht Treaty. Replaced by the ECB in 1998.

European System of Accounts (ESA 1995) ESA 1995 defines the accounting rules such that the economies of the member states can be described in quantitative terms in a consistent, reliable and comparable manner.

Eurostat The Statistical Office of the EU based in Luxembourg.

Factor cost A measure of national income or output based on the cost of factors of production rather than of market prices. This allows the effect of any subsidy or indirect tax to be removed from the final measure.

FISIM Financial Intermediation Services Indirectly Measured. An estimate of the value of the services provided by financial intermediaries such as banks, for which no explicit charges are made. Excluded from HICP.

Framework Regulation The first HICP regulation (2494/95) which set out the main themes of the HICP.

GDP Deflator Measures changes in the prices of goods and services produced in a country including those exported to other countries. Prices of imports are excluded.

Geometric mean An alternative to the arithmetic mean defined as the *n*th root of the product of *n* numbers. Used in the Jevons Index (see below).

Harmonized Index of consumer prices (HICP) EU national consumer price indices designed for use in setting the EU interest rate and monitoring EU price stability. The subject of this book!

Hedonic regression A type of regression analysis used to predict the influence of various features on the price of a product. Thus price changes due to changes in the specification of certain features can be estimated and removed from the actual sale price.

Higher-level price index A price index for a grouping above the level of elementary aggregate.

Household Budget Survey (HBS) A sample survey conducted among households to determine their annual expenditure on a wide range of specified goods and services. Results are used to provide weights for the HICP. Also referred to as Family Budget Survey or Household Expenditure Survey.

Household Final Monetary Consumption Expenditure (HFMCE) A national accounts measure which defines the expenditure coverage of the HICP, in particular the exclusion of non-monetary "expenditure" such as imputed transactions.

Implementing Regulations The detailed regulations based on the Framework Regulation concerning mainly the technical implementation of the general rules for the HICP.

Interim Index of Consumer Prices (IICP) The initial and temporary version of the HICP used for the first assessment of convergence.

International Labour Organisation (ILO) A UN organisation originally established in 1919, responsible for protecting rights at work and related issues. Based in Geneva, it maintains a global database of consumer price indices.

Implicit Quality Index (IQI) An index formed as the ratio of an index of prices unadjusted for quality change to an index of prices adjusted for quality change. It provides an approximate measure of the aggregate quality change for which allowance has been made.

Index reference period The period for which the value of the HICP is set at 100.

Institutional households A group of individuals staying in an institution for long periods of time such as retirement homes, military accommodation and boarding schools, and sharing resources.

Jevons index An elementary price index covering two periods to be compared, being the ratio of the geometric mean of the price relatives for each element between the two periods, or the ratio of the geometric means of the prices in each of the two periods. These give identical results.

Laspeyres index A higher-level weighted price index covering two periods to be compared in which the basket of products comprises the quantities of goods and services in the earlier of the two periods.

Lowe index A higher-level weighted price index that measures the change in the value of a basket of products between two periods where the basket does not necessarily have to consist of the actual quantities in the same periods.

Maastricht Treaty The EC Treaty of 1992 which set out the plans for Monetary Union.

Missing observation An unobservable price due to the absence of a product from its usual situation such as a particular retail outlet.

Monetary expenditure (See Household Final Monetary Consumption Expenditure (HFMCE)).

Monetary Union Index of Consumer Prices (MUICP) A subset of the EICP restricted to those countries which are members of the Monetary Union.

National coverage The use of weights covering the expenditure of national residents of a country regardless of where the expenditure is made (see also "Domestic coverage").

NSI National Statistical Institute: an official national organisation given the task of obtaining, processing and publishing the main body of official statistical data. Sometimes referred to as National Statistical Office (NSO).

Outlier A term used to describe any extreme value in a set of data such as a price or a price relative that requires further investigation or has been verified as correct.

Own consumption Goods produced by households for their own consumption such as food or clothing. Excluded from the HICP.

Paasche index A higher-level price index covering two periods to be compared in which the basket of products comprises the quantities of goods and services in the later of the two periods.

Plutocratic index Also known as an "expenditure-weighted" index. A form of CPI in which the weights are based on total aggregated expenditure values rather than average household expenditure proportions (see "Democratic Index").

Price stability An economic situation where inflation is moderate and predictable.

Price updating A procedure whereby the quantities in an earlier period are re-valued at the prices of a later period, using the components of the price index.

Producer Price Index (PPI) An index which measures inflation from the perspective of costs to industry or producers of goods and services.

Purchasing Power Parities (PPPs) The rates of currency conversions that equalise the purchasing power of different currencies by taking account of the differences in price levels between countries.

Pure Price Index An index (such as the HICP) in which it is only changes in prices (and not in "utility") that are reflected in the measure between the current and the base or reference period.

Quality Adjustment (QA) An adjustment to the change in price of a product of which the characteristics or specifications change over time, designed to remove the contribution of the change in characteristics to the observed price change.

Quantities Quantities of products are the physical weights numbers, etc., of the products. Given that these are not directly additive, expenditures on the quantities are used instead, in particular for the purpose of calculating weights.

Rebasing Refers to changing the weight reference period price reference period or index reference period. The timing of these reference periods may be changed separately or at the same time.

Regulation An EU regulation is a legal act that applies directly at the national level. Member states do not need to create their own legislation to bring a Regulation into force.

Rothwell index A type of "variable weights" index used for dealing with seasonal products.

Scope The set of products for which the index is intended to measure the price changes. The scope of the HICP will generally be defined in terms of a designated set of consumption goods and services purchased by a randomised set of households.

Seasonal products Products showing a strong seasonal variation in one or more of the following: prices, monthly expenditures, quantities sold, quality, demand or supply.

Social transfers in kind A national accounts category "household actual final consumption" includes social transfers in kind, such as the provision to households of free or subsidised health and education services.

Statistical Programme Committee (SPC) An EU Regulatory Committee comprised of NSI heads responsible for ensuring that the actions to be undertaken are consistent with those decided upon in the national statistical programme. Now replaced by the European Statistical System Committee (ESSC).

Statistical units Organisations (shopkeeper, shop owner, government department, etc.) which provide, or allow officials to gather information on prices and sales volumes for the NSIs (see Reg 696/93 of 15 March 1993).

Sub-indices A general name used in the context of the HICP which relates to a relatively detailed product or other stratum level.

Superlative index A type of index formula that can be expected to approximate to a cost of living index.

Symmetric index A price index that makes equal use of the prices and quantities in both of the periods compared and treats them in a symmetric manner.

Tariff A list of pre-established prices and conditions for the purchase of certain goods or services containing differentiated prices and conditions of sale.

Tariff Price A price within a tariff that applies to a component element or unit of consumption of the good or service in question.

Task Force (TF) A sub-group of a Working Party charged with examining specific aspects of a future regulation.

Uprating index See "Compensation index".

Walsh index A basket index in which the quantities are geometric averages of the quantities in the two periods. It is both a symmetric index and a superlative index.

Web scraping A technique employed to obtain large amounts of data from websites whereby the data are extracted and saved to a computer.

Weight The weight of a product in the HICP is the proportion of total household expenditure which is spent on that product during the weight reference period.

Weight reference period The period for which the expenditure shares serve as the weights for the HICP.

"Whereas" clauses In the preamble to a Regulation, the "whereas clauses" explain, down to the required level of detail, why the regulation is needed and how its content can be justified.

Working Party (WP) Informal name for Working Group: a group of national experts meeting regularly to make proposals for regulations chaired by Eurostat.

Index

J. Astin, *Measuring EU Inflation*,
https://doi.org/10.1007/978-3-030-68806-6

The manufacturer's authorised representative in the EU is Springer Nature Customer Service Centre GmbH, Europaplatz 3, 69115 Heidelberg, Germany. If you have any concerns regarding our products, please contact ProductSafety@springernature.com

Printed and bound by CPI Group (UK) Ltd, Croydon, CR0 4YY
30/09/2026
02225451-0009